Chains of Empire

Also from Westphalia Press

westphaliapress.org

Chains of Empire

English Public Schools, Masonic Cabalism,
Historical Causality, and Imperial Clubdom

by P. J. Rich

WESTPHALIA PRESS
An imprint of Policy Studies Organization

Westphalia Press
An imprint of Policy Studies Organization
1527 New Hampshire Ave., NW
Washington, D.C. 20036
info@ipsonet.org

ISBN-13: 978-1-63391-078-2
ISBN-10: 1633910784

Cover design by Taillefer Long at Illuminated Stories:
www.illuminatedstories.com

Daniel Gutierrez-Sandoval, Executive Director
PSO and Westphalia Press

Rahima Schwenkbeck Director of Media and Marketing
PSO and Westphalia Press

Updated material and comments on this edition
can be found at the Westphalia Press website:
www.westphaliapress.org

Chains of Empire

English Public Schools, Masonic Cabalism,
Historical Causality, and Imperial Clubdom

Front Endpaper: Sir Pertab Singh's visit to Haileybury.

Back Endpaper: Arrival at Aligarh College of The Prince of Wales (George V).

Westminster School Entrance.

Chains of Empire

English Public Schools, Masonic Cabalism,
Historical Causality, and Imperial Clubdom

P. J. RICH

And nothing on earth shall sever the chain that is round us now. –
Eton Boating Song

Some residual public-school thing, quintessential to Clubs, infected the atmosphere. –
Allan Hollinghurst, *The Swimming Pool Library*

Regency Press (London & New York) Ltd.
125 High Holborn, London WC1V 6QA

Remembering Laura Wirtner Miller,
knowledgeable about life's rituals and graces

and

For mother and father, good humoured
observers of far places and strange customs

*Creativity is ultimately
mysterious. It raises the
question of causality in a
particularly strong, striking,
and probably insoluble manner.
- Rupert Sheldrake*

The trilogy ENGLISH PUBLIC SCHOOLS AND RITUALISTIC IMPERIALISM

ELIXIR OF EMPIRE *English Public Schools, Ritualism, Freemasonry, and Imperialism*

CHAINS OF EMPIRE *English Public Schools, Masonic Cabalism, Historical Causality, and Imperial Clubdom*

RITUALS OF EMPIRE *English Public Schools, Imperial Baubles, Masonic Magicians, and Morphic Resonances*

Paul John Rich was a Kinsmen Scholar at Tonbridge School and received the AB and EDM from Harvard and the PhD from The University of Western Australia. A longtime adviser in the sheikhdom of Qatar, Dr. Rich is a member of the Royal Society of Literature, the Royal Institute of Philosophy, the Royal Institution, the American Philosophical Association, and the Kant Society. He belongs to the Psychohistorical Association and the Group for the Use of Psychology in History. In 1990 he was awarded the Cameron Medal for contributions to educational research in Western Australia. He is a Life Governor of Manchester College, Oxford University.

CONTENTS

LIST OF ILLUSTRATIONS

ACKNOWLEDGEMENTS

Adequately acknowledging the support of Associate Professor Donald Leinster-Mackay of The University of Western Australia would require full use of an unabridged dictionary. He exemplifies the scholar-educator. Discussions with him provide grist for the mill – if not fodder for the cannon!

John Thorpe of Regency Press showed exemplary patience and stoutly supported the idea of a trilogy about ritualism and the public schools. I am indebted to the Sterling and Francine Clark Art Institute in Williamstown, Massachusetts, for permission to reproduce the Gérôme canvas, *The Snake Charmer*, and to Ms. Martha Asher, the Registrar of the Institute, for correspondence concerning the painting. Mrs. P. Hatfield, the Archivist of Eton, has generously answered questions about Melville Macnaghten, the author of *Sketchy Memories of Eton*.

Thanks go to Dr. Paul D. Wiebe, principal of the Kodaikanal International School in Tamil Nadu, India; so does gratitude to the Master of Dulwich College, Mr. A. C. F. Verity, for conversations whilst he was on a visit to Qatar. Dr. David Walton, formerly of Qatar University lent an informed ear. Ms. Nora Mitchell, author of *The Indian Hill-Station*, was a welcome correspondent. Drs. J. A. Mangan, Rupert Sheldrake and Rupert Wilkinson have been generous in replying to letters. Dr. W. A. Reid's review of *Elixir of Empire* in *The Journal of Curriculum Studies* (Vol. 22, No. 1, 1990) was especially helpful.

Appreciation goes to Mrs. Ann Murray, formerly of the Doha Club and now on the staff of the Guards and Cavalry in London, and to the staff at the Doha Club in Qatar – especially to T. Jeyasothy, then its Librarian and now of Western Australia. Mr. Robert Burnet, historian of the Royal and Ancient Golf Club of St. Andrews, has provided photocopies and ideas. Mr. Brian Devlin offered tea and sometimes sympathy, while Professors Ramez Kutrieh and Marcia Kutrieh, now in Riyadh, provided coffee and advice. During the writing of the book, an 'office mate' was Dr. Seddik Afifi, the Adviser to the Crown Prince of Qatar. Our association was intriguing, to say the least.

A debt to various works is apparent in the notes, but there are two books to single out: James Gleick's *Chaos: Making a New Science* (Heinemann, 1988) is an intellectual adventure that should be read by historians. Christine Heward's *Making a Man of Him: Parents and Their Sons' Education at an English Public School, 1929-50* (Routledge, 1988) illustrates what can be hoped for in contributions to social history from public school studies, challenging the view that the English public schools are an exhausted subject.

Thanks go to Mr. Arthur Ellis, Librarian of The University of Western Australia and Ms. T. A. Barringen of the Royal Commonwealth Society Library. Mrs. Penelope

Tuson of the India Office Library in London is a longtime correspondent. I have enjoyed the hospitality of the Institutes of Historical Research and of Commonwealth Studies, of the Library of The United Grand Lodge of England, of the Royal Society of Arts, of the Guildhall Library, of the Society of Genealogists, and of the Heraldry Society. Rev. John Cardell-Oliver provided news of "scholars; sinuous sentences and Maginot lines of obscure references".

Dr. Ben Darbyshire, Warden of St. George's College, The University of Western Australia, and Mr. Trevor Wigney of the university's alumni office were cheerful sounding boards. Finally, I wish to single out friends at the Department of Education, The University of Western Australia – including Professor John Hattie, Dr. Felicity Haynes, and Dr. Clive Whitehead. I take pride in our association.

The emergence of the "grant maintained" or "opt-out" schools, which are freed of local council control and have resemblances to the old direct grant schools, may create opportunities to overcome the social divisions that the public schools help to maintain. If this book contributes to an understanding of the "public school problem" and a solution, it will fulfil a purpose. I agree with the former headmaster of Winchester, John Thorn, when he remarks that "The important task is so to arrange the funding that it does not create division."

P. J. Rich
The University of Western Australia
June 1990

PREFACE

I salute the people who discover causes, and do not only write about causation 'Felix qui potuit rerum cognoscere causas.' – Dorothy Emmet, *The Effectiveness of Causes*, 1984.

It was indeed a continuation of the public school system at its best. – Sir Ronald Storrs regarding Cambridge University, *Memoirs, 1937.*

I suppose that when a savage dresses himself up with paint and feathers on some state occasion he is only obeying the same ineradicable instinct of human nature which prompts the custom of the Freemason to don aprons and ribbons, – Gilbert Coleridge, *Eton in the Seventies, 1912.*

This book concerns causality and the extraordinary manifestations of British Imperial rule by ritual as encouraged by the English public schools. It is part of a trilogy about the public school culture, and follows on *Elixir of Empire* (Regency, London, 1989). The thesis put forward is about a 'reality' that the Victorians created and in which to an extent we still live, one of remarkable ritualism which the English public schools played a major part in producing. The story is of glittering decorations and convincingly choreographed ceremonies, but more importantly concerns the political confidence that such phantasmagoria produced. (See *Prince of Wales setting Cornerstone of Reading Grammar School, 1870,* page 14.)

Chapters focus on problems in the historiography of Imperialism and of the public schools. Prosopography (collective biography) is discussed, as well as the 'new' tools of social history. Gentlemen's clubs are used as an example of the institutions which extended the ubiquitous public school influence in the Empire, leitmotifs spread by what Anthony Quinton has called "the old imperial club-haunting male ruling class".

Chains of Empire, as the second in a series entitled *English Public Schools and Ritualistic Imperialism,* supports the contention that the public schools inculcated a peculiarly ritualistic outlook. The final volume, *Rituals of Empire,* will discuss how the artifacts of rule achieved a totemistic power.

There is a distinction, albeit often ignored, between imperialism and colonialism. Emphasized here is the proposition that institutions such as the schools and clubs were the surrogate of both, and that colonialism was if anything more dependent on the public schools than were the more inclusive phenomena of Imperialism. In a possible second series, *Magicians of Arabia,* the insights developed about public school ritualism will be applied to one part of the Empire, the Arabian Gulf. The entire project confirms the distinctive English public school contribution to Imperialism in both general and specific terms, establishing a new paradigm for Imperial and public school studies.

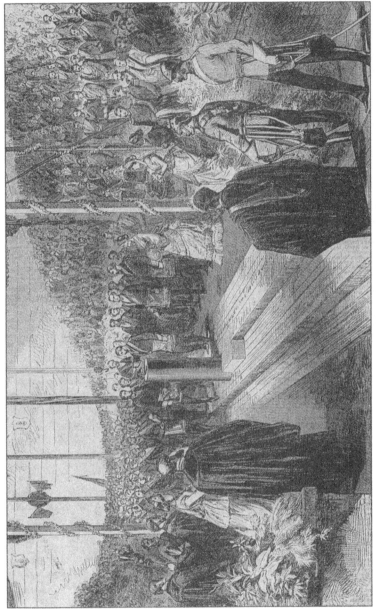

The Prince of Wales, as a Freemason, setting the Chief Stone of the new Grammar School at Reading. (Reading becomes grant maintained in 1991.)

Not surprisingly, this has led to considering causality, a subject that has caused as much controversy amongst historians as any issue. Adrian Wilson remarked ("Whig History and Present-Centred History", *History Journal*, 1988) that historians of ducks see ducks while historians of rabbits see rabbits. Sometimes they see mites on the ducks and rabbits. The debate *reductio ad absurdum* discourages even the intrepid. There are always more alternatives to consider. Dr. Michael Tooley comments with understatement in his book *Causation* that, while many accounts of causation have been advanced, none has been greeted with anything approaching general acceptance.[1] When causal considerations are combined with discussion of the English public school, which has generated more literature than any other educational institution in British society, the dimensions of the problem truly become daunting.

The plan was to begin with a consideration of Fichte's *Grundlage der gesammten Wissenschaftslehre* of 1794, outlining the contribution that he made indirectly to speculation about causality, and then originally included a lengthy consideration of the ways in which French historians and their appreciation of iconology constitute a *crucial* rather than *antiquarian* contribution to historical studies. For reasons of space much of this has been put aside, and the emphasis is solely on the continuing influence of the English public school in British history. For the same reason it has been necessary to postpone till the third volume consideration of the possible origins of Victorian school ritual in the earlier Gothic Revival, and discussion of *ritology* and the controversy over the contributions of exponents of symbolic analysis such as Victor Turner: "Turner is an academic fool. He has stood on his head and told us that rituals are hot seedbeds of change; that rituals not only control process, they generate it; that rituals not only mark boundaries, they evoke phasic motion in a culture."[2]

The subject of rituals is so vast that it easily could impinge on the historiographic issues that prompted the book. Particular mention should be made of the pioneering work of Peter McLaren, who in *Schooling as a Ritual Performance* testified to a belief "that schools serve as rich repositories of ritual systems: that rituals play a crucial and ineradicable role in the whole of the student's existence; and that the variegated dimensions of the ritual process are intrinsic to the events and transactions of institutional life and the warp and woof of school culture."[3]

Cockfighting and Peasants

History cannot be exempted from the proving exercises that apply to other disciplines just on the grounds that it deals with inexactitudes. So does meteorology. The subject of causality is not for the feckless. One historian's totem is another's taboo. In his novel *The Power-house*, John Buchan (Lord Tweedsmuir) offers the advice that "the world is full of clues to everything, and . . . if a man's mind is sharpset on any quest, he happens to notice and take advantage of what otherwise he would miss." A good deal of historical writing does miss the unimpeachable importance of causality. In remedying this, "good" history will seek to straddle the divide between the holistic and individualistic. Historians approach the causality problem in several ways: as imaginative reconstruction, or as requiring research methods different from other discourses, or as akin to that of nature, having a similar structure but different subject matter.[4] The last approach is the most promising but most contentious. Nevertheless, specialized studies produce excellent insights into broader issues.

There is no reason why being specialized should mean being pedantic. The study of fruitflies sounds pointless unless one knows that such studies shed light on genetic mechanisms.[5] Nothing sounds more obscure than Clifford Geertz's study of Balinese cockfighting or Natalie Zemon Davis's study of one French peasant of the sixteenth century. But the former is a crucial enthnographic contribution to understanding alien cultures, and the latter is is a landmark in social history. Succeeding chapters are a *reclama,* seeking to show that specialized cross-disciplinary and interdisciplinary approaches are praxes fundamental to the advance of history.[6]

The subject is not unrelated to a current debate over EMPATHY in history. Empathy requires drawing on a wide variety of perspectives. The recent introduction of empathy to the British secondary school history curriculum, making it part of the GCSE National Criteria for History, has given something of an official stamp to developments in social history and minority studies. Adolescents being introduced to history as a discipline are to be held accountable for an awareness that some historians lack.

Pondering *The Satanic Verses*

The furore in the Middle Eastern press over Salman Rushdie's *The Satanic Verses* included innuendos about the effects of his schooldays at Rugby, which were viewed as contributing to his apostasy. For his part, Rushdie has only admitted to unpleasant memories of Rugby breakfasts while the other boys watched his frustrated attack on kippers. The incident appears in *The Satanic Verses.* If Rugby did influence Rushdie, he was hardly the first author to have been influenced by a public school education. The public schools have been culturally significant for generations. This book aims to put them in the centre of discussion of Imperialism.

Jonathan Gathorne-Hardy remarked in *The Old School Tie* that "Public schools have often been criticised as crude agents of British Imperialism . . . (but) the picture is not totally clear, partly because little research has been done." J. A. Mangan comments in *'Benefits Bestowed?': Education and British Imperialism,* that "One fact emerges with great force from this set of essays – the close and continuing association between British imperialism and the public-school system . . . it must be recognised that the history of upper-class education and imperialism has scarcely been exhausted."[7] Dr. Mangan's books have helped to renew interest in the relationship of public schools with the Empire, albeit with a focus on athleticism and manliness.[8]

He and others have been concerned with how the association of the schools with Imperialism was contracted and continued, and with what it had to do with the genius of the British Empire. What was the precise nature of the tie between the schools and

Imperialism? *In Farewell the Trumpets*, the summation of the *Pax Britannica* trilogy, James Morris wrote: ". . . as in all great historical movements, the fundamental purpose was not a purpose at all, but simply an instinct. The British had reached an apogee. Rich, vigorous, inventive, more than 40 million strong, they had simply spilled out of their islands, impelled by forces beyond their own analysis." An uneasiness about the explanations so far offered led to suggestion in *Elixir of Empire* that understanding the Empire required an appreciation of public school ritualism. *Elixir* cites the public school Masonic lodges as an unappreciated aspect of the vaunted public school *ethos.*

'That Council School Boy'.

The influence was diffuse, and not limited to those who attended the public schools. A vast amount of Victorian and Edwardian ephemera points to the universal interest in public school life. The working class avidly followed the adventures of boys such as Tom Speedie, the hero of the *Chums* stories about "That Council School Boy". Could a lad of humble background make good at Repington? (See 'That Council School Boy', above.) Speedie offered working class readers the vicarious public school experience, and so did other heroes such as stalwart Jack Graham, a *Chums* favourite who makes good at exclusive Whitborough School despite having been abandoned as a baby to a workhouse. As for the Empire, it was in good hands with public school boys, although they had narrow escapes. (See *The Human Sacrifice*, page 18.) The old school tie always triumphed, and in the pages of *Chums* and similar magazines, schoolmates on holiday easily routed the natives – or as in D. H. Parry's stories about St. Osyth's, restored to the throne a worthy Indian boy who had been a compatriot at school back in England. Even in countries not part of the Empire, such as Thailand, the English public schools exercised an influence through the native élite that they had educated.[9]

THE FOURTH FINGER OF LI CHAN SUEY

BY
FRANK H. SHAW

The human sacrifice to the Chinese Idol.

The Great Hall, United Service Club.

Causation and Causality

There remained after writing *Elixir* much about the causal relationships between the schools and the Empire that seemed worth pursuing. The very word 'causality' required attention. Dorothy Emmet in *The Effectiveness of Causes* argues for 'causation' but here 'causality' is preferred. The distinction, which seems to hinge on the former term suggesting *relationships* while the latter suggests *processes,* is not crucial.

There does not seem to have been a previous full length treatment of causality as far as the public schools are concerned. *Chapter I* considers the complexities inherent in considering causality. *Chapter II* explains how quickly such a topic acquires metaphysical dimensions and perplexities. In *Chapter III*, problems of prosopography as an adjunct to the search for causal factors are considered. With the advent of the computer, the time is not distant of being able to amass and tabulate completely the educational backgrounds of Imperial services such as the Indian Civil Service. A detailed prosopographical approach to any one of the Imperial services may confirm that the small number who ran the Empire were not only public school products, but were related by family to those who ran the public schools, to the headmasters and to the influential assistant masters. *Chapter IV* reviews the influences other than schooling in a man's life. *Chapter V* looks at the darker implications of the public schools for Imperial careers.

Chapter VI and *Chapter VII* emphasize that the schools affected other institutions, taking as a case the gentlemen's clubs – opinion-making institutions whose culture was "old school tie". The connections between the Empire, the clubs, and the schools have not been extensively explored, despite the omnipresence of the clubs in Victorian life and their importance as the settings of Imperial ceremony and intrigue. (See *The Great Hall, United Service Club,* page 19.) *Chapter VIII* looks towards the possible future developments in Imperial and public school scholarship.

Illustrations should not be a tea break from the text. Photographs and pictures are not wrapping paper. For example, in the case of those that show buildings, it should be emphasized that architecture was an ingredient of Imperialism. The ornamentalism of the Victorians may seem non-utilitarian and wasteful, but in a subtle way confirmed Veblen's stricture that respectability depends on being wasteful. The visual record is as much part of history as written documents.[10]

Similarly, footnotes are INTEGRAL to a narrative and are HEURISTIC as well as bibliographical. With the computing interest in hypertext and the linking of files in hierarchical and lateral pathways, footnotes in the compendious Victorian fashion are being electronically revived. As with badminton, they can induce a stiff neck in the reader – but although a Harvardian, this writer is unreconciled to the much misused Harvard citation method which enigmatically inserts in the text such cryptograms as *"Tolstoy, War and Peace"*. It was interesting to see the pungent comments of Harry Slade in the *Times Literary Supplement* (10 March 1989) about how ". . . the Harvard system, in which the text is peppered with surnames and dates, was devised for archaeological or technical papers where the writers have little to say and less facility for saying it." Writers about public schools have much to say!

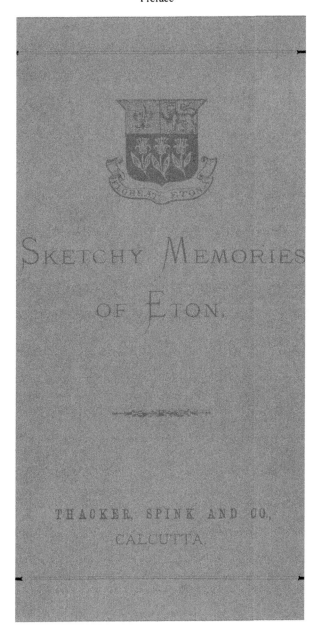

SKETCHY MEMORIES

OF ETON.

THACKER, SPINK AND CO.,
CALCUTTA.

Chains of Empire – P. J. Rich

Citing *Sketchy Memories of Eton*

There are many shelves of books about the public schools, but there is at least one book which is cited here frequently which is not cited elsewhere in the literature. That is Sir Melville Macnaghten's *Sketchy Memories of Eton*. (See *Sketchy Memories*, page 21.) Mrs. P. Hatfield, the Archivist of Eton College, has rightly pointed out in correspondence that *Sketchy Memories* is not referred to by Edward Mack in his monumental and inclusive two volume work on the public schools. It should have been, because it is an outstanding example of a number of books by old boys overseas whose memories of school grew more emotional as the distance from England increased. An enterprising publisher could market reprints of some of this material in editions that focus on the importance of the genre, in a format resembling that of Professor B. Clark's recent Oxford University Press edition of Evelyn Sharpe's *The Making of a Schoolgirl*.

Macnaghten came from a family of Etonians who wrote a number of school reminiscences, yet *Sketchy Memories* is not mentioned in *any* book about the public schools. Macnaghten's use of the Eton boating song written by William Cory Johnson, with its reference to binding chains, gives this book its title. Richard Ollard remarks in *An English Education* that Cory epitomises Eton "in his universality as in his limitations, in his scepticism as in his ardour". He was a strange combination of radical, rationalist, and romantic, and he was one of those Victorian schoolmasters who worshipped youth and sacrificed everything to be near it; his part in creating the public school mystique was considerable.

Metaphors about chains are frequent in writings about causality. As Dr. Donald Leinster-Mackay notes, the word brings to mind Arthur O. Lovejoy's germinal *The Great Chain of Being*. In discussing Jung, F. David Peat remarks, "Causality is defined as 'a chain of cause and effect'. This suggests a CHAIN or series of links, in which each one is firmly locked into its two neighbours so that the whole chain is able to stretch out indefinitely in both directions. In this way every event in the universe is causally linked to an event that comes before it, and to one that comes afterward."[11]

Britannia

Because the *English Public Schools and Ritualistic Imperialism* trilogy deals with symbolism in education and government, the books appropriately are graced by jackets sporting Mr. Kevin Smart's sardonic vision of Britannia, a heroine who changes from the cynical lady on the cover of *Elixir* into the bespangled strumpet adorning *Rituals*. Appropriately, it was an Old Etonian, Edward Arne, who composed the music for "Rule Britannia".

Britannia has been invoked in many causes, as shown by the threatening *Punch* cartoon of 1911 depicting the emaciated lady that would be produced by a reduction in Royal Navy appropriations. (See *Britannia*, page 23.) Her trident is blunted and her shield is second-hand, and she sums up a point of view. Rupert Sheldrake asserts in

A Little-Navy Exhibit.
Design for a figure of Britannia, as certain people would like to see her.

Chains of Empire – P. J. Rich

The Guardian ("Myth Taken", 10 February 1988) that Mrs. Thatcher is a true heir to Britannia. Which of the ladies has the more attractive figure is left to others, but Mother Britain has been around a long time. She parades as a Roman provincial goddess in the second century A.D. Her trident is eighteenth-century, and her Athenian helmet is a nineteenth-century addition. Mr. Smart's additions to her wardrobe include a schoolmaster's mortar-board adorning the lion for *Elixir,* a Masonic apron and schoolboy's boater for *Chains,* and the 'gongs' of the imperial orders for the forthcoming *Rituals.* It is noteworthy that the British embraced Britannia as a national patroness rather than Lady Godiva!

Totems added to Britannia's wardrobe through the years testify to the myth-makers' versatility. The merits of Britannia, Germania, and Marianne can be endlessly debated. The ladies acquired clothing as the nineteenth century progressed, and noticeable is Marianne's lamentable change from a fetching bare-breasted and attractive activist into a pudgy schoolmistress. French friends claim that the politics of towns can be determined by the amount of clothes that Marianne has on. The scantier representations are in the socialist bastions. Presumably changes will occur to the ladies' appearance in years to come. Each age has its controlling images. A reminder was the appearance in Peking's Tiananmen Square of a thirty foot high "Goddess of Democracy", a challenge to the huge picture of Chairman Mao which had hitherto dominated the Forbidden City.

The controversy about *quality* and *equality* in education is very much alive. Plans to allow state maintained schools in Britain to 'opt-out' and acquire considerable autonomy should heighten debate over what course secondary education should take in the twenty-first century. Dr. John Rae, longtime Harrow teacher and then headmaster of Westminster, has captured the headlines by denouncing the "malign spell" of the public schools and urging that they be abolished or turned into sixth-form colleges. Claiming that they "stifle at birth" the opportunities of those who do not attend, Dr. Rae accuses them of obstructing efforts to educate the general population.[12] There are those who would assert with justice that imperialism of one sort or another is not a dead issue.

Ritualistic propping-up of the state can be dangerous. Britannia's lion, as well as Uncle Sam's eagle and Ivan's bear, must be kept in bounds. Rupert Sheldrake has remarked ". . . if we forget it, then there is no alternative to the cult of a monetaristic Britannia, complete with her nuclear Trident." History's perspective helps to keep the would be guardians and their predatory mascots enchained.

NOTES – PREFACE

Publications at London unless otherwise noted.

1. Michael Tooley, *Causation: A Realist Approach,* Clarendon Press, Oxford 1987, 5. "In a sense, all historians are revisionists, for unless they merely tell the same old story in different words, each tries to make some contribution that changes our understanding . . .". Donald Kagan, "The First Revisionist Historian", *Connections,* Vol. 85, No. 5, May 1988, 43. "Perception is very important – but we will see Rutland in different ways: is there a native view as opposed to a commuter's view? Is there an internal as well as an external view? Is there an official view? Is there an R.A.F. view? Is there a public schools'

view?" *Rutland Review*, No. 9, 1989, 298. See L. Jonathan Cohen, "Grounds for Realism", *Times Higher Education Supplement*, 2 February 1990, 20. Invaluable for background is Peter Novick, *That Noble Dream: The Objectivity Question and The American Historical Profession*, Cambridge University Press (hereafter CUP), 1988.

2. Christopher Lloyd, *Explanation in Social History*, Basil Blackwell, 1986, 8. *Cf.* Bob Jessop, "Poulantzas and Foucault on Power and Strategy", *Ideas and Production*, Issue Six, 1987, 61, 79.

3. Enid Welsford, qtd. Peter McLaren, *Schooling as a Ritual Performance: Towards a Political Economy of Educational Symbols and Gestures*, Routledge & Kegan Paul, 2. This of course relates both to how authority is created and maintained. See, *e.g.*, Tom Pitt-Aikens and Alice Thomas Ellis, *Loss of the Good Authority: The Cause of Delinquency*, Viking, 1989, esp. 2, 32, 70, 106, 119.

4. See McLaren, *Schooling as a Ritual Performance*, 2-3. *Cf.* Theodore S. Hamcrow, *Reflections on History and Historians*, University of Wisconsin Press, Madison, 1987. Also see Paula Miller, "Education and The State: The Uses of Marxist and Feminist Approaches in the Writing of Histories of Schooling", *Historical Studies in Education*, Vol. 1, No. 2, Fall 1989, 283-306.

5. George Levine, *et al.*, *Speaking for the Humanities*, American Council of Learned Societies Occasional Paper No. 7, New York, 1989, 6.

6. *Ibid.*, 7. "There should be no monopolies in the humanities . . . Cross-disciplinary work provides critical corrections of the assumptions of disciplines and generates new insights, as well as errors that can lead specialists to rethink what needs to be said to prevent them." *Ibid.*, 8.

7. J. A. Mangan ed., *'Benefits Bestowed'?: Education and British Imperialism*, Manchester University Press, 1988, 6, 8.

8. See Peter Cunningham, "Educational History and Educational Change: The Past Decade of English Historiography", *History of Education Quarterly*, Vol. 29, No. 1, Spring 1989, 90-91.

9. Thailand is a good example, as many of the ruling élite went to English public schools. The longtime Minister for Education, Prince Dhani Nivat, was a devoted Old Rugbeian. See M. L. Pin Malakul, "Education During the Time When His Highness Prince Dhai Ninvat was Minister of Public Instruction", *Siam Society Journal*, Vol. 63, June 1975, 9-27. Also *The Siam Society Under Five Reigns*, n.a. The Siam Society, Bangkok, 1989, 189-90. Also, *Collected Articles by H.H. Prince Dhani Nivat*, The Siam Society, Bangkok, 1976.

10. Placing illustrations in a segregated section implies that they are incidental. Their significance should be emphasized by integration in the text. See Maurice Sendak, *Caldecott & Co.: Notes on Books & Pictures*, Reinhardt, 1988. The illustrations in this book are ones that were popular and common in their day and hence were an *influence* as well as a reflection of the times. They were obtained from London print dealers, primarily those in the shops of Cecil Court. They appeared in magazines such as *Punch, Illustrated London News, Illustrated Times, Chums*, and *Boy's Own Paper*. For an introduction to such *meubles* as history, see James Lever, *Victoriana*, Ward Lock, 1966. As for photographs, "In the recording of exotic cultures in the nineteenth century, the photographer was producing a vivid image of people who had little idea of what preconceptions for a 'good likeness' were . . . [resulting in] portraits of rare dignity, psychological intensity and revealing penetration." Ken Jacobson, "Exotic Portraits", *The Photo Historian*, No. 86, Autumn 1989, 48.

11. F. David Peat, *Synchronicity: The Bridge Between Matter and Mind*, Bantam, 1987, 35-36. Indeed, Victorian ritualism was based on considerable previous ritualistic revivalism: ". . . (the) pattern of development of the medieval revival in the fields of heraldry – its last use on the fields of the tournament in the reign of Charles I; its ultimate decline and apparent extinction in the 1730's; its reappearance and steady return to fashion amongst the upper classes from about the accession of George III in 1760; its final restriction to a state of universal national popularity in the reign of William IV and the early years of Queen Victoria – this cycle over the period of two centuries was the same for all other branches of the whole Gothic movement and thus for the movement as a whole." Ian Anstruther, *The Knight and The Umbrella: An Account of the Eglinton Tournament 1819*, Alan Sutton, 1986, 84.

12. Qtd. in *The Daily Telegraph*, 5 June 1989, 7.

CHAPTER I

Preludes

To render unto Fettes the things that are Fettes. – W. Wallace, *Fifty Years of Fettes,* 1931.

Every college, except Magdalen and the House which were dominated by Eton and Westminster, who wear their ties with a difference, was in its corporate aspect an appendage of the Public School system. – Sir Charles Petrie, *Scenes of Edwardian Life,* 1965.

The tradition of preserving traditions became a tradition. – Jonathan Gathorne-Hardy, *The Old School Tie,* 1978.

Arrogance and Condescension, feelings of superiority and male chauvinism are not the virtues of a democratic society. But even today people are being brought up in this spirit, in 'public schools' during youth or in gentlemen's Clubs during adulthood. – Werner Glinga, *Legacy of Empire,* 1986.

Enthusiasts of Conan Doyle will recall Dr. Watson's troubles in understanding the significance of a dog that didn't bark, until Sherlock Holmes explained that it was precisely the lack of barking that was important. What Watson missed was a subtlety of causality, but just as perilous as overlooking causes is attributing them to phantasies. (Holmes was allegedly a boy at Winchester College, where in 1869 at the age of fifteen he solved 'The Case of the Devil's Hoofmarks', an episode recounted in a Cambridge University Press book by Allen Sharp.) The eighteenth-century conviction that combustion was due to a mythical substance, phlogiston, exemplifies reliance on imagination rather than reality.

The search for historical causality continues to be frustrating because its offshoots and possibilities persistently proliferate. As a consequence, there are numerous approaches to studying the British Empire. The biologist J. B. S. Haldane, asked to state his idea of God, replied, "He is inordinately fond of beetles." (There are 350,000 catalogued species.) He is also fond of causes. New ones appear with alarming frequency. Genetic mapping may eventually point to an 'Imperial personality'. Currently historical epidemiology is reviewing how pandemic influenza may have created opportunities for Imperial political penetration. As if historical climatology was not specific enough, the wind has become a focus of speculation as far as its Imperial consequences, involving topics such as trade routes, irrigation and windmill technology. The future will produce more of such insights and demand more 'rethinking' of Imperialism than anyone can anticipate. The wise

27

will keep their options open, but agreement is not in sight. One man's scarab is another's beetle.

Speculation about an emotional subject such as Imperialism has produced dilemmas in distinguishing reality from illusion. While the growth of the British Empire was matched by a growing pride in PATRIA, the causes have led to considerable debate.[1] What is clear is that the growth of Imperialism paralleled a revived ritualism in British life, a gallimaufry of contrived rites. The metaphors that were summoned up to serve the Empire were astonishing. In 1897 *Punch* was able to combine Roman, Teutonic, Indian, and other motifs in its tribute to Queen Victoria. (See *For Queen and Empire!!*, below.) This enthusiastic ritual-making has been somewhat ignored because ritual is supposed to have more to do with 'natives' and with 'primitive' culture than with sophisticated political scenarios.[2] Ritualism has supernatural and magical connotations that make historians uneasy. Nevertheless, ritualism has always been at the heart of political activity, and the British Empire was no exception. The Empire was bolstered by an elaborate ceremonialism whose mundane origins were sometimes conveniently forgotten.[3]

What more can a historian today add to the discussion of Imperialism? It seems that attention should be given to the resonances of the ritualism taught by the English public schools. The schools are near the epicentre of the Empire. J. A. Hobson, the author of the classic work *Imperialism* (1901) that influenced Lenin, thought that the Empire's iconography owed something to the "dominant and aggressive personality" of schoolmasters who were "deceived as to the inner meaning and effects of the services they render to reaction".[4] Imperial history was affected by the totems and talismans that the English public schools employed from "the lumber room of rubbish which goes by the name of history".[5]

'For Queen and Empire!!'

Preludes

Not everyone is astringent about the borrowed sources of ritual's imagery. Jung for one writes at length about the treasures which humankind draws on, and it is hard to conceive of a society without adornment and ceremony.[6] However, the schools' part in this, when noted at all, has been treated either as a whale or a weasel – as immense, ill-defined, and sited only in passing, or to be ferreted out of hiding by a painful particularism. Histories of schools politely avoid political implications. Public school historians in the main have resembled "a legion of gradgrinds . . . wound up like mechanical rabbits and set to running about in ever-smaller circles".[7] Most discussion that has taken place has been deadly dull. But no consideration of Imperialism can be considered to be thorough without discussion of the public schools. The schools' topic should be tackled neither metahistorically, thus offering an easy mark for critics of holism, nor in such detail as to recall Macaulay's jibe that "if history were written thus, the Bodleian library would not contain the occurrences of a week".[8] This makes for a difficult assignment, but the pitfalls are more easily avoided than other conundrums, those raised by causality.

A Search for Imperial Paradigms

Writing history about the Empire (or any other subject) *should* require thinking about causal theories.[9] A single sentence can reveal a host of assumptions. The short statement that "Thomas Arnold reformed Rugby School" disguises numerous theories about an individual's part in institutions. The search of educational historians for successful PARADIGMS[10] has been long, wide-ranging, and exasperating. Keeping up with the revisionists daunts the most voracious readers. To make matters more confusing, the mind itself has been proclaimed by neurophysiologists as really consisting of several minds.[11] Rather than alarming, this perhaps should be welcomed as a handy explanation for human indecisiveness. But whether ultimately humans are found to house one mind or several, their behaviour is the product of a coalition of complex causes.[12]

Investigating causality means weighing these causes, and leads to proposals that often are too inclusive or too exclusive: too inclusive because they attribute to multiple and esoteric reasons what can be accounted for by more commonplace causes, and too exclusive because in enumerating the reasons a simplistic approach can exclude the less obvious. Recent social history has taken causal concerns to extremes. The exploration of permutations has verged on nit-picking. While digging into causes has always been part of writing good history, and while heuristic argument is part of that process, the excesses have justly been censured.[13]

Still, putting aside whether or not social history is such a revolutionary enterprise, and granting that criticism is warranted if the historian ignores political history or other 'older' approaches, much of the criticism is unwarranted. Social historians have contributed to a constructive swing towards the REHISTORIZATION of the social sciences. A trend is emerging for relating the history of education to political history, thus buttressing the argument for relating the English public schools to Imperialism

29

and putting the history of education into the mainstream of historical discourse.

A contention in this volume, and in the trilogy generally, is that the schools' connection with the Empire arises out of the fact that they were intensely ritualistic institutions. However, ". . . few people recognize how important ritual is in modern politics. Because ritual is usually identified with religion, and since modern Western societies have presumably separated political affairs from religious life, there is an assumption that ritual remains politically significant only in less 'advanced societies'."[14] For this and allied reasons, the rituals of Empire and their associations with the public schools have not been fully explored. When they have been noticed, detailed consideration has been disdained on the grounds that a low-visibility underclass was being overlooked and deserved the bulk of attention.[15]

Neither the proponents of *Meisterwerk* nor friends of the downtrodden should question the relevance of ritualism and the public schools, because the schools influenced not only their own students but British culture. This is evident in the mass youth movements: "The Boys' Brigade and the Boy Scouts drew on the deep reserves of Charterhouse, Clifton and Wellington at a time when the *ars militaris* was at least being practically developed in the public school cadet corps."[16] One reason that this has not been emphasized is that Dr. Harold Silver and Sir Arthur Bryant are unlikely soul mates.

Indiana Jones and Kurt Hildebrandt

The proliferation of historical specialities is redolent of medical specialities, a further instance of PARTICULARIZATION helping with diagnosis. A corollary is that, just as the general practitioner has been routed by the medical specialists, the proliferating historiographies complicate synthesis by historians and deny history an audience of intelligent lay people. *The general approach to history is still needed.* This book endorses the approach taken by the theorist Kurt Hildebrant, the consequences of which were evident in successful work such as Paul Wittek's 'ghazification' of Ottoman history, *e.g.* the extension of Ottoman studies to include social history, without losing a political perspective.[17]

As anodine, rash, or romantic as *general approaches* may be, the *general reader* cannot wait generations for the smoke of academic battle to clear and a glimpse of the past to emerge. She wants a panoramic view and enjoys the musings of the metahistorians. There is a place for what Michael Oakeshott calls, not always approvingly, the contemplative mode.[18] Happily there has been a revival of historical romanticism – encouraging because despite the value of writing criticisms about history there is a need to write history. Without jumping on the bandwagon and flaying Oakeshott, who concededly is an unlovable writer, it should be noted that his failure to write history is as noteworthy as his ability to write about the writing of it. His criticisms taken to a logical conclusion would bring historians to a full stop.

On the other hand, while historians need to be prodded into moving away from minutiae, any rectifications 'under the romantic influence' need to be made cautiously. Oakeshott warns, "In short, the word 'cause' in historical discourse is commonly a loose, insignificant expression . . .".[19] A discussion of causality is always in danger of becoming arcane. The Germans, with a seeming ability to have a juicy word for every condition, refer to *Verstehen, the notion that history had to be* emotionally felt. Perhaps locked inside every bespectacled academic there is an Indiana Jones yearning to be a Toynbee, or *vice versa,* with sometimes disastrous results.

History does have emotional underpinnings, and ritual involves manipulating the emotions. *Elixir of Empire* put forward the thesis that many rituals of British Imperialism originated in the English public schools. If the elixir of Imperialism was ritual that sustained morale *(esprit, élan)* and gave the Imperial ruling élite its cohesion,[20] the ritualism can be traced back to the ways in which those schools "presupposed an adult way of life quite startlingly unlike the 'natural' life of people at most times, in most societies".[21] The attitudes inculcated by the public schools were an expression of what is sometimes called SOCIAL IMPERIALISM. Let it be repeated that the working classes were given an ample dose through popular novels and magazines, and through organizations such as the Lads' Drill Association and Federation of Working-Boys' Clubs.[22]

Secret Passwords

The public schools developed their own vocabulary and were identified with a famous or infamous accent. This is a reason, though not the only one, why the startling developments in semiotics should be incorporated in discussion of the schools, including the work of Umberto Eco. *The Name of the Rose* brought Eco to popular notice, but in a successor novel that is much more a reflection of his research, *Il Pendolo di Foucault (Foucault's Pendulum)*, he examines alchemistic movements such as the Freemasons, Templars, and Rosicrucians, and the consequences of secret ritualistic cultures. The three movements had their public school supporters and their Imperial versions which spread throughout the Empire.

Fraternal orders are not the only evidence supporting the hypothesis of public school 'rule by ritual', or the sole instance of school ritualism inspiring important social and political developments. John MacAloon in *This Great Symbol* claims that the Olympic movement with all its mythical images recovered its impetus from the indelible impression the public schools made on its founder, Pierre de Coubertini. David Kertzer in *Ritual, Politics and Power* (1988) remarks:

> The role of ritual in impressing foreign political powers is also much in evidence in colonial administration, where great emphasis was placed on ritual display as a means of communicating the authority and power of the rulers. This typically took the form of local ritual display of colonial superiority, but occasionally it involved bringing local indigenous rulers to

the colonial homeland for a ritual lesson . . . It would be difficult, though, to top the Aztecs in the use of ritual to intimidate the emissaries of other peoples. On special occasions, such as the dedication of a new temple, Aztec rulers invited kings and notables from neighbouring societies to observe their rites, which always included human sacrifice.[23]

Imperial and public school ritualism was equally distinctive, although usually less dramatic (except in the pages of *Chums* and the penny dreadfuls). Ritology as a discipline challenges entrenched political and educational presumptions – particularly those that view Imperialism as the product of causes which are more 'physical' than ritualism, such as the need for markets or military security. (The day is past when physicalism is acceptable to physicists, but not to some historians.) Consideration of the school influence not only means revising ideas about Imperialism and the Third World, but also modifying notions about the motives of the Imperial rulers. It is a matter of understanding the collective mentality of a public school cadre that sought *communitas* throughout their lives: "The Group attempts to span the gap separating self from others positively and directly. It believes in natural solidarities which it reinforces with appeals to tradition and trust, and in ritual."[24]

Cunning Causality

The questioning of causality brings one to a crossroads meeting of speculations about philosophy, science, history, and education. Any more than a cursory discussion invokes metaphysics. Contributing is the accelerating decay of the Copernican world of the physicists where causes and effects were demonstrable. Mario Biagioli refers in a study of the philosopher of science Emile Meyerson to the "cunning of causality", and comments wistfully, "To see a law in nature is an act of will or – as Meyerson puts it – a limited miracle that the scientists perform to perceive the identity of causes and effects."[25]

Scholars display, despite the obstacles, a stubborn determination to explain events – but their explanations must constantly be revised to have any validity.[26] A lesson that should have been learned by now is that the mechanistic explanations of the last hundred years are in doubt. As a corollary, evidence has accumulated that social history is not a visionary voyeurism but a necessary corrective to the over-emphasis on political history. This involves causal explanations that go beyond traditional boundaries. Mary Warnock remarks, "No one has heard a three year old lately able to utter only single words, saying things like 'The difficulty with me is, I don't *want* to go to bed', or 'it looks to me as if my brother has been at it' can fail to toy with a Chomskian or Cartesian notion of innate ideas, the deep structures of language being in us from before birth."[27]

In respect to arguments for a more mysterious world than many are comfortable living in, contributions of Rupert Sheldrake may prove to be significant. Sheldrake in *A New Science of Life* and *The Presence of the Past* has revived vitalism, the

Aristotelian notion of a life force. In a critique of Richard Dawkins, a modern defender of Darwinism, Sheldrake claims that biology, after a long period of opposing VITALISM, (the doctrine that organisms are organised by purposive principles) has purposive organising principles of its own: GENETICS.[28] As Sheldrake would be the first to admit, his work was anticipated by Henri Bergson and by a Harvard psychologist, William McDougall. Dr. McDougall in the 1920s conducted experiments in which it seemed that rats performed better in mazes *because previous generations of rats had encountered the same maze.* This suggested that nature's laws were habits. Sheldrake's theory is not confined to the behaviour of living things – for that matter neither is the geneticism of Dawkins, who has proposed the existence of *memes,* units of cultural inheritance comparable to genes: "Examples of memes are tunes, ideas, catch-phrases, clothes fashions, ways of making pots or of building arches. Just as genes propagate themselves in the gene pool by leaping from body to body via sperm and eggs, so memes propagate themselves in the gene pool by leaping from brain to brain via a process which, in the broad sense, can be called imitation . . ".[29]

While Dawkins has stirred ample controversy with his notion of a causal chain starting with genes, [30] Sheldrake goes further than Dawkins in upsetting conventional causality. He postulates that there are 'morphic fields', a memory of nature which shapes events. These are organising patterns that can re-appear physically when conditions are appropriate: "The process by which the past becomes present with morphic fields is called MORPHIC RESONANCE. Morphic resonance involves the transmission of formative causal influences through both space and time."[31] This is grist for Jungian mills, offering explanation for the collective unconscious.

Sheldrake himself is cautious, and feels that his ideas should be proved or disproved by experiments. For example, some compounds that are synthesized for the first time do not readily crystallize. If a morphogenetic field is created, according to the Sheldrake hypothesis the amount of time required for crystallization should gradually diminish. There are other possible tests of the theory. The suggestion has been made that in Australia, where cattle-stops are common to prevent livestock from crossing roads, that there is a significance to the fact that ranchers find that fake guards which are merely painted on the road stop the cattle just as well as real ones. If that is the case, is it because cattle in the past learned to avoid getting their feet tangled in real guards? Thus morphic resonance would be at work. Or do Australian cattle dislike stripes, and not just ones resembling the grids that their ancestors fell into?

Melville Macnaghten

Possibly one turns with relief to more conventional ideas – including those of a number of truly Victorian old boys. Melville Macnaghten (1853-1921), who was to become head of Scotland Yard, wrote anonymously *Sketchy Memories of Eton, 1866-1872.* The son of a chairman of the East India Company, he was managing the family estates in Bengal when he produced the little book, which was printed in Calcutta in

1885. His brother Russell was a master at Harrow and his brother Hugh became a master at Eton and author of highly assorted Eton hagiography.

Macnaghten was at Eton in 1868-1872, at the start of the important headmastership of James Hornby (1868-1884) and at the abrupt end of the tenure of Eton's most important teacher of the period, Johnson Cory (1845-1872). In describing the typical Old Etonian, Macnaghten wrote that, ". . . whenever and wherever he hears our grand old boating ballad sung . . . (he) chimes in with 'And nothing on earth shall sever the chain that is round us now' with a truthful intensity that comes straight from his heart." As noted, Macnaghten's invocation of Cory's *Eton Boating Song* with its reference to chains suggested the title for this book and is representative of the nostalgic overseas old boy culture. Coincidentally, J. A. Mangan comments in *The Games Ethic and Imperialism* about Etonians in Calcutta at a time shortly after publication of Macnaghten's miscellany:

> Links between school and Empire were also maintained through the curious expedient of the regular provision of reports of nostalgic old boy dinners in obscure and less obscure parts of the Empire. One Old Etonian writing from Calcutta, for instance, described the table there for the Fourth of June celebrations of 1880 as 'arranged with the exquisite harmonies of Eton blue'. The servants wore complementary costumes and the evening was filled with reminiscences of days past interspersed with toasts to 'Cricket' and 'The Boats' and rounded off, of course, with 'The Boating Song'.[32]

These chains of what Macnaghten called "steadfast feeling of love" that lasted "as long as life itself" became the chains of Empire. Evidence for this is provided by an 'archaeological perspective' of rituals which although often described as if they were the lighter side of Imperialism were far more than its random twitches and spasms. Derek Verscholye remarked in his essay for Graham Greene's collection *The Old School,* that "It would be interesting if some social critic with full knowledge of the underworld of education and Imperial politics in the eighteenth and nineteenth centuries would plot the graph of cause and effect that unites the two systems . . .".[33] This writer hardly claims to be so knowledgeable, but this book does consider the causes and effect of public school ritualism.

Macnaghten writes about the *Boating Song* as if it were hoary with age. It was not, but the desire to believe that it was illustrates of what was happening to embellish the public schools and to link them to the Empire. In this connection, one should recall that when he wrote the song in 1863, Johnson Cory did so with Etonians serving the Empire in mind: "I thought of young men quartered in Indian hill-forts, droning in twos, or singly through a steaming night, miserably remembering their last row at Eton, pining and carving for lost youthfulness."[34] Cory as an Eton master profoundly influenced the boyhoods of Rosebery and Curzon, and in testimony to the Clarendon Commission and the book *Eton Reform* took on the mantel of defender of Eton's traditions. His dismissal for writing an affectionate letter to a young friend only enhances his significance: a biography is long overdue. Sir Henry Newbolt celebrated him, and poetically invoked (might one remark?) morphic resonance, in *Iconicus:*

> *Beyond the book his teaching sped,*
> *He left on whom he taught the trace*
> *Of kinship with the deathless dead,*
> *And faith in all the Island Race.*

The careers in the *Eton School Register* of those who were Macnaghten's contemporaries in the 1860s and 1870s demonstrate how Imperially-connected the old boys were. One schoolmate was James E. C. Welldon, headmaster of Dulwich and Harrow and Metropolitan of Calcutta. Another was John Broderick, the Secretary of State for India whose altercation with Curzon contributed to his resigning as Viceroy. Nor to be forgotten is Henry Sandbach, "who died unmarried at Aden of wounds by a lioness in Somaliland, in trying to save a native attendant"; William McAdam Steuart, District Traffic Superintendent of the Southern Mahratta Railway, Dharwar, India; Major The Hon. Charles Winn, who "died unmarried at Umballa from an accident at polo"; or Heywood Seton-Kerr who "Discovered the Prehistoric Flint Mines in Somaliland and in Egypt, and the Egyptian Emerald Mines".

There were legions of Etonian tea-planters and winners of medals and clasps in now forgotten campaigns *(Egypt 1882 including Tel-el-Kebir Med. with clasp, 5th Cl. Medjidie, Khedive's Star)*. Others included Herbert Paul, the legal member of the Council of India; Melville Portal, the explorer who died accompanying his brother in Uganda; Henry Streatfeild, who set something of a record by being aide to the Governor-General of Canada, the Viceroy of India, the Lord Lieutenant of Ireland, and Field Marshal Earl Roberts; Stephen Burrows, director of education in Ceylon; and Thomas Harvey, Wellington College master and tutor to the children of the Maharaja of Baroda.

Imperialist Educationists

The public school STYLE was spread by old boys who became teachers as well as by those who became colonial administrators. Teaching in a public school was socially acceptable at home as well as overseas. Eton contemporaries of Macnaghten who took up schoolmastering include the Eton masters Raymond Radcliffe, James Joynes, Edward Impey, and Henry Salt; Frederick Armitstead, master at Uppingham; Arthur Tabor, headmaster of Cheam preparatory school; Edward Selwyn (who married Thomas Arnold's daughter), headmaster of Uppingham; George Sayer, master at Bradfield; John Charles, headmaster of Newcastle preparatory school; Alfred Cooke, headmaster of Aldenham; Clement Bryans, master at Fettes and Dulwich; Henry Calthrop, Bursar of Eton; Edward Lyttelton, the headmaster of Haileybury and Eton (an account of his sacking as head of Eton in 1916 would itself make a good book about schools and power); and Charles Crowder, master at Bromsgrove and Cheam.

In short, schools produced numerous Imperialists and educationists and these interests often were combined in one and the same individual. Moreover, the chains were strong not only between the schools and their students but between them and those who were not entitled as old boys to sing the boating ballad or any other public school song, but venerated the institution. The public school spirit became the spirit of British society and the Empire. Writers such as J. G. Cotton Minchin in *Old Harrow Days* (1898) and *Our Public Schools* (1901) celebrated the union.

Notwithstanding these *primae facie* indications of the influence of the public school ethos on society at large, the effects were two way.[35] At about the same time that Cory's lyrics were being sung by Etonians in Calcutta, other Imperial enthusiasts were at work – Charles Dilke's *Greater Britain* appeared in 1868, John Robert Seeley published *The Expansion of England* in 1883, and James Anthony Froude's *Oceana, or England and Her Colonies* appeared in 1886.[36] The public school influence can be connected with such efforts, but it really comes into its own in the many manifestations of popular culture which are still unexplored. As John MacKenzie points out in his useful *Propaganda and Empire: The Manipulation of British Public Opinion, 1880-1960:* ". . . there has been little attempt at a synthesis of studies of education, juvenile literature, the theatre, youth organisations, and propagandist movements . . .".[37]

Considering the neglect of the subject, this book may be described not as a redescription of a well understood phenomenon but rather as a different approach – not as a **fuller description** of what happened but rather as a **fresh explanation** of what happened. It undoubtedly will surrender to fuller explanations. Peerages these days are for life only, rather than hereditary.[38]

Rough Ashlars

Freemasonry and the public schools enjoyed close associations. Masonic lodge rooms, including those of the school lodges, display a rough ashlar by the master's throne as a physical reminder that the institution shapes men. (See *Masonic Rough Ashlar,* page 37.) Near the rough ashlar there is placed a finished stone representing the polished result of Masonic activity, a forceful indication of a causal relationship – or of a hoped-for relationship.

Historians have been less confident than the Freemasons about the influence of institutions. Few have offered more than passing analysis of the consequences on lives of schooling or lodge and club membership. Despite the voluminous literature on the public schools, the reader seldom encounters any consideration of the significance of the schools to general history. The other side of the coin is that historians have been reticent about giving a place in general histories to educational history, let alone to a specific topic such as the public schools. They 'get by' with a nod towards education (and other social topics).[39]

This is a deficiency, because *successful* political rule has depended less on force than on, in Antonio Gramsci's much-quoted phrase, *cultural hegemony.*[40] There is

Rough Ashlar and Pedestal.

VISIT YOUR SONS AND DAUGHTERS !

" Monthly Return " Tickets at 1d.-a-Mile (3rd Class), and 1½d.-a-Mile (1st Class) are issued throughout the year between any two stations (minimum fares 7/6 1st class, 5/- 3rd class), available for return any time up to one month. Following are some specimen Fares between London and the principal School-towns served by the

SOUTHERN RAILWAY

TOWN.	From or To	RETURN FARE.		TOWN.	From or To	RETURN FARE.	
		1st.	3rd.			1st.	3rd.
ASHFORD (KENT)..	Charing Cross	14/9	9/9	HORSHAM	Victoria ..	9/9	6/6
BATTLE	Charing Cross	14/9	9/9	HOVE	Victoria ..	13/3	8/9
BEXHILL	Charing Cross	16/3	10/9	HYTHE (KENT) ..	Charing Cross	17/9	11/9
BIRCHINGTON-ON-SEA.	Victoria ..	18/-	12/-	LANCING	Victoria ..	14/9	9/9
BOGNOR REGIS ..	Victoria ..	17/-	11/3	LYNDHURST	Waterloo ..	21/6	14/3
BOURNEMOUTH (CENTRAL)	Waterloo ..	27/-	18/-	MAIDSTONE (EAST)	Victoria	10/6	7/-
BRIGHTON	Victoria ..	13/3	8/9	MARGATE	Victoria ..	18/9	12/6
BROADSTAIRS ..	Victoria ..	19/6	13/-	PARIS	Victoria {	Ask at S.R. Stations.	
BURGESS HILL ..	Victoria ..	10/6	7/-	RAMSGATE	Victoria ..	19/6	13/-
BUXTED	Victoria ..	11/3	7/6	RYE	Charing Cross	18/9	12/6
CANTERBURY (EAST)	Victoria ..	15/9	10/6	RYDE	Waterloo ..	21/9	14/6
CHRIST'S HOSPITAL	Victoria ..	10/3	6/9	ST. LEONARDS ..	Charing Cross	16/3	10/9
DEAL	Charing Cross	21/6	14/3	SEAFORD	Victoria ..	15/-	10/-
DOVER	Charing Cross	20/3	13/6	SHOREHAM-BY-SEA	Victoria	14/3	9/6
DROXFORD	Waterloo ..	16/3	10/9	SIDMOUTH	Waterloo ..	42/-	28/-
EASTBOURNE	Victoria ..	16/3	10/9	SOUTHAMPTON ..	Waterloo ..	20/-	13/3
EXETER	Waterloo ..	43/3	28/9	SOUTHSEA	Waterloo ..	18/9	12/6
FARNHAM	Waterloo ..	9/9	6/6	SWANAGE	Waterloo ..	33/-	22/-
FOLKESTONE (CTL.)	Charing Cross	18/6	12/3	TAVISTOCK	Waterloo ..	53/9	35/9
GODALMING	Waterloo ..	9/-	6/-	TONBRIDGE	Charing Cross	8/-	5/3
HASTINGS	Charing Cross	16/3	10/9	WAREHAM	Waterloo ..	30/6	20/3
HAWKHURST	Charing Cross	12/-	8/-	WESTGATE-ON-SEA	Victoria ..	18/6	12/3
HERNE BAY	Victoria ..	16/3	10/9	WORTHING	Victoria ..	15/-	10/-

nothing illusory about hegemony: its results are as evident as the Freemason's ashlar. Of the institutions devised to shape opinion and turn the 'rough ashlars' into leaders, the English public school must be reckoned as one of the most effective, exerting its hegemonic influence on all of Imperial education and on more besides.[41]

Publication in 1972 of Correlli Barnett's feisty *The Collapse of British Power* made it rash to discuss any Imperial topics without considering the controversies about the public school's allegedly 'Jesuitical' influence. There is no lack of evidence. Since E. C. Mack produced what at the time seemed a definitive two-volume survey *The Public Schools and British Opinion* (1938, 1941) hundreds of additional titles have been produced. Reviewers will continue to groan and authors will continue to apologise, because the topic is not exhausted. Long before Barnett's polemics, it was evident that the public school occupied a remarkable niche in British culture. The former Southern Railway's locomotive series 900-940 named after famous schools are a large example of how much of a place. There is symbolic significance to naming such behemoths 'Harrow' and 'Tonbridge'. (See *Visit Your Sons and Daughters!*, page 38.)

Regarding the proliferation of books about the public schools as the mere belabouring of a historical byway ignores that the schools are as outstanding an example of education's influence on history as a historian can find. Sensing this, Barnett did for the public schools and political history what Cyril Connolly's "theory of Permanent Adolescence" did for the schools and social history by showing that links existed between the schools and Britain's economic and technical fortunes. The expansion of the schools in relation to the growth of the Empire were discussed in *Elixir of Empire,* which offered examples of how the most farouche outposts of the British Empire felt the influence of ritualistic voyeurism. (See *Prince of Wales Views Native Beauty,* page 40.)

The growth of the schools and at the same time of an Imperial **fervour** are associated. Although Imperial ambitions were a longstanding part of British politics, they intensified as the schools' involvement with the Empire became important – approximately during the era of Disraelian Imperialism. The term 'imperialism' changed its meaning from a pejorative one that was used derisively against Napoleon III in the 1850s to the proud assertion of the 1880s. Although J. Gallagher and colleagues have demonstrated that this late Victorian Imperial enthusiasm was not such a sudden volte-face in attitude as has been claimed, it remains that there was an outpouring of enthusiasm for the Empire in the later nineteenth century.[42]

An important argument in subsequent chapters is that the public school spirit profoundly influenced other institutions such as those bastions of 'The Establishment', the gentlemen's clubs. The clubs have been selected as an example of how what appeared to be independent agencies took on a public school colouring. They are an accepted and obvious part of the British scene, and blend into the landscape as if they were the post office or a government office. But there is little evidence that an independent club ethos was a force in the Empire, while there is considerable evidence that the influence of the clubs, and of regiments, learned societies and other social organisations, reflected the schooldays of members.[43] If an institution is a strong

mythic resonance — a strong pattern

one, it stands to reason that it will have a part in shaping other institutions. This was the case *par excellence* with the public school. In the gentlemen's club: ". . . they behave like a lot of adolescents – oh, very well brought up adolescents – with the run of the tuck shop."[44]

On King Edward's way to South Africa,
a native beauty dances for him at Freetown, Sierra Leone.

40

Preludes

"You Naturally Begin to Explain"

Causality *per se* is always appropriate as a subject of historical discussion – and in life: "If you live a daily life and it is all yours, and you come to own everything outside your daily life besides and it is all yours, you naturally begin to explain. You naturally continue describing your daily life which is all yours, and you naturally begin to explain how you own everything besides."[45] Unfortunately, no matter how natural it is to explain, as more causal influences have been 'discovered' by historians, the problems of causality have grown more complicated. The competition between different explanations may account for the light way in which schooling has been treated both by biographers and by historians in general.

They understandably have too much on their plate to give a primacy to any one cause, but how the twelve year old tyros of the third form turned into twenty-two year old tyrants of a native district deserves more thought than the topic has been given. To appreciate the neglect of the subject, the struggles of social history should be recalled, as this helps to explain why it is the *political* historians feel they have the proper perspective for writing 'general' history and why it is the *political* historians who feel qualified to be generalists.

Accounts of causality invariably include a mention of how David Hume in *Treatise of Human Nature* asserted that causality amounted to objects being contiguous to each other. The sequential conjunctions seemed to Hume to be simply that – and despite his interest in history and the success of his own *History of England,* he felt no obligation to show in any detail the significance of the proximity of events or if juxtaposition meant that one happening depended on another. Matters could scarcely have been left to rest there, and they were not. Pestalozzi, who of course was more a practitioner than a philosopher, in his *Inquiry into the Course of Nature in the Development of the Human Species* (1797) rhetorically asked if men would live as they did had they not been moulded and coerced. Obviously – he answered himself – men were the product of compulsion. Pestalozzi was unwilling to accept that history was a gigantic accident. For him and others after him, causality has been a continually provocative conundrum.

The effort to find laws midst coincidences has contributed to the proliferation of specialities, a process generating irritation amongst the politically-oriented historians previously dominating the scene. The political view was criticized as 'the Oxford attitude', personified in the holder of the Regius Chair, Edward Augustus Freeman (1823-92). The robinsonade approach was more successful in fiction than in history, and its counterpart in historical writing, political chronicle, had grave deficiencies. Another Regius professor, John Richard Green (1837-83) demonstrated a sensitivity to the problem by claiming in his *Short History of the English People* (1874) that he had devoted more pages to Methodism than to the escape of the Young Pretender.

Green was exceptional. The majority saw the 'higher' history as political. Auguste Comte (1798-1857) would be reckoned a historian had his contemporaries been more open-minded. They were not, and sociology has stolen attention that might have gone into historical studies. *This is hindsight producing insight, but the consequences for historical studies have been profound and negative.* The recent realisation that there is no such thing as a non-socialized person has consequences in so far as the historiography of Imperialism is concerned. Even at this date Imperialism is mainly studied as a political movement, which is patently inexcusable. Be it the British or any other variety of imperialism, political-economic explanations cannot suffice – particularly those chiliastic ones purporting to explain all but based only on evidence of diplomatic ambitions or economic avarice. (In retrospect, by the time Wilhelm Dilthey emphasised intellectual culture in his much translated and reprinted *The Study of the History of Science of Man, Society and the State* (1875) it should have been obvious that COLLECTIVE SYMBOLISM was a force in the construction of culture.)

There has been no decade since Dilthey without insights into ritualism's place in history, although there has been little effort to fit these developments into a view of causality. Social history has generally avoided challenging the prevailing Humean perspective that permeates political history – despite the unfriendly criticism levelled at social history by political historians.[46] This has begun to change.

The Networks

In fact, there are further changes on the horizon. The discussion of historical causality that has gone on over decades has expanded its horizons with the rise of psychohistory and an interest in the more nefarious aspects of social history. The founding of the International Society of Political Psychology and of its journal *Political Psychology* is an assault on the temple. Another example is the best-selling accusations made by the feminist Barbara Rogers, who blames the secret "network" for discrimination against women, taking to task not only the old boys but also the Freemasons and the "upmarket large city clubs": "I began to see very clearly how thoroughly the social clubs, where the British establishment, very often public school and Oxbridge educated men, meet, are a mechanism for enforcing inequality." Rogers alleges that the network includes societies such as the Knights of Malta, Freemasons, and the Livery Companies in the City of London. She explains, "The possibilities of manipulation which these men-only structures, claiming the backing of 'tradition' (the Freemasons' claim to date back to Babylon is nonsense and the knights aren't knights at all) are breath-taking . . . There are caucuses within caucuses: Masonic Lodges within Livery Companies which in turn control the powerful Corporation of the City of London."[47]

These fears perhaps go to an extreme. Issues such as the balance of payments and views of gender cannot be laid solely at the door of the lodges, clubs, and schools, no matter how influential they are – but Roger's point is well taken about an alliance between the schools and like organisations. There is a desirable medium between scoffing at the idea of 'the network' and blaming everything on its consequences. *The Tatler* (July 1986) put the case for having a good laugh at the old boys and Masons:

42

Library of the Reform Club.

43

So they all trot off with their little suitcases! and do their silly prep and chant their silly chants! silly Daddy and his boys' night out! still, it gets him out of Mummy's hair! Given the right level of amused condescension, Freemasonry can be risible. One is used to seeing Prince Michael of Kent, for example, looking strong, silent and supportive. It is a public image that suits him. One might be a little less straight-faced about a masonic image of the gallant Prince, mightn't one? Left trouser leg rolled up, chest exposed, blindfold on, hangman's noose about the neck? Chanting prep-school gibberish? *Very silly indeed*, Daddy.

Ridiculous as they appeared to some, working together these institutions provided an education in rituals which were used in governing the Empire. The lodges and the clubs can be regarded as educational institutions in their own right. Besides their informal role as a place where information was exchanged, they provided useful libraries and even map rooms that were valuable to Imperial opinion makers. (See *Reform Club Library*, page 43, and *United Service Club Map Room*, page 45.) The libraries formed by some clubs and lodges would be the envy of any academic, if they were open to the uninitiated. Their existence implies a more serious dimension to club and lodge life than is usually recognised.

If such institutions as public schools, clubs, and lodges were as negative in their consequences as critics shrilly claim, then they also must be credited with a responsibility for British success over the last hundred and fifty years. *They cannot be held to have contributed to failures if it is not admitted that they influenced British triumphs as well – a point that many seem unwilling to entertain.* Whatever the implications of generations of the ruling élite going to public schools, it is almost self-evident that at times the life of the Empire resembled an extension of adolescent schooldays.

Imperial politics involved the reappearance throughout careers of adolescent animosities and amicuses. In 1934 Leo Amery, who was Secretary for the Colonies (1924-29), Secretary for the Dominions (1925-29), and Secretary for India (1940-45) exuberantly claimed that in besting Winston Churchill in a Commons debate that he had finally got 'one up' for Churchill pushing him into the Harrow swimming pool in 1889. "School life," wrote Robert Graves, "becomes the reality, and home life the illusion." The title of his book, *Goodbye to All That*, conveys the irony. The public school old boys seldom said a final goodbye to adolescence.[48]

Rituals and Power

Nearly seventy years ago Marc Bloch's *Les Rois Thaumaturges* (1924) established how ritual helped maintain royal power. David Kertzer has taken up this theme in *Ritual, Politics, and Power*, complaining that the subject is regarded as only pertinent to 'primitive' societies: "Historians, especially in the past couple of decades, have provided many valuable descriptions of political rites, but these, too, are commonly

The United Service Club map room.

dismissed by readers as the quaint customs of a bygone era."[49] The rituals in the schools and Empire had an importance that came closer to *mores* than to what has been considered *folkways*.[50] The rituals may have been 'folkish', but they had a profound impact.

A salient but unanswered question has been how did the Imperial rites originate? While the public schools were not the only influence, the rituals of 'competing' bodies were affected by them. Observers noted that clubs built rambling edifices overseas that at times managed to resemble public schools physically, surrounded as they were by cricket pitches and adorned with rose windows and spires that could have graced a school chapel. The symbiotic relationship is illustrated by the fact that after Arnold Lunn published *The Harrovians,* an innocuous novel whose chief revelation was that boys crib, he was forthwith compelled to resign from his five

London clubs on the grounds that by letting down the public schools, he had let down his clubs.

The schools were related to much in Victorian and Edwardian life that at first appears distant from them. A Borstal governor asserted that "a distinct tradition was growing up amongst the boys, and they looked forward to a time when the traditions of Borstal would be at least equal to those of Eton and Harrow."[51] The buildings of Colonial College in Suffolk, which between 1887 and 1900 prepared public school boys for agriculture overseas, have survived as a borstal. Whether old boys of the original foundation have visited is unrecorded.[52]

Kibroth-Hathaavah

An instance of the twists and turns that causality takes is **homo-eroticism,** an undercurrent of nineteenth-century society that partly owed its existence to the public schools. Kibroth-Hathaavah, the Bible's burial-ground for those who have lusted, was invoked by Frederic Farrar in his much reprinted school novel *Eric, or Little by Little.* Not only homosexuality, but flagellation and other dark themes were part of the school experience. They will be considered in Chapter V.

There is a compelling case to be made for the schools' influence on lifelong conduct, as indicated in the title of Desmond Coke's Shrewsbury novel, *The Bending of the Twig.* Coke's hero goes off to Shrewsbury armed with advice from novels purchased for him by his mother. *Tom Brown, Eric, The Hill, and Stalky & Co* are acceptable, but she confiscates *Jack Joker,* whose fictional headmaster is Jack the Ripper. (Dr. Donald Leinster-Mackay considers the case for a prep school master having been the Ripper in *The Rise of the English Prep School.*) The thousands of novels about schooldays suggest that attending public school was thought to be an abiding influence on a man's life. Nor were the botanical analogies confined to secondary schools. In 1894, *Blackwood's Edinburgh Magazine* advised that preparatory schools were the public schools' "nursery for hardening young cuttings".

Decades later the memories of school could raise blood pressures. Roald Dahl looked back fifty years to give a graphic account of sufferings at the hands of his headmaster. This was the subsequent Archbishop of Canterbury, Geoffrey Fisher:

> The Headmaster, while I was at Repton, struck me as being a rather shoddy bandy-legged little fellow with a big bald head and lots of energy but not much charm . . . it was he himself who had the task of crowning our present Queen in Westminster Abbey with half the world watching him on television. Well, well, well! And this was the man who used to deliver the most vicious beatings to the boys under his care! . . . At the end of it all, a basin, a sponge and a small clean towel were produced by the Headmaster, and the victim was told to wash away the blood before pulling up his trousers. Do you wonder that this man's behaviour used to puzzle me tremendously? He was an ordinary clergyman at the time as well as being

Headmaster, and I would sit in the dim light of the school chapel and listen to him preaching about the Lamb of God and about Mercy and Forgiveness and all the rest of it and my young mind would become totally confused.[53]

Greedy Institutions

To believe Correlli Barnett, Dr. Arnold's 'stained-glass obsessions' spread from Rugby to the Empire. It is not that simple, and it is not clear that the late Victorian schools were anything like what Dr. Arnold envisaged. What is clear is that they were greedy of loyalty and had a part in shaping the behaviour of the British created *crème-de-la-crème*. The Empire was run by public school boys who made their background painfully evident, and not by grammar school men. The schools produced, to use Gathorne-Hardy's phrase, 'frustrated benevolent dictators'.

The failure to adopt the Taunton Commission's proposal in 1868 that the schools' endowments be used to finance a truly national and comprehensive system was as important in Britain's development as any other single event of the nineteenth century. The Empire required administrators. Rather than a national system of education providing them, it was the public schools that filled the need. The schools influenced not only the personal lives of those who attended them but Imperialism itself: "The old adage that in the beginning God created the world, the Church of England and cricket might well be extended to include the 'public' or church school, for many believed that in its absence the last two of the trilogy would not survive, and some had a sneaking suspicion that the first would also soon crumble."[54]

So the public schools were far more than a system of education, and the investigation of their influence takes one far from the classroom and playing field. It has not been appreciated just how manifold were the consequences of the export of the adolescent rituals of the Victorians and Edwardians. An unfortunately neglected study that does appreciate the subtleties of this 'Imperial ecosystem' is Nora Mitchell's highly original account of Indian hill stations, enclaves which inevitably included schools, clubs, and lodges. She quite rightly concluded that these concentrations of institutions were far more important in the Imperial landscape than had been realised, and that they had considerable ramifications as far as social change was concerned.[55] Her efforts to plot the social implications of the hill stations are an illustration of how causality can and should be approached as a multi-dimensional subject.

Chaos

An appreciation of the need for an analysis that cuts across disciplines has utterly changed the way data in the physical sciences are being understood. The concept in the sciences of *chaos*, brings with it the realisation that what have been thought to be apparently unrelated and random events mask order and meaning on a vaster scale than hitherto believed. (Of course, the re-employment of a word which to the laymen means disorder is itself confusing.) Chaos studies in the sciences deserve to be related forthwith to historical studies. They cross the lines that separate disciplines, bringing together thinkers from diverse fields.[56] Such insights could and should be applied to social history, and to the problems presented in Imperial studies by increasing historical specialization. Unfortunately, they have been ignored by historians.[57]

Since this book crosses disciplinary lines in its concern for the social history of an élite, it presumably is eligible for criticism from both the defenders of 'classical' history who spurn social history and from those who advocate a specific brand of social history such as black or gay studies as a corrective to élitism. In the face of such confusion it is useful to recall that while historians quarrel about particularism as a route to holism and synthesis, the notion of less is more is no longer a vice in the sciences.[58]

Chaos if properly understood as a *modus operandi* will suggest analogies to game theory as well as the use by sociologists of the term 'strategy'. Its popularity amongst scientists calls attention to the problems in describing the dynamic nature of the environment and to the difficulties in calculating effects. Just as chaotic studies (and social history) suggest the presence of patterns where only confusion has previously been perceived, sociologists' 'strategic studies' affirm an unambiguous order.[59] A seminar of the most devoted practitioners of chaos, social history, and strategic studies would be illuminating: not very much is clear amongst those who seek to explain society, past or present.

For historians, one of the most helpful exercises in dealing with this confusion would be to re-emphasize the necessity of discussing causality. Causal analysis needs to be revived as a means of understanding complex scenarios, despite the objections from ". . . action theorists, phenomenologists, ethnomethodologists, and interpretative sociologists for whom exercises in causal deduction or causal inference represent the worst sort of neopositivism . . .".[60] So there are patterns, whether we are presently aware of them or not.[61] The way that we look at the world is changing more rapidly than ever before, but "The choice is always the same. You can make your model more complex and more faithful to reality, or you can make it simpler and easier to handle."[62] The complex model may be closer to reality, but there are perils inherent in an expansive historiography – as the next chapter further explains.

NOTES – CHAPTER I

1. See J. H. Grainger, *Patriotisms: Britain 1900-1939*, Routledge & Kegan Paul, 1986, 7. Also, Andrew Blake, "Life in Doctor Wortle's Schools", *Trollopiana*, No. 7, November 1989, 5-7. For revisionist discussion of empiricist ideas of causality, see Tooley, *Causation*. Nevertheless, "I believe that one can say that almost all current discussions of the nature of laws, and particularly of causation, however much they may differ from Hume's views in various respects, are fundamentally Humean in inspiration." *Ibid.*, 31. The issue of causality is not confined to philosophers of history. Spirited debate goes on amongst lawyers. See David Rosenberg, "The Causal Connection in Mass Exposure Cases", *Harvard Law Review*, Vol. 97, No. 4, February 1984, 848-930. Motivation research also involves causal questions. "Economic Mobility", *Institute for Social Research Newsletter*, University of Michigan, Autumn 1985, 3. *Cf.* E. H. Dance, *History*

the Betrayer: A Study in Bias, Greenwood Press, Westport (Connecticut), 1960, *Passim*.

2. Peter McLaren, *Schooling as a Ritual Performance*, 16. "The crucial question of course, is *what kind of meaning* is being conferred by the use of certain symbols – what stands to be gained, what lost, and by whom." Michael Baigent, Richard Leigh, Henry Lincoln, *The Messianic Legacy*, Corgi, 1987, 175. See Roger Andersen, *The Power and The Word: Language, Power and Change*, Paladin, 1988, 52.

3. Peter Berger and Thomas Luckmann, *The Social Construction of Reality*, Allen Lane, Harmondsworth, 1967, qtd. Anderson, *The Power and the Word*, 87. Regarding Eton's tail coats, "This costume, which has come to be regarded as hallowed by tradition, is of no great antiquity; nor, strangely enough, is there any written regulation regarding it, beyond a vague meeting of 'School Dress'. Giving evidence before The Public Schools Commission in 1862 the Headmaster, Mr. Balston, stated that the boys were not compelled to wear any particular dress . . . in 1862, therefore, there was no fixed definition of school dress and none exists today; it depends entirely on a kind of common law . . .". J. W. Hill, *Eton Medley*, Winchester Publications, 1948, 5.

4. Qtd. Grainger, *Patriotisms*, 37. Note continued interest in and confusion about Antonio Gramsci's and Louis Althusser's theorizing concerning social apparatus whose influence is exerted informally. This is evidence that the informal relationships between education and Imperialism need reconsideration. "How deeply school teaching of the patria, such as it was, went we cannot now tell", Grainger notes. He contends that lower-middle- and working-class schools "were starved of patriotic signs and symbols", suggesting that Imperial ritualism was upper class, *i.e.* public school, in origin. *Ibid.*, 38.

5. *Ibid.*, 39. "A distinctive civilization must be brought home by ritual symbol." *Ibid.* "Might there be ermergent *processes* as well as emergent *properties?*" Richard Dixey, "Science: Knowledge Through Causes", *Noetic Sciences Review*, No. 12, Autumn 1989, 7.

6. In the forthcoming *Rituals of Empire*, Jung is discussed in relation to Imperial and public school ritualism. See the review of *Elixir of Empire* in *The Coat of Arms*, N.S. Vol. VII, No. 147, Autumn 1989, 100-101.

7. David Hackett Fischer, *Historians' Fallacies: Toward a Logic of Historical Thought*, Harper, New York, 1970, 25. But would a ferret chase a weasel?

8. Qtd. *Ibid.*, 67.

9. ". . . causal relationship is reputed to be the exemplar of all significant relationship, the sovereign release from chance and accident . . . ". Michael Oakeshott, "Historical Events: The fortuitous, the causal, the similar, the correlative, the analogous and the contingent", Michael Oakeshott, *On History and Other Essays*, Basil Blackwell, 1983, 72.

10. For differences between **rationalistic and naturalistic paradigms** see Egon G. Guba and Yvonna S. Lincoln, "Epistemological and Methodological Bases of Naturalistic Inquiry", *Educational Communication and Technology*, Vol. 30, No. 4, Winter 1982, 233-52. "The search for causality is the mainspring that drives conventional research . . . the question is not whether to entertain a concept of causality but which concept to accept." *Ibid.*, 241. *Cf.* John B. Davis, "Explicating the Normative Content of Economic Theory", *Forum for Social Economics*, Vol. 19, No. 1, Spring/Fall 1989, 1-7. An *older* discussion, that by medieval schoolmen of "Intentionality", is avoided here. However, it seems to have re-emerged, involving DNA and neuroscience! See J. Z. Young, *Philosophy and the Brain*, Oxford University Press, hereafter OUP, 1988, 51-60. For "hegemony" see Garland Cannon, "Chinese Borrowing in English", *American Speech*, Vol. 63, No. 1, Spring 1988, 7, 21.

11. "The idea that we have one rational mind seriously undersells our diverse abilities. It oversells our consistency, and it emphasizes the very small, rational islands in the mind at the expense of the vast archipelago of talents, opportunities, and abilities surrounding them." Robert Ornstein, *Multimind: A New Way of Looking at Human Behaviour*, Macmillan, 1988 (1986), 17.

12. ". . . most of us, for most of our lives, do not try to determine the causes of things." *Ibid.*, 21. See *e.g.* Anne Sommers, "Nursing a Grievance", *Times Literary Supplement*, 4 January 1990, 1443. "Keynes Unmasked", *The Economist*, 11 November 1989, 101.

13. "Social history, in devaluing the political realm, devalues history itself. It makes meaningless those aspects of the past which serious and influential comtemporaries thought most meaningful. It makes meaningless not only the struggle over political authority but the very idea of legitimate political authority . . . of principles and practices that do not merely reflect (as Antonio Gramsci would have it) the

49

'hegemony' of the ruling class . . . The truly radical effect of the new enterprise is to **devalue** not only political history but reason itself, reason in history and politics – the idea that political institutions are, at least in part, the product of a rational, conscious, deliberate attempt to organize public life so as to promote the public weal and the good life." Gertrude Himmelfarb, *The New History and the Old,* Belknap Press of Harvard University Press, Cambridge (Massachusetts), 1987, 16. In contrast: "The most fruitful change in historical attitudes in my time, I think, has been the emergency of 'history from below' – the realisation that ordinary people also have a history, perhaps that they played more part in determining the shape of the historical process, whether for change or for continuity." Christopher Hill, *History and the Present,* 65th Conway Memorial Lecture, South Place Ethical Society, 1988,12. *Cf.* Peter Costa, "A Conversation with Charles Maier", *Harvard University Gazette,* Vol. LXXXV, No. 8, 20 October 1989, 5.

14. David I. Kertzer, *Ritual, Politics, and Power,* Yale University Press, 1988, 2.

15. *Cf.* Steadman Upham, "Archaeological Visibility and the Underclass of Southwestern Prehistory", *American Antiquity,* Vol. 53, No. 2, April 1988, 245- 61.

16. Grainger, *Patriotisms,* 41. Public schools themselves have and had still have scout troops. The current list is short and the leading schools are notable by their absence – suggesting that uniforms, awards, and training are redundant in a public school atmosphere. See J. F. Burnett ed. *Independent Schools Yearbook 1987,* A. C. Black, 1987, 909. (Despite discussion of scouting as a disseminator of Imperial and public school values, research remains to be done in this as in other areas relating to how the old boy 'message' was propagated.) Notwithstanding the emphasis in this book on the difficulties that are created by the proliferation of approaches to historical causality, the variety of suggestions as to what has influenced Imperial history attests to the subject's vitality rather than its demise. See Carl N. Degler, "Is the New Social History Threatening Clio?", *Organisation of American Historians' Newsletter,* Vol. 16, No. 3, August 1988, 5. On scouting see Stanley Reynolds, "From Boers to Boys' Own", *The Guardian,* 5 November 1989, 26. Paul Fussell, "A Radical Road to Happiness", *Times Literary Supplement,* 19 October 1989, 119.

17. Consider Colin Heywood, "Wittek and the Austrian Tradition", *Journal of the Royal Asiatic Society* 1988, No. 1, 7-25, esp. 18, 23. Also, critically, Colin Heywood, "'Boundless Dress of the Levant': Paul Wittek, The George-*Kreis* and The Writing of Ottoman History", *Journal of the Royal Asiatic Society,* 1989, No. 1, 32-50. A dose of social history improves the quality of history teaching. See Phyllis A. Hall, "Teaching Analytical Thinking . . . and *The Return of Martin Guerre*", *Perspectives,* Vol. 28, No. 1, January 1990, 14.

18. In Oakeshott's view, the 'practical' attitude sees the past in terms of the present, working backward from the present to find the roots of the present. On the other hand, the scientific attitude attempts to impose general laws. The contemplative attitude verges on *literary* imagery. See Himmelfarb, *New History and the Old,* 173-74. Oakeshott is suspicious of efforts to make sense of the past. He employs an image of history as a mistress, and claims that for the historian ". . . the past is feminine. He loves it as a mistress of whom he never tires and whom he never expects to talk sense." qtd. *Ibid.,* 175. Himmelfarb, whose *The New History and the Old* defends what she claims is the mainstream of historical activity, chastises Oakeshott for his scepticism, accusing him of being more of a nihilist that Nietzsche. *Ibid.,* 182. "In fact, the most striking thing about Oakeshott's theory is how little hope it holds out, either for the future of English historiography or for the past." *Ibid.,* 181. See Rein Staal, "The Irony of Modern Conservatism", *International Political Science Review,* Vol. 8, No. 4, October 1987, 344-46. Whiggery?

19. Oakeshott, *"Historical Events",* 85. "Is there such a thing as natural necessity, some necessity in the sequence of natural events?" Roland Hall, "Causal Powers", *Times Higher Education Supplement,* 17 November 1989, 20.

20. ". . . we define military cohesion as the bonding together of members of a unit or organisation in such a way as to sustain their will and commitment to each other, their unit, and the mission." John H. Johns, *Cohesion in the US Military,* National Defense University Press, Washington 1984, iv. Cohesion was achieved gradually: ". . . slowly, a change in Imperial attitudes begins to take place in the second half of the nineteenth century. Religion, for instance, played little part in Henty's work, though women did show a tendency to pray while battles were surging about them." Bob Dixon's *Catching Them Young* (2): *Political Ideas in Children's Fiction,* Pluto, 1977, 88. *E.g.* the Imperial ethos *replaced* religion.

21. Isabel Quigly, *The Heirs of Tom Brown: The English School Story,* OUP, 1984, 7.

22. See Frank Martin Brodhead, "Social Imperialism and the British Youth Movement, 1880-1914", PhD dissertation, Princeton University, 1978, esp. 23- 27, but also 39-40, 64-65, 68, 91, 100, 147-50, 200, 260 n. 33.

23. In *Ritual, Politics, and Power*, 33.

24. Graham Little, *Political Ensembles: A Psychosocial Approach to Politics and Leadership*, OUP, 1985, 8. When it is understood that the physical withdrawal of the British and other imperial powers did not bring an end to imperialism – and that imperialism never completely suppressed other hegemonies – the historiography of the European empires changes radically in its approach. There is urgently a need for sensitivity to the 'native' structures: "Culturally, the causes as well as the effects of this shift can be rapidly evoked. We think about the Third World in a different way today, not merely because of decolonization and political independence, but above all because these enormously varied cultures all now speak in their own distinctive voices." Frederic Jameson, *Nationalism, Colonialism and Literature: Modernism and Imperialism*, Field Day, Derry (Northern Ireland), 1988, 9. But there is also a growing and impressive sophistication in approach: "I am reluctant to repeat here the obligatory knee-jerk condemnations of causality and so-called linear history, although I do not particularly feel that the situation/response model (drawn from Sartre) is a 'causal' one in that stereotypical sense." *Ibid.*, 11, n.7. "Symbols are given increased attention – 'Miss' or 'Ms', 'black' or 'negro', the flag and the anthem, the powers of titular offices . . . what was fearful and tabooed is brought down to the level of a problem to be rethought . . .". *Ibid.*, 165.

25. Mario Biagioli, "Meyerson: Science and the 'Irrational'", *Studies in History and Philosophy of Science*, Vol. 19, No. 1, March 1988, 16. For an educationist's view of explanation in education see Diego Gambetta, *Were They Pushed or Did They Jump? Individual Decision Mechanisms in Education*, OUP, 1987.

26. "Animals (and positivists) do not seek explanations and do not perform or believe in miracles." Biagioli, "Meyerson", 16. See Willis Harman, "Spirituality, Science and the Transformation of Consciousness", *World Goodwill Newsletter*, 1989, No. 3, 2-4. *Cf.* Stephen T. Worland, "Etzioni's 'Denontogolical Paradigm': A New Direction for Social Economics?", *Forum for Social Economics*, Vol. 19, No. 1, Spring/Fall 1989, 10.

27. Mary Warnock, *A Common Policy for Education*, OUP, 1988, 50. *Cf.* John R. Searle, "Is the Brain's Mind a Computer Program?", *Scientific American*, Vol. 262, No. 1, January 1990, 50 *ff.* Consider R. W. Beardsmore, "Autobiography and the Brain: Mary Warnock on Memory", *The British Journal of Aesthetics*, Vol. 29, No. 3, Summer 1989, 261-69.

28. Rupert Sheldrake, *The Presence of the Past: Morphic Resonance and the Habits of Nature*, Collins, 1988, 86-87.

29. Dawkins, *The Selfish Gene*. 290, qtd. Sheldrake, *Presence of the Past*, 242. See and *cf.* Lynn Devenport, "Sampling Behavior and Contextual Change", *Learning and Motivation*, Vol. 20, No. 2, May 1989, 97-114.

30. M. Hampe and S. R. Morgan, "Two Consequences of Richard Dawkins' View of Genes and Organisms", *Studies in History and Philosophy of Science*, Vol. 19, No. 1, March 1988, 127-28. Consider R. Williamson, "DNA Technology in Diagnosis and Genetic Counselling", *Triangle*, Vol. 28, No. 3/4, 1989, 91-96.

31. Sheldrake, "Introduction", *Presence of the Past*, n.p. n.

32. J. A. Mangan, *The Games Ethic and Imperialism*, Viking, 1986, 65.

33. Derek Verschoyle, "Indian Innocence, Ltd.", Graham Greene ed., *The Old School: Essays by Divers Hands*, Jonathan Cape, 1984 (1934), 201.

34. qtd. Paul Johnson, "Education of an Establishment", George Macdonald Fraser ed., *The World of the Public School*, Weidenfeld & Nicolson, 1977, 25.

35. "In order to retain these links the schools had to respond positively to the demands of their increasingly powerful institutional allies or alternatively accept the fact that they would decline as vehicles of upper-class reproduction." Brian Slater and Ted Tapper, *Power and Policy in Education: The Case of Independent Schooling*, Falmer Press, 1985, 8.

36. J. H. Grainger is decidedly unimpressed: "In so far as they acknowledged the rationality of existing social institutions, endorsed the world of fact and deed, accepted ancient violence and sanctified it, went to

the vulgar for unreflecting patriotism, Oxford idealists may have provided assurance for activists at work within Greater Britain. Yet they rarely came into the open. **The work and dramaturgy of Empire were only faintly illuminated by them.**" *Patriotisms*, 126.

37. J. M. Mackenzie, *Propaganda and Empire: The Manipulation of British Public Opinion*, 1880-1960. Manchester University Press, 1984, 9. Mackenzie makes a significant contribution but is not alone in believing that the schools are an unappreciated factor in politics. Rupert Wilkinson in *The Prefects* saw their influence as crucial in the formation of the British political character. John R. Reed in *Old School Ties: The Public Schools in British Literature* (Syracuse University Press, 1964) writes: "A study of the effects of the private educational system upon British literature might stress the importance of education on the writers themselves or the result of this influence in literary works", but he preferred to deal with the treatment of the schools themselves by a number of writers. Jonathan Gathorne-Hardy in *The Public School Phenomenon* (Hodder & Stoughton, 1977) baldly claimed that the key to understanding British character was understanding the public schools. Tapper and Salter comment that "Although there are distinctive national educational traditions within the United Kingdom, the private sector has at the upper reaches of the class structure helped to create a common national culture. Its influence has extended beyond national boundaries with the creation of replicas in most Commonwealth countries . . .". *Power and Policy*, 55.

38. Stephen Bann, "History and Her Siblings: Law, Medicine and Theology", *History of the Human Sciences*, Vol. 1, No. 1, May 1988, 20.

39. Although education has vast social implications, historians of education have been late to join the debate over the truth of "what women, minorities, and working-class students have always known: the precincts of higher learning are not for them, and the educational system is meant to train a new mandarin class." Stanley Aronowitz and Henry A. Giroux, "Schooling, Culture, and Literacy in the Age of Broken Dreams", *Harvard Educational Review*, Vol. 58, No. 2, May 1988, 180. This is particularly sad because the history of education shows that education has had a vital role "in age after age, to solidify the social hierarchy, norms, and beliefs of the elite". James Paul Gee, "The Legacies of Literacy: From Plato to Freire through Harvey Graff", *Harvard Educational Review*, Vol. 58, No. 2, May 1988, 205. See the articles on intellectual history in *The American Historical Review*, Vol. 29, No. 3, June 1986.

40. See Carl Levy, "Antonio Gramsci: Selections from Cultural Writings", review article, *History of European Ideas*, Vol. 9, No. 1, 1988, 75-78.

41. See *A Round Table: Labor, Historical Pessimism, and Hegemony* with articles by Leon Fink, Jackson Lears, John P. Diggins, George Lipsitz, in *Journal of American History*, Vol. 75, No. 1, June 1988. "In Thomas L. Haskell's wickedly funny formulation, **Gramscianism is to Marxism as Unitarianism is to Christianity:** a 'feather pillow' to catch those falling from the true faith. From this point of view, the concept of cultural hegemony is too soft but also too volatile. 'Like dry ice,' Haskell writes: '. . . hegemony always tends toward sublimation, becoming merely a diffuse aspect of the human condition rather than a distinct feature of particular societies that one could ever point to in explanation of specific events and actions.'" qtd. Jackson Lears, "Power, Culture, and Memory", *Journal of American History*, Vol. 75, No. 1, June 1988, 137. *Cf.* Thomas L.Haskell, "Convention and Hegemonic Interest in the Debate over Antislavery: A Reply to Davis and Ashworth", *American Historical Review*, Vol. 92, No. 2, October 1987. *Ritualism is hegemony on display:* "It was only in the last quarter of the nineteenth century that royal ceremonial re-acquired its public magnificence, its pomp magnified for the masses . . . The non-royal élite could whole-heartedly support the symbolic re-creation of the sacred ruler, which helped prop up the hierarchical society structure." Kertzer, *Ritual, Politics, and Power*, 176.

42. *E.g.* by 1906 the Primrose League had over one and a half million members.

43. This is one of the rationales behind Chapters VI and VII.

44. Richard Gordon, *A Gentlemen's Club*, Arrow, 1988, 95.

45. Gertrude Stein, qtd. Jameson, *Nationalism, Colonialism and Literature*, 18 n. 13.

46. Tooley, *Causation*, 28-31. *Chains* however is not an attack on political history. Dieter Senghaas, for example, has gone to extremes with *Wissenschaftsimperialismus*. But, while explanations of causation that invoke ritualism and symbolism are tentative, the effort in this area produces a more successful analysis than does a bare chronicle or solely political approach. "Even those historical writers who have no conscious thoughts on the principles of historical causation (the vast majority, one suspects) do have to be

aware of the distinction between explanation and description (itself a useful, but inevitably less taxing, function) or, indeed, disguised narration." Arthur Marwick, *The Nature of History*, 2d ed., Macmillan, 1985 (1970, 1981), 156.

47. Qtd. in a review by Angela Neustatter, "The Boys' Own Club", *The Guardian*, 18 October 1988.

48. Robert Graves, *Goodbye to All That*, Penguin, Harmondsworth, 1986 (1029), 24.

49. Kertzer, *Ritual, Politics and Power*, x. ". . . *ritual represents the creation of a controlled environment* . . . There is an 'agnostic' dimension to ritual." Jonathan Smith, *Imagining Religion: From Babylon to Jonestown*, University of Chicago Press, 1982, 61.

50. "Folkways are standardised practices, matters of dress, leisure habits, etiquette, which though observed as a matter of tradition and custom need not necessarily be observed by ever individual; more are patterns of behaviour upon which the survival of society is held to depend . . . and which are enforced by very strong social pressures, often amounting to legal sanctions." Marwick, *The Nature of History*, 128. ". . . attitudes in the public school stories were carried over into the ideology of Empire." Dixon, *Catching Them Young* (2), 95. See Erika Mann, *School for Barbarians: Education Under the Nazis*, Lindsay Drummond, 1939. "It is significant that Hitler used them (the English public schools) as a model when he set up the notorious Adolf Hitler School for leaders . . . ". G. C. T. Giles, *The New School Tie*, Pilot Press, 1946.

51. Stephen Humphries, *Hooligans or Rebels? An Oral History of Working-Class Childhood and Youth, 1889-1939*, Basil Blackwell, Oxford, 1981, 224.

52. Interview with Dr. Patrick Dunae, 12 June 1988.

53. Roald Dahl, *Boy: Tales of Childhood*, Penguin, Harmondsworth, 1986, 144- 46. *Cf.* "The Importance of Teaching", *The Royal Bank Letter*, Vol. 70, No. 5, September/October 1989, 42.

54. Norman G. Curry, "Anglican Educational Enterprise", John Cleverley ed., *Half a Million Children: Studies of Non-Government Education in Australia*, Longman Cheshire, Melbourne. 1978, 47.

55. Nora Mitchell to P. J. Rich, 31 March 1989. See Nora Mitchell, *The Indian Hill-Station: Kodaikanal*, University of Chicago, Department of Geography, Research Paper No. 141. Consider Linda Hughes, "Turbulence in the 'Golden Stream': Chaos Theory and the Study of Periodicals", *Victorian Periodicals Review*, Vol. XXII, No. 3, Fall 1989, 117-25.

56. James Gleick, *Chaos: Making a New Science*, Heinemann, 1988, 5. See A. A. Tsonis, "Chaos and Unpredictability of Weather", *Weather*, Vol. 44, No. 6, June 1989, 258-63.

57. Thomas Bender, review of *The New History and the Old*, *Journal of American History*, Vol. 75, No. 3, December 1988, 909. Biagioli, "Meyerson".

58. Gleick, *Chaos*. 7. See *e.g.* Sharon E. Nicholson, "Long-Term Changes in African Rainfall", *Weather*, Vol. 44, No. 2, February 1989, 46-56.

59. Graham Crow, "The Use of the Concept of 'Strategy' in Recent Sociological Literature", *Sociology*, Vol. 23, No. 1., February 1989, 1-24.

60. A. Michael Huberman and Matthew B. Miles. "Assessing Local Causality in Qualitative Research", David N. Berg and K. K. Smith eds., *The Self in Social Inquiry: Researching Methods*, Sage, 1988 (1985), 352. See Galen Strawson, *The Secret Connection: Causation, Realism and David Hume*, Clarendon Press, Oxford, 1989.

61. Huberman, "Assessing Local Causality", 352-53. *Cf.* (!!) Edward A. Dyl and John D. Schatzberg, "The Super Bowl Phenomenon. Does the NFL Drive the Market?", *AAII Journal* Vol. XII, No. 1, January 1990, 7-9.

62. Gleick, *Chaos*, 278. *Cf.* Alan Ryan, *The Philosophy of the Social Sciences*, Macmillan, 1988 (1970), 10, 15, 17, 22, 40, 113, 128, 188-89, 214, 221-22, 238. Also *cf.* Charles Levin, "Art and the Sociological Ego: Value from a Psychoanalytic Perspective", John Fekete ed., *Life After Postmodernisms: Essays on Value and Culture*, Macmillan, 1988, 22-63, esp. 31. Thomas S. Edwards, "'Reconstructing' Reconstruction: Changing Historical Paradigms in Mississippi History", *The Journal of Mississippi History*, Vol. LI, No. 3, August 1989, 165-80.

CHAPTER II

Perplexities

As in the making of whisky or sherry the new wines are added to a vat in whose depths lurk older liquors. – Richard Ollard, *An English Education: A Perspective of Eton,* 1982.

These are the sort of people who, if they met you one Saturday afternoon with a fishing-rod, creel, and campstool, walking towards the river, would ask, "Going fishing?". – R. G. Collingwood, *An Autobiography,* 1982.

There is no need for writers, young or old, to say to headmasters, in the words of Isaiah, 'set thine house in order, for thou shalt die and not live,' for the system is growing and changing and will, therefore, continue, in a changing world, to live. Rather should we say to them with T. E. Brown, 'suffer no chasm to interrupt this glorious tradition. Continuous life – that is what we want.' – Sir Arnold Wilson, *More Thoughts and Talks,* 1939.

Little results from cacophonous debate *reductio ad absurdum* about causality, at least as far as the Empire and public schools are concerned. The pursuit *per se* presents perplexities, and perils. The philosophizing about history can become a substitute for writing it. A preoccupation with a single cause produces a highly biased picture and the search for causes can result in the findings being distorted to fit the solution – as Karl Popper, amongst others, warned.

The public schools did not hide their light under a bushel. They gladly took the credit for influencing boys and Empire. Their growth provides intriguing parallels with that of the Empire. Nathaniel Woodard's numerous foundations seemed similar to colonies – Lancing was the jewel in the crown, the India of the empire. Woodard schools such as Hurstpierpoint, Ardingly, Bloxham, Denstone, Ellesmere and Worksop were lesser colonies. Just as the railway helped in the growth of Imperial administration it helped to incorporate obscure schools into the burgeoning system. Similar anologies abound, and the anecdotal material overwhelmingly confirms an influence so ubiquitous and taken for granted that it is reminiscent of Umberto Eco's remark that the Victorian bourgeoisie were formal because of stiff collars. Yet, while the parallels and the *bon mots* concerning the schools and Empire are numerous, there is no unanimity about their significance. This is partly because hegemony (as Gramsci emphasized) is always contested. Presented with such riddles, historians divide into lions and tigers:

Perplexities

Lions, by nature, are idle beasts. Provided they have enough to eat, they can easily accept a lazy way of life, happily dozing their days away in the shade of a convenient tree. Tigers are much more demanding. They have nervous systems that object to inactivity and make it impossible for them to relax for very long, no matter how well fed they may be . . . Most animal species fall into the lion category. They are inherently conservative, seeking out the old and the usual, the comfortable things.[1]

Causality, with all its ramifications, is unendingly complex. New conundrums arise out of any 'answers' brought forth. Findings can be turned into the 'proof' of further reinterpretations. A case in point is that evidence offered of influences in the public schools such as athleticism which has been incorporated by this writer into a hypothesis of *rule by ritual.* This in turn, and in time, will undoubtedly be incorporated into another construct. Any "final" synthesis is *inevitably* premature.

Genius Loci or Morphic Resonance?

Sheldrake suggests that history has a "real" existence, a physical existence which exerts a "morphic resonance" on events. In fact, he maintains that "Chemical and biological forms are repeated not because they are determined by changeless laws or eternal Forms, but because of *causal influence from previous similar forms.* This influence would require an action across space and *time* unlike any known type of physical action."[2] The idea is not so startling when put into perspective. In *Sketchy Memories* Macnaghten invokes the influence of Eton's *Genius Loci:* **"I think that there are good honest feelings of many centuries which the *Genius Loci* hands down from generation to generation . . .".** The issue is not a presence of the past in the present, which most would agree does exist, but whether it really has a separate *physical existence* and consequent *effect.* **Macnaghten's *Genius Loci* is a folkloric version of Sheldrake's morphic resonance.**

Nor does Sheldrake claim that his hypothesis is completely original. As mentioned, the experiments that he cites of W. McDougall were carried out at Harvard as early as 1920. Generations of white rats were confronted with exits from a tank of water. Over a period of fifteen years and thirty-two generations of rats, the experiment continued. There was a pronounced increase in the ability of the rats to solve the tank problem. Further experiments along similar lines were carried out by F. A. E. Crew of Edinburgh, and W. E. Agar of Melbourne. Sheldrake hypothesizes that *the experience of the rats in solving the tank problem has a continuing existence.* Drawing on this 'living memory', succeeding generations were able to reduce the time taken to solve the problem.

These are startling assertions because of the difficulty of envisaging an independent existence of ideas or forms which are metaphysical, but twenty years *after* McDougall and twenty years *before* Sheldrake's publications, the philosopher Kenneth Boulding

55

was tempted to give tradition not only an independent causal role but also *existence* just as real as the weather or diet. In *The Image*, he nearly steps over the line to pre-empt Sheldrake's hypothesis of morphic resonance by referring to the way that the constant reiteration of values acquires almost a biological status, and describing how the ceremonial life of society centres around the reinforcement of value systems through investitures, coronations, graduations, reunions, and festivals.[3] Boulding hesitated, perhaps realizing the furore that would be roused.

The tumult caused by Sheldrake's notion of "FORMATIVE CAUSALITY" has, to the intense discomfort of many, moved from the pages of *New Scientist* and *Nature* to the *Times Literary Supplement*.[4] Sheldrake has put more than a gloss on Proust's astonishment in *Swann's Way* over a madeleine dipped in tea recalling a childhood in Combray, Arnold Toynbee's musing in *Study of History* (Volume X) about how a sense of reality about the past 'comes' to a historian, or Gibbon's experience in Rome that led to writing *Decline and Fall*. Whatever the antecedents, Sheldrake's theory is one of the most controversial hypotheses in many years.

The Lasting Love

According to Sheldrake, the repetition of an action or thought reinforces future behaviour. In this light, the intense emotions about the old school take on special interest. At the end of *Sketchy Memories,* Macnaghten exclaims "And so, my dear old pals, as the Blue Peter is flying at the foremast, let us westward ho! and away, but one cup at parting; once more let us drink the toast beloved of all others - FLOREAT ETONA." On his rather more dramatic departure, James Barrie's Captain Hook in *Peter Pan* exclaimed '*Floreat Etona*' as the crocodile ate him. Barrie wrote: "To look at, these schools are among the fairest things in England; they draw from their sons a devotion that is deeper, more lasting than any other love."[5]

Imperial administrators staged rites that recalled adolescence. This theatrical enthusiasm for adolescent ritualism spread throughout the Empire and had ideological consequences, reinforcing hierarchical views about human nature. The public school had golden opportunities to impart a bias, and the means to do so.

The consequences according to a line of thinking based on Hume can be challenged. Humeans, if not Hume himself, have contended that nothing 'proves' causality, and that it depends only on conjunction.[6] The notion is philosophically interesting, but not convincing enough to overcome the overwhelming evidence that the public school shaped lives. A Humean rejoinder might be that the schools fitted into life rather than affected life,[7] but discussion then succumbs to a variation on the chicken-or-the-egg dilemma.[8]

No matter how apparent it is that the schools contributed to the outlook of Imperial administrators, investigation will leave unexamined causes that could have contributed. The number of causes involved with any historical situation is almost numberless. Another caveat is that history's premises never remain in place for long.

56

Rapidly new lines of investigation become available and quickly the search moves on.[9] No one can be complacent about the adequacy of an outlook.

What would now appear to be a hopelessly antiquarian approach to historiography characterized the confident writings of the Imperial administrators, belonging as they did to learned bodies such as the Royal Geographic and Royal Asiatic Societies – societies that can themselves be considered as an influence on Imperial thought and as subjected to public school influence. The historical writings of Imperial administrators reflected a distinct view, one encouraged by such societies, and the reminiscences and recollections of the time can hardly be accepted at face value. The son of Robert Hamilton (later Lord Belhaven and the Kuwait Political Agent in 1916-18), warned about personal Imperial memoirs such as his father's that: "No author can write such a chapter about himself with any truth."[10]

Searching for a 'truer' history, educational historians in tandem with historians from other disciplines have produced an ever-proliferating number of hybrid approaches, each dependent on which disciplines are amalgamated. Women's history and gay studies have in turn had to give way to gender history. Agricultural history and forest history barely acquired their societies and conferences before genetic history claimed its place. The better part of valour is to *suggest* rather than to attempt to *prove* the centrality of the history of the schools to Imperial political development.

As far as the surviving documentary evidence is concerned, scholarly disciplines such as quantitative, medical, demographic, climatological, and agricultural history, emerged *after* the Empire was at its zenith. Consequently the biographical and autobiographical documentation from the period was generated without a sensitivity to issues that the new specialities have engendered.[11] An understanding of behaviourism and psychology was lacking in the Victorian era, and it can be assumed that some evidence was irretrievably lost not because it was burnt or suppressed but because it was not noticed.

Fortunately, the lack of evidence which is often a problem is less of a problem with the public schools. During the period of high Empire from 1850 to 1950 they were a highly visible and self-conscious institution, and this resulted in a large number of records surviving.[12] **Observers were sensitized to the schools' importance.** Proof of this abounds, extending to documentation of physical differences between public school boys and others. In 1926, Christ's Hospital boys at age thirteen were 2.4 inches taller than council-school boys; at age seventeen they were 3.8 inches taller than a similar group of working class youths.[13] This raises other questions, such as those about diet or smoking habits, but at least indicates the range of materials available for studying the schools.

Theories such as Rupert Sheldrake's that bear on social rituals have a better chance of being tested in the public school sphere than in the less documented area of maintained education. No other kind of schooling has had its painful rites of initiation more painstakingly recorded or has striven as vigorously to differentiate its members from the 'outsiders'. "There at Westminster School," wrote Sir Peter Ustinov in *Dear Me* (1977), "I was given the clothes of an undertaker, together with a furled umbrella, in order, we were told, to distinguish the boys from City of London bank messengers."

When Mother Was Matron

The schools not only supplemented other institutions but supplanted them.[14] This even applies to the family, as will be seen in Chapter IV. Robert Graves noted that boys would slip into calling their mothers "Matron" and address their fathers as if they were masters.[15] The schools were in *loco parentis,* a fact celebrated rather than condemned by Henty and lesser potboiler laureates. After school, the separation from family continued when men went overseas and what was called the 'long silence' began, dissolving eventually most connection.[16]

The heyday of the Henty heroes was the heyday of old boy influence abroad. The paladins of schoolboy novels make the transition from schoolhouse to Government House with ease, and the 'natives' provide as suitable a foil for adventures as did the 'townees'. Both underclasses are depicted with little affection and look as if they are "being charged with stealing a postal order".[17] That some evidence is derisive is a tribute to the influence, but Sir Arnold Wilson, one of the most famous of British Residents in the Arabian Gulf, castigated the critics: ". . . the old and popular game of 'damning the old school', followed, as often as not, by sneers at 'the old school tie' in which some of the best of life's minor loyalties are turned to jest."[18] His irritation shows how close to his heart Clifton was. The old boys, J. M. Barrie wrote to Lady Cynthia Asquith, had a "something" that he had difficulty describing: "The nearest thing to it must be boot polish."

The White Rose in Shrewsbury Market-place

Incomprehensibility seems one explanation of the failure to give the schools their historical due. The fault is not slothfulness on the part of historians, who to give them credit for intellectual curiosity are often found surreptitiously examining other possibilities than those they have embraced. The difficulty is that public schools are a topic requiring considerable ability in the art of social deciphering. The consequences of "Pop" are more unfathomable than those of the Trent affair.

Nevertheless, not all historians ignore the subject. A measure of the schools' impact is how historians have viewed their own schools.[19] Arthur Bryant, whose first published work was his *History of the Harrow Mission* (1921), wrote about his Harrovian tie: "It gives me the same prickly and glowing feeling that a sober eighteenth-century squire must have felt when occasionally in loyal Hanoverian days he sported – after dinner – the white rose in Shrewsbury market-place."[20] A public school educated historian such as Bryant will look where he knows the ground. Bryant's viewpoint reflects Harrow. R. G. Collingwood has something of Rugby about him. The surprise would be if he had gone to Bedales. (That is, if he had gone to Bedales during its unconventional height before World War I.)[21]

Arnold Toynbee, on the other hand, was a Wykhamist and included Winchester's long-time headmaster, Montague Rendall, in *Acquaintances.* When Toynbee was at Winchester from 1902 to 1907, Rendall was his housemaster and not yet headmaster.

His influence according to Toynbee was "powerful and permanent".[22] Contrasting Bryant, Collingwood, and Toynbee – the Harrovian, Rugbeian, and Wykhamist – *there is a suggestion of their schools in their work.* Harrow as a Whig citadel, Rugby as the castle of Imperial Christian chivalry, and Winchester as a college of Victorian scholasticisms give pause when considering causality.

If causal questions related to schooling stubbornly remain 'which-came-first' questions, and if the issue's 'vitals' are elusive, there is evidence that at least some parents wanted schools to take over the responsibility for their children.[23] At the same time, it has to be reiterated that the school influence was but *one* influence. A bad meal should have been cited causally far more times than it has been. Carrying further the Collingwood epigraph at the start of this chapter, research in causality resembles fishing. What is eventually consumed depends on where one fishes and the tackle used – and not on what is caught but what is kept.

Easily overlooked is that part of the school influence was *negative causality,* the effect of what was not done rather than what was done. One can argue that because the schools encouraged an élite view of education, popular education was not encouraged by the colonial administrator. Furthermore, the schools exerted considerable causal influence via *imitation.* As already mentioned, scouting is increasingly recognized as an instance of the affect of the public schools on other movements, reflecting Robert Baden-Powell's idea that the Scouts would take the place for the lower classes of the public school.[24] When school rituals shape those of other institutions or are adopted by mass movements, Sheldrake's hypothesis about morphic resonance comes forcefully to mind. In support of the power of this resonance, whether morphic or mundane, the recollections of Colin Shrosbree are apt:

> Like many English children, my education was formed by the public schools before I knew they existed. The grammar school which I attended as a scholarship boy in 1949 – with its gowns, its formality, its staff largely from Oxford and Cambridge, its games, its prefects and the classics for the brighter boys – had all the appearance and tone of a very minor public school, without the boarders.[25]

Myth, Fantasy, and Legend

A catalogue of the experiences of the Empire's rulers should give pre-eminence to their initiation into clan rituals when at public school, which were places of 'myth, fantasy and legend'.[26] The influence of public school sports was part of the story, but ritualism based on schooldays included much more.[27] The contention of this book and its companions in the trilogy is that the public schools indirectly helped to provide the pattern for Imperial organization. This largely has escaped the attention of historians of education, but of course it is unlikely that a bird was the discoverer of air. Once attention is focused on educational ritualism, the amount of collaborative documentation that accrues is awe inspiring. A great deal of what has sustained other

Lodge Equipment.

interpretations of the public school experience, such as notions about the bourgeoisie, athleticism, chivalry, and the English gentlemen, is subsumed. A reference to morphic resonance is pertinent. Sheldrake's hypothesis of formative causation proposes that morphogenetic fields play a causal role in the development of systems. He offers an architectural analogy: "In order to construct a house, bricks and other building materials are necessary; so are the builders who put the materials into place; and so is the architectural plan which determines the form of the house. The same builders doing the same total amount of working using the same quantity of building materials could produce a house of different form on the basis of a different plan."[28]

The unnoticed building blocks of the ritualism of school and Empire were innumerable seemingly insignificant talismen and tokens, although sometimes they could be conspicuously literal as well as metaphorical. Prince Alfred College old boys in Adelaide, South Australia, had an elaborate metal badge that they wore, and which were dutifully reclaimed from those unworthy of it. The old school tie was a less gauche sign of this identity. The values that wearing the tie represented could be subtle, but "The glue was a cultural style in its broadest sense."[29] The Masonic lodges, displayed a similar *love of totems*, as a picture of a typical lodge's hoodwinks, gavels, candles, ceremonial slippers, and other paraphernalia illustrates. (See *Lodge Equipment*, page 60.) The physical manifestations of belonging – not only the neckties but the blazers and buttons – had a status that are explored in *Rituals of Empire*.

The dissemination of the public school tradition was not only through British enthusiasts but by 'natives' fuelled by a desire for the knowledge of how to manipulate Imperial symbols and thus acquire power, an acknowledgement by the ruled that an expertise in ritualism conferred political status. Notwithstanding recent attention to how public school athleticism spread throughout the colonies, sports were not emphasized to acquire an expertise in cricket *per se*. Sports were a ritual skill. The unhappy native beneficiaries of this emphasis often display more of a resemblance to fledgling soldiers at drill than boys enjoying happy schooldays. (Compare *Gordon College Khartoum* and *P.T. at Sherborne*, page 62.)

Because the English public school was so obviously an ingredient of the Empire's success, pseudo-traditions were created by overseas schools in hopes that they would aid in turning out governors and generals. Other types of schools might offer sports but lacked the convincing ritualism. Curriculum, too, played a part, *yet the genius of public schools was not in academics but in rites*. Schools such as Bedales and Abbotsholme, which boasted of a relaxed and less ritualistic style, illustrated by their deliberate informality, well understood that much more was expected for fees than what was acquired in the classroom.

Implicit in ritualism is repetitiveness. In Sheldrake's words, ". . . according to the hypothesis of formative causation, the form of a system depends on the cumulative morphic influence of previous systems."[30] A lifelong formalized male chauvinism which clubs enshrine and reinforce will be considered at length in Chapter VI. Another result of a public school education (to give Correlli Barnett his due) may have been a prejudice against technical education, reflecting the way the schools

Gordon College, Khartoum.

P.T. in Quad at Sherborne School.

looked down on specialists and glorified generalists. The all-rounder was incarnated in fiction's Henty hero, an idealized stereotype that helps explain the unembarrassed pontifications that British in charge handed down to their colonial subjects about motorcycles, leprosy, fire-fighting, banking, artesian wells, and opium.

Deference to the old boy's authority was not limited to brown and black colonial subjects. If the Empire accepted the old boys as oracles, it is also true that the British working class often unquestioningly accepted public school boys' *bona fides*. Whatever the arguments against the schools, they produced men who exacted respect. Rather ominously for those who believe in free will, Sheldrake points out that "the larger the number of animals in the past which have learned the task, the easier it should be for subsequent similar animals to learn it."[31]

Surviving artifacts suggest that the process involved *competition*. Since the schools' relationship with the Empire was symbiotic, it is not surprising that public school museums literally housed heathen idols and other totems of failed ritual systems. A dissertation deserves to be written on the phenomena of the Victorian public school museums as well as of general museums stuffed with artifacts donated by old boys. (See *United Service Museum*, below.)

Less conspicuous but more influential than the museums were the backgrounds of the teachers and students. Every school sheltered those with experience abroad.[32] Describing Allhallows' second master, a school yearbook remarked: "There has

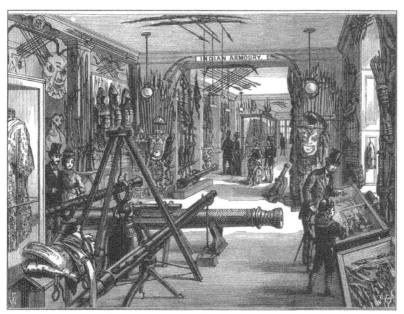

United Service Museum.

63

always been a touch of the Raj about Bill – he was born in Assam . . .". School magazines described Imperial exploits, reminding boys of the deeds of their predecessors. It was hardly a critical press, and was flavoured with a heady *noblesse oblige* – a boy recruited to India dies doing his duty in a polo match, another returns to describe his triumphs: "Major Sinclair talked on his part in the recent expedition to Ashanti (1896)." A Lawrentian in West Africa in 1898 boasted of an expedition against the Emir of Lapai at Gooloo: "Our loss was nil, while theirs was considerable." Cadet corps news was a staple, enlivened by recollections of the North-West Frontier from the grizzled sergeant-majors who seemed a fixture in school armouries.

Public School Culture

The issue of public school influence antecedes the 'second' Empire of Victoria's reign. Concerning the eighteenth century, Donald Leinster-Mackay in *The Educational World of Daniel Defoe* (University of Victoria, 1981) states, "Where

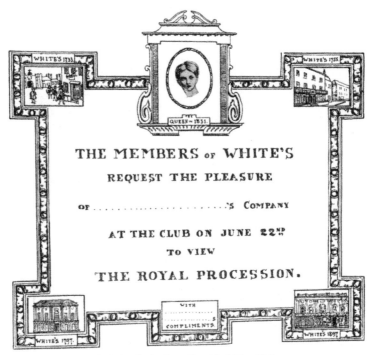

Invitation Card – Queen Victoria's Jubilee. 1897.

White's Club.

Defoe breaks new ground in his criticism of educational institutions is in his condemnation of the endowed public schools for being the seed-beds of disaffection for the universities. Westminster, Eton, Canterbury and Winchester are mentioned by name as being responsible for this early 'tainting' of youth." Nevertheless, the issue comes to the fore in the nineteenth century. What developed can be best described not as an Imperial culture nor Victorian culture nor Edwardian culture, although those descriptions have a utility, but a *public school culture*.

Defoe emphasizes that society has patterns that are inseparable from the heritage of that society. This is suggestive of Sheldrake. Children come under the influence of social morphic fields, and "tune in" to the culture. Learning is facilitated by morphic resonance.[33] This is all well and good, but as Sheldrake admits it presents its full share of perplexities and perils. There has to be considerable investigation before the hypothesis takes on flesh. At present the idea is vague, and about as helpful as explaining arson by noting that oxygen was present at the scene of the crime.

The public schools' cultural influence to those unfamiliar with British education may seem minor alongside economic or political explanations, but the case is strengthened by the schools' input into other institutions such as gentlemen's clubs and Freemasonry.[34] Whilst old boys were part of an *ad hoc* fraternity bound by secret signs, they were with monotonous regularity members as well of real fraternities, the selective clubs and lodges which became bastions of the Imperial social structure.

Three institutions discussed here – the schools, the clubs, the lodges – were infused with an Imperial pomp. A member could sit conveniently in his club and watch the ceremonials of Empire, as the members of White's did in comfort for Queen Victoria's Jubilee procession in 1897. (See *Royal Jubilee Invitation*, page 64, and *White's*, page 65.) In that instance, status won an **actual**, as opposed to **figurative**, seat at the Imperial performance.

Harbouring strong feelings for their school, club, and lodge, the British had correspondingly less time for local customs and imposed their own. This was not always a case of Imperial ritual being substituted for local ritual. There also was a ritualization of local affairs which heretofore had **not** been regarded as ceremonious occasions by the natives. The public schools had taught boys how to apply ritual to what in other countries was unstructured and private.

Besides these innovations, in many cases the indigenous society's own totems and taboos were jettisoned. While the British ruthlessly tampered with local customs, tampering with tradition in Britain itself (or what was *believed* to be tradition) was taboo. The old boys felt that "to tamper with the school is to tamper with their own childhoods".[35] Schooldays and the Imperial punctilio shared sacrosanctity, although both had been invested with a pseudo-antiquity by administrators in much the same way as a designer sprays fake cobwebs around a film set. Anthony Parsons, a former Bahrain Political Agent and distinguished Arabist, recollected a school visit in Sudan where ". . . the adolescent Sudanese girls, in powdered wigs and elaborate English eighteenth-century costumes, vigorously acted out this comedy of manners."[36]

Nor was it obvious that what was going on was a play. Naive natives were unenlightened about the distinctions between the political and the theatrical. Victorian "crèche-ifications" applied a bogus antique finish to Imperial edicts. The antiquity amounted to a hijacking of history, cultivating assumptions that the Imperial idiom dated back to time immemorial. Fakery was endemic. The public schools, like the Imperial government, energetically sought to become as old as possible. As will be seen, foundations with church associations simply appropriated the history of the nearby parish.[37] This was commonplace.[38] Nor was energy spared as far as the actual physical foundations were concerned. When Charterhouse moved to Godalming, stones from the original building were carted along to give the requisite atmosphere. Shrewsbury mounted a similar effort when it moved, but the effort was less evident, as those of Charterhouse were handsomely carved while the Shrewsbury blocks only displayed graffiti.

As Whitehall and the schools grew moss and affected medievalism, Freemasonry was also busily burying its origins in a mythical past. There is a parallel between lodge masters pushing lodge origins back in time and headmasters doing the same for their schools: "A recent investigation of the ancient records in York Minster has shown that the Royal School of St. Peter existed in the sixth century."[39] What appeared out of the confusion seemed an ". . . eclectic ramshackled structure, swarming with Knights Templars, Rosicrucians, alchemists, Masonic initiates . . . mixing up Rene Gueron and Conan the Barbarian, Avalon and the Kingdom of Prester John . . . fascinating for the happy few who stand proof-tight, philology-

66

resistant, bravely ignorant of the Popperian call for the good habit of falsification."[40]

The "restoration" of ritual present problems even to the most scrupulously honest, because denouncement out of hand is inappropriate. Should the etiquette of the past be preserved when it is in deteriorated condition, or should it be revamped or reproduced? The dilemma exists in the case of social mores as much as it does for wallpaper in a historic house. When restoring starts, where should it stop? Like the 'reconstruction' of the Palace of Westminster, much of the Imperial ritualism was built out of pure conjecture. Put most politely, the rituals were misleading in their historical claims.[41] It is no surprise to encounter the schoolmaster in E. M. Forster's novel *The Longest Journey* who is engrossed in manufacturing school rituals: "The school caps, with their elaborate symbolism, were his; his the many-tinted bathing-drawers, that showed how far a boy could swim; his, the hierarchy of jerseys and blazers. It was he who instituted Bounds, and Call, and the two sorts of exercise paper, and the three sorts of caning . . .".[42] (See *Home for the Holidays,* below.)

Customs were cooked-up out of thin air. As mentioned in *Elixir,* Westminster resuscitated pancake greezing: the school cook, superintended by a beadle bearing the mace (How many state schools had beadles and maces?), tossed a pancake high in the air, boys scrambling for the largest piece and a guinea prize.[43] Dr. Patrick Dunae recounted to this author his surprised delight that on a visit to British Columbia's Shawnigan Lake School in 1987 the boys held a greeze, a 'tradition'; instituted by an Old Westminster headmaster. After greezes, Old Westminsters overseas would not have lacked the confidence to concoct their own ritual dishes for native consumption.

Home for the Holidays.

67

The old boys encouraged Imperial subjects to seek honours. Maharajahs and shaikhs competed for gun salutes instead of a pancake: ". . . many princes would sell their souls to have a couple of guns added to their salutes".[44]

Intangibles Made Tangible

The public school instilled a lifelong interest in 'gongs'. Robert Birley's interference while headmaster with the selection of Eton's élite inner circle, Pop, led later to his knighthood being sidetracked by influential Old Etonians, and possibly to his being denied a peerage.[45] There was a tremendous expansion in ceremonious prize giving in the Victorian era. Clubs and learned societies shared in the enthusiasm. The Victorians had their own versions of the contemporary television game shows, only proceedings had more dignity and the gifts were not as prosaic as toasters and electric blankets. In the Empire, the prizes included knighthoods and medals and epitomized Imperial hierarchicalism by minute nuances. Ritualism sustained class. Imperial awards remained élitist in nature during wartime: public school boys were almost all officers and received the Military *Cross* or Distinguished Service *Order*. The deserving, the enlisted men, got the humbler Military *Medal* or Distinguished Service *Medal*. The careful distinctions demonstrate how honours demand deference from the recipients while enhancing the ego of the donors. Too often honours are thought about in terms of the recipients, when it is the donors who gain the most status.

The meaning of such tokens and the singular importance of costumes, decorations, and other apparent trivia should not be minimized. Ataturk understood the significance of totems when abolishing the fez in Turkey. The Scottish nationalists understood it when they stole the Stone of Scone. Walpole was aware of it when the kilt was embargoed in the Hanoverian era. The talismans are the SUBSTRATUM of ideology, and ideology could not persist without being celebrated in ritual. Ritual is the intangible made tangible. Its successful employment in the Empire has implications for anyone concerned with the Victorian and Edwardian eras. Exploration of its rôle should improve perceptions of what 'really' happened, and roll back a fog of cultural amnesia that has given rather recently conceived traditions an appearance of immemorial antiquity.[46] Truly we "labour endlessly to discover who is running the game, the secret motives, the algorism, finally, of this enigmatic tumult, now gay, now somber, often meaningless but always in quest of meaning . . .".[47]

The story of historiography in the last few decades is a version of the old 'man bites dog' story: scientists confirm the findings of social historians! Only the historians remain unaware of the irony. However, the question of how metaphysical the consideration of historical causality should become or how much the natural sciences can contribute to understanding history will not be settled here, or perhaps anywhere. What is maintained is that the philosophy of science should have more of a place in the history of education that it has had.

Morphic resonance is only one of the possible causal influences: "We have to choose, because we could never cope with the universe as it really is. Its booming, boisterous confusion is too much for us, so we carefully elect just those bits of environmental information that make immediate sense . . .".[48] Fortunately, worrying about causes and education is different from worrying about the cosmos. *Something can be done about education.*

Thomas Arnold's Reappearance

In the United States, where everything seems possible, the growth of cryonics institutes which immerse the dead in liquid nitrogen has raised the possibility that historians will someday be confronted with the **ultimate revisionist argument,** the men and women of the past revived to defend themselves. The newsletter of one such organization, the Immortalist Society of Oak Park, Michigan, points out, "What do you have to lose? From a medical standpoint, you have nothing to lose by being frozen immediately after clinical death. At worst, you will simply remain dead. But if we are right, you will return to consciousness and youthful good health in the future." This is bland compared with claims that eventually human beings will be regenerated from the genetic codes deciphered from a finger-nail or lock of hair. The reappearance of Thomas Arnold or Edward Thring would be a nightmare for dogmatic historians of education.

Be that as it may, the reappearance of metaphysics in educational discussion is much to be desired. The dogma that belief-states are never physical-states cannot be sustained.[49] Sheldrake's is only a hypothesis, but ideas such as morphic resonance and chaos are full of implications for education. Scientists realise that complex results mean a search for complex causes. A corollary is the appreciation that small differences in input can become overwhelming differences in output.[50] Educators take note.

As will be seen, the search for causal factors in individual lives relates to broader educational issues. Havelock Ellis asserts that: "A biographer should concentrate upon the curve of life that has its summit at puberty and ends with the completion of adolescence: **whatever else there is to make is made then.** The machine has been created; during these years it is wound up to perform its work in the world. What follows counts for something but always for less."[51] Determining the school influences on individuals is crucial, but there is no sense in considering an influence such as the public school influence on Imperialism if those involved did not attend public school.

The history of education offers new possibilities for Imperial studies. Melodies have been left unrecognized because the rhythm has been unfamiliar.[52] That is why EDUCATIONAL PROSOPOGRAPHY is a powerful instrument of discovery, and why the value of its use comes next in the discussion.[53]

1. Lyall Watson, *Neophilia: The Tradition of the New*, Sceptre, 1989, 11-12. "Neophilic species . . . are determined nonspecialists." *Ibid.*, 12. See William Outhwaite, *New Philosophies of Social Science: Realism, Hermeneutics, and Critical Theory*, Macmillan, 1987, 8-9.

2. Rupert Sheldrake, *A New Science of Life*, Paladian, 2nd ed. 1987 (1981), 96. Consider James Lovelock, *The Ages of Gaia*, OUP, 1988. Also Norman Cousins, "Intangibles in Medicine: An Attempt at a Balancing Perspective", *JAMA*, Vol. 260, No. 11, 16 September 1988, 1610-1612.

3. Kenneth E. Boulding, *The Image: Knowledge in Life and Society*, University of Michigan Press, Ann Arbor, 1961 (1956), 72-73. The importance of similar matters is evident in the work of Michel Foucault, Dorind Outram, and other social historians. See Richard Griffiths, *"Jours de Gloire"*, *Times Higher Education Supplement*, 1 December 1989, 22.

4. Lois Wingerson, "Ideas That Stick in the Wind – The Theory That Refuses to Go", *New Scientist*, 2 October 1985, 56-57. *Cf.* Stephen R. F. Clark, "A Matter of Habit?', *Times Literary Supplement*, 24 June 1988, 702.

5. Andrew Birkin, *J. M. Barrie & The Lost Boys*, Constable, 1986, 196.

6. Notwithstanding *Critique of Pure Reason*, the prevailing question has not been whether causality was a fact, but how to determine it. "Everything has a cause." Adolf Graunbaum, "The Pseudo-Problem of Creation in Physical Cosmology", *Philosophy of Science*, Vol. 56, No. 3, September 1989, 379.

7. On the related question of the schools being part of the 'milieu', see Daniel Calhoun, *The Intelligence of People*, Princeton University Press, New Jersey, 1973, vii. Hereditarian thinking leads to a pessimism about the effects of education. *Ibid.*, 3-4. *But*, as Calhoun admits, "the whole subject is open". *Ibid.*, 19.

8. See Jack Nobbs, Bob Hine, and Margaret Fleming, *Sociology*, 2nd ed. rev., Macmillan, 1983, 377. Also R. B. Braithwaite, *Scientific Explanation*, OUP, 1953, 320, qtd. Adam Schaff, *History and Truth*, Pergamon Press, Oxford, 1976, 201. Braithwaite is appropriately invoked by Rupert Sheldrake in *The Presence of the Past*. *Cf.* David Sapire, "Determinism, The Remote Past, and the Causal or Determinal Structure of The Universe", *Philosophy of Science*, Vol. 56, No. 3, September 1989, 474-83. Also *cf.* Mark Wilson, "John Earman's *A Primer on Determinism*", *Ibid.*, 502-32.

9. See Francois Furet, *In the Workshop of History*, University of Chicago Press, 1982, 57-58. Also John Bintliff, ed., *Extracting Meaning from the Past*, Oxbow, Oxford, 1988, esp. James Lewthwaite, "Living in Interesting Times: Archaeology as Society's Mirror", 86-98. *Cf.* José Havet, "Cartoons - A Neglected Source of Insight Into International Development", *Development Dialogue*, 1987, No. 2, 128-48.

10. Lord Belhaven, *The Uneven Road*, John Murray, 1955, 8. Yet, "the best scholarship these days develops in a self-conscious way." Jonathan Clark in his savage review of Paul Langford's *New Oxford History of England*, *The Times*, 18 September 1969.

11. See Emmanuel Le Roy Ladurie, *The Territory of the Historian*, Harvester Press, Brighton 1979. The past is *always* being reconstructed. See Peter Biller, "Medieval Waldensians' Construction of the Past", *Proceedings of the Huguenot Society* Vol. XXV, No. 1, 1989, 39-54.

12. Martin J. Wiener, *English Culture and the Decline of the Industrial Spirit, 1850-1980*, Penguin, Harmondsworth, 1985, 21.

13. Correlli Barnett, *The Audit of War: The Illusion & Reality of Britain as a Great Nation*, Macmillan, 1986, 192-93. Obviously there could have been many contributing factors. Reports on new pharmaceuticals warn that "where a causal relationship could not be established . . . it cannot be excluded."

14. See Oscar Browning, *An Introduction to the History of Educational Theories*, Kegan Paul, Trench, Trubner, 1903, 191.

15. Graves, *Goodbye to All That*, 24.

16. See John Beame, *Memoirs of a Bengal Civilian*, Chatto & Windus, 1961, 189.

17. A. P. Thornton, *The Imperial Idea and Its Enemies: A Study in British Power*, 2nd ed., Macmillan, 1985, 93-94.

18. Arnold Wilson, *More Thoughts and Talks: The Diary and Scrap-book of a Member of Parliament from September 1927 to August 1939*, Right Book Club, 1939, 62.

19. *E.g.* A. J. P. Taylor, *A Personal History*, Hamish Hamilton, 1983, 45. Also David Plante, "Profiles: Sir Steven Runciman", *The New Yorker*, 3 November 1986, 69.

20. Pamela Street, *Arthur Bryant: Portrait of a Historian*, Collins, 1979, 44. *Cf. Ibid.*, 46, 50.

21. *Some* historians seem to have found public schools a congenial place to work. D. C. Somervell did his best-selling abridgement of Toynbee while housemaster of Judde House at Tonbridge, this author's old house.

22. Arnold Toynbee, *Acquaintances*, OUP, 1967, 37, 40.

23. J. E. Barton, contributor, *The Headmaster Speaks*, Kegan Paul, 1936, 43.

24. Michael Rosenthal, *The Character Factory: Baden-Powell and the Origins of the Boy Scout Movement*, Collins, 1986, 90-91, 104.

25. Colin Shrosbree, *Public Schools and Private Education: The Clarendon Commission 1861-64 and the Public Schools Acts*, Manchester University Press, 1988, vii.

26. *Ibid.*

27. John A. Armstrong, *The European Adminstrative Elites*, Princeton University Press, 1973, 122.

28. Sheldrake, *A New Science of Life* 75. "Our ultimate objective included . . . To identify the building blocks of culture – what we later came to call the isolates of culture, akin to the notes in a musical score." Edward T. Hall, *The Silent Language*, Fawcett, 1969 (1959), 36. Anticipations of Sheldrake's hypothesis are discussed in this author's PhD, "The Rule of Ritual in the Arabian Gulf, 1858-1947: The Influence of English Public Schools", The University of Western Australia, 1989, available from University Microfilms, 300 North Zeeb Road, Ann Arbor, Michigan 48106.

29. Tapper and Salter, *Power and Policy*, 64.

30. Sheldrake, *New Science of Life*, 107.

31. *Ibid.*, 189.

32. However, see T. W. Bamford, *Rise of the Public Schools*, Nelson, 1967, 239.

33. Sheldrake, *Presence of the Past*, 343. *Cf.* Daniel Lerner, "The Transfer of Institutions", William B. Hamilton ed., *The Transfer of Institutions*, Duke University Press, Durham (North Caroline), 1964, 14.

34. "Anyone who has been to an English public school will feel comparatively at home in prison." Evelyn Waugh, *Decline and Fall*, 1928. "Perhaps the greatest virtue claimed for public schools in the past was that they equipped their pupils for a life which could hardly ever be as bad as Marlborough. That is why public school boys always did well in prison." John Mortimer, "Training for a Life in Prison", *Sunday Times* 29 May 1988, G2.

35. Geoffrey Walford, *Life in Public Schools*, Methuen, 1986, 212.

36. Anthony Parsons, *They Say the Lion – Britain's Legacy to the Arabs: A Personal Memoir*, Jonathan Cape, 1986, 83.

37. See *Rousdon Mansion: Present Home of Allhallows Schools*, Allhallows School, 1978. By similar logic, schools near Salisbury could claim to be Druidic! At the same time, churches were also "re-inventing" traditions. See, *e.g.* Mary and Charlotte Thorpe, *London Church Staves*, Elliot Stock, 1895, passim.

38. Better still if there was an adjacent Cathedral as in the case of King's School, Canterbury.

39. Charles Knightly, *The Customs and Ceremonies of Britain*, Thames and Hudson, 1986, 147.

40. Umberto Eco, *Travels in Hyperreality*, Picador, 1987, 71.

41. Parallels in the arts include Robert Craft's invented conversations of Stravinsky, Ralph Schoenman's manipulations of Bertrand Russell's image, and Walter Hooper's manufactured writings attributed to C. S. Lewis. See David Bratman, "C. S. Lewis", *Mythprint*, Monthly Bulletin of The Mythopoeic Society, Vol. 26, No. 2, 7-8.

42. qtd. Jeffrey Richards, *Happiest Days: The Public Schools in English Fiction*, Manchester University Press, 1988, 170.

43. Knightly, *Customs and Ceremonies*, 207.

44. Charles Chenevix Trench, *Viceroy's Agent*, Jonathan Cape, 1987, 9. See Ann Morrow, *Highness: The Maharajahs of India*, Grafton Books, 1986, 234.

45. Arthur Hearnden, *Red Robert: A Life of Robert Birley*, Hamish Hamilton, 1984, 254.

46. See Ruth Perry, "Some Methodological Implications of the Study of Women's Writings", *Harvard Library Bulletin*, Vol. XXXV, No. 2, Spring 1987, 230-48. An excellent account of the vicissitudes of royal ritualism is Jeffrey L. Lant, *Insubstantial Pageant: Ceremony and Confusion at Queen Victoria's Court*, Hamish Hamilton, 1979.

47. Jacques Berque, *Cultural Expression in Arab Society Today*, trs. Robert Stookey, University of Texas Press, Austin, 1978, 305-306. Despite any small success, history taunts us with enigmas and the thought that we have not really broken the code. Christopher Lloyd, *Explanation in Social History*, Basil Blackwell, Oxford, 1986, 8.

48. Watson, *Neophilia*, 61.

49. Sheldrake notes that "The question of form has been discussed by Western philosophers for well over two thousand years, and the same kinds of arguments have reappeared century after century and are still alive and well today." Sheldrake, *Presence of the Past*, 59.

50 Gleick, *Chaos*, 8.

51. Havelock Ellis, *An Open Letter to Biographers*, Oriole Press, Berkely Heights (New Jersey), 1938, 11. the questions of formative influences involves taking a position: ". . . the insistence that individuals just are social, historical agents, the other that they just are social historical products." W. Watts Miller, "Durkheim and Individualism", *The Sociological Review*, Vol. 36, No. 4, November 1988, 647.

52. Phyllis E. Wachter, "Biography of Works about Life-Writing for the Latter 1980s", *Biography*, Vol. 11, No. 4, Fall 1988, 316. Not everyone agrees: "'The connection between Imperialism and the public schools that Rich now substantiates has been acknowledged in passing only'? But this connection has been long accepted, *e.g.* Gathorne-Hardy in *The Public School Phenomenom* (1977) devotes some 17 pages to a discussion of the matter." G. R. Batho reviewing *Elixir of Empire*, *Comparative Education*, Vol. 26, No. 1, March 1990, 155.

53. *The Journal of the Society for Psychical Research* comments frequently on the "mysteriousness" of causation involved in clairvoyance, adding "all causation is mysterious". Frank B. Dilley, "Making Clairvoyance Coherent", *Journal of the Society for Psychical Research*, Vol. 55, No. 814, January 1989, 244. Quite.

CHAPTER III

Prosopography

Do Wykehamists become Wykehamists through going to Winchester, or do they go to Winchester because they are already potential Wykehamists? – Anthony Lejeune, *Strange and Private Wars,* 1986.

'Where did you go to school?' is notoriously the most strategic question that one Englishman can ask of another – Paul Delany, *The Neo-pagans,* 1987.

The importance of the English Public Schools to the major civil and military services and even to business would be difficult to exaggerate. Their grip on the national imagination is not equalled by that of comparable institutions in any other country among the Western democracies – Robert Heussler, *Yesterday's Rulers,* 1982.

Prosopography, collective biography spiced with analysis, is closely associated with the problem of causality. It comes into play because before causality can be considered, the causes have to be sorted out. However, while gathering the biographies of a group is a start, that is not enough. Facts do not have motives – the falling apple had no intention of demonstrating gravity to Newton, whereas Newton had considerable purposes. Nevertheless, before causes are weighed and valued, their very existence has to be confirmed. This is where prosopography has importance. Only when the 'life-facts' have been gathered can the arguments start over the relative significance of each factor. The material uncovered may be so much trivia.

The employment of prosopography itself constitutes a causal assertion, a claim that individuals do make history. That does not render the task of interpreting events any easier. History advertises, like a Broadway review, 'a cast of thousands':

> Within the *histoire totale* of Empire, lumbering along with no concluding chapter in sight, there are recurring characters: able statesmen, unaccountable energumens, strategist clerks, atavistic aristocrats, company promoters, 'civilians' with principles, elect Englishmen, well-mobilized Scots, Anglo-Irish soldiers, gentlemen and merchant adventurers, evangelizers of the earth, peripheral activists, men on the spot, Mannoni's Robinson Crusoes and Prosperos, *makers of milieus and relationships.* It is possible to put a hook in the nose of any one of these characters and tow it safely to shore. But how can philosopher, political scientist, economist, even comic spirit, ever comprehend within one single theory all these

73

Like Tom Bennet's paver cut assemblage

diverse agencies, all the asymmetries, all the disjunctions in time and space?[1]

Should a biographical exercise reveal that the subjects in the group are Puseyites or Benthamites or Freemasons or Old Boys, the implications can be considered. It is useless to discuss *a priori* what may turn out to be non-existent – for example, the influence exerted by Greek Orthodox monasticism on a group of Danish Lutheran school children. (Of course, despite the inherent implausibility, only a prosopographical investigation would show that the Danish children had no contact with Greek Orthodoxy.)

Causal factors can be uncooperative about declaring their presence. Scholars in their difficult search may enviously recall Sherlock Holmes' remark in *The Red-Haired League* (1892): "Beyond the obvious fact that he has at some time done manual labour, that he takes snuff, that he is a Freemason, that he has been in China, and that he has done a considerable amount of writing lately, I can deduce nothing else." Nonetheless, the need to understand the commonalities of a group, to explore the similarities and differences between its individuals, does make prosopography a helpmate.

To mention prosopography is to call to mind Sir Lewis Namier (1888-1960), the Polish-born and Balliol-educated historian. In *The Structure of Politics at the Accession of George III* (1929) Namier showed the technique's effectiveness and garnered his share of honours as a result, but lately his stock has declined. He has been accused of denuding politics of ideas, and of pretending that politics did not exist.[2]

The criticism of statistically-oriented foraging can be well justified concerning smokescreens of tables and averages whose use should be (to borrow an expression of the Macaulay enthusiast John Burrow) like a necessary visit to the washroom. At any rate, the technique has not been as effectively employed by historians as it could have been. This especially holds true for educational history and the history of the public schools. Despite the amount of biographical material represented in public school registers, there has been little done in terms of collective studies of old boys. Historians of individual schools have given the scantiest attention to the prosopography of their schools' old boys, more generally providing stilted chronologies that ignore a goldmine of primary resources available in alumni archives.

Prosopography is less easily applied when seeking affilictions that are pertinent to rule by ritual, such as membership in a Masonic lodge. Obviously membership in a secret society is one of the hardest bits of information to ferret out, but is an extremely important indication of a person's interests and helps in understanding the symbols by which he lived.[3] Lodge membership is an indication of the symbols that were cherished, as is the school attended.

Educational history has as much or more original material at its disposal for prosopography as any historical speciality. That the technique is used so sparingly is symptomatic of a major problem in the history of education itself. Its historians seem, at least at times, to avoid approaches which are employed as a matter of course in writing general history. Freud and Gramsci belong to a ghostly purlieu as far as many historians of education are concerned, and frissons generated by juxtaposing paradigms seem to be regarded as 'poor form'. How much remains to be fashioned out of the voluminous school records is shown by Christine Heward's recent (1988) *Making a Man of Him: Parents and their son's education at an English Public School, 1929-50*, drawing on over 2000 letters to the headmaster of Ellesmere College. From this correspondence, she was able to develop themes hitherto unnoticed by public school scholarship: the plight of widows as far as education, changing views of the professions in England between the world wars. Particularism can be productive of historical explanation, and prosopography despite being a specific technique can produce broad insights.[4]

What Can Go Wrong?

Prosopography has certain difficulties that should cause anyone using the technique to be cautious, the most serious being **to claim too much on the basis of too small a group.** By illustration, Stanley Elkins and Eric McKitrick's study of the American Revolution, *The Founding Fathers: Young Men of the Revolution*, has been faulted as "sans fear and sans research". It expounds a generational thesis about the adoption of the American constitution, based on a sample of Federalists and and Antifederalists. The arithmetic has been denounced as "slovenly" and the sample as "absurdly small".[5]

There is a fairly long history to the publishing of public school statistics – Prince Lee's successor at King Edward's Birmingham had compiled in 1857 an interesting study of the parental backgrounds of boys, and one that David Newsome cited in his masterful *Godliness & Good Learning*. The *Public Schools' Yearbook* decision in 1899 to abandon using its criteria for admitting schools and to include all schools that belonged to the Headmasters' Conference was a watershed as far as deciding which schools were "public". Efforts to estimate the contribution of individual schools by the use of figures include Alick Henry Maclean's *Where We Get Our Best Men* (1900), *Public Schools and the War in South Africa* (1903), and *Public Schools and the Great War, 1914-19: Some Figures* (1923). Along with such statistically-occupied studies, public school literature contains generalizations about the characteristics of individual schools. Richard Ollard in *An English Education* claims about Winchester, Rugby, Wellington, and Marlborough, that "If these were the names of characters in a Restoration comedy and not of great public schools we should know at once that the four were plain, bluff, old-fashioned gentlemen, a little coarse, perhaps but essentially good-hearted, while Eton would be the man of fashion, selfish, cynical, and predatory."[6] The connection between schools and Imperial service has also been long noted: the *Lahore Civil and Military Gazette* in 1900 carried an article on "Which Public School sends out the most men to India". At the time, Clifton headed the list, followed by Winchester, Charterhouse, Marlborough,

Cheltenham, St. Paul's, Rugby, and Eton.

Arguably though, it was in 1977 with the publication of John Honey's *Tom Brown's Universe* that the welter of figures available about old boy lives and the notions about the cachet imparted by individual schools were given full pride of place. T. J. H. Bishop and Rupert Wilkinson had used statistics extensively but with limited aims in a study of the Winchester school lists, *Winchester and the Public School Elite: A Statistical Analysis*. Others as mentioned had also used statistics, but Honey excelled in categorizing schools by the use of numerous tables, based on what he considered the prestige-gauging measures as games fixtures. He was preoccupied with the schools' status, offering innumerable 'facts' but little theoretical framework. Professor Honey's results were then taken up by Dr. J. A. Mangan, a much published and prominent historian who has written at length about school athleticism. Dr. Mangan latched on as well to the work done on the Sudanese Political Service by Antony Kirk-Greene of Oxford's St. Anthony's College. Kirk-Greene tried to show that the SPS was made up of Oxbridge blues, thus confirming the cliché that the Sudan was a 'country of blacks ruled by blues'. He did not go into the award of blues in historical depth and perhaps did not emphasize emphatically enough the implications – a half blue in canoeing or croquet was hardly the same as a blue in Rugby Union or rowing, and (to use extreme examples) a half blue in Rugby League or ballroom dancing might do more harm to a reputation than good. One Oxonian has remarked that rather than catalogue blues, Kirk-Greene should have investigated who was in a crew that was Head of the River or had success at Bumps: bumping could confer as much status as winning a blue.

Dr. Mangan took the information Kirk-Greene had turned up about SPS blues and set out to show what he could from the results by using what he called Honey's "novel and sophisticated process of analysis", applying Honey's categories such as "The Early Lesser Schools" and "The Early Leading Schools". He concluded that "If his groupings are collapsed and adapted with the early leading and lesser schools grouped together and labelled 'Early Established Public Schools', and juxtaposed with the 'peripheral', 'recent' and 'more recent' schools similarly grouped together and labelled 'Later Public and Peripheral Schools' we have two broad categories of schools."[7]

The reference to **collapsing categories** is unfortunately reminiscent of **collapsing balloons**. Honey's were already miniscule divisions and Dr. Mangan's collapsing categories did not represent an advance. A fixation with sporting fixtures as the way to determine status ignores other aspects of the status question. As an example, the deliberate strategies to achieve status practiced by governing bodies and headmasters have to be considered more than they have been. (See *The Choice of a School*, page 77.)

T. W. Bamford points out in his classic *Rise of the Public Schools* just how cold-blooded were the admissions policies of schools.[8] Evans Prosser, headmaster of Ellesmere College, ". . . sold school places with the smooth bonhomie of the secondhand car salesmen", and realized that Ellesmere would be judged on its ability to place its boys in successful careers. Consequently, "Sound wickets had a lower

The Choice of a School.

priority at Ellesmere than an ample supply of bunsen burners."⁹ The quote is ironically from Dr. Mangan's *Times Higher Education Supplement* review in 1988 of Heward's *Making a Man of Him*. In the same review, Dr. Mangan concedes that ". . . the classroom was more important than playing field, a state of affairs increasingly typical of the public school system of the Thirties and later, as my own research has indicated." One agrees with Dr. Mangan that there could be matters more important than the playing field, but his contention that there was a sea change in the 1930s as to what determined a school's popularity is by no means proven. *A school's position always had depended on far more than games.*¹⁰ G. C. Turner in his distinctive investigations of Marlborough history insisted that "in Victorian days a school's success was often measured by its scholarship".¹¹ Efforts such as Honey's to read into athletic fixtures a host of conclusions are doomed to frustration.

A Pastime for Snobs

Categorization compels distorting generalizations. Colour is an example. There are literally millions of colours. A Macintosh computer can produce 16.8 million shades of colours. We reduce them in discussion to a few hundred at best. Public schools may not exist in such multi-hued diversity, but they are diverse enough to make their categorizations perilous. Nevertheless, categorizing has been a favourite pastime of snobs, old boys, and novelists. James Hilton in *Goodbye Mr. Chips* describes Brookfield: "It was, nevertheless, a good school of the second rank. Several notable families supported it; it supplied fair samples of the history-making men of the age – judges, Members of Parliament, colonial administrators, a few peers and bishops . . . It was the sort of school which, when mentioned, would sometimes make snobbish people confess that they rather thought they had heard of it."

This sort of comment is fair enough in a novel or in the *Tatler,* but is fraught with dangers in serious history.[12] In Dr. Mangan's case, his categories seem, if anything, more confusing than Honey's – Glasgow Academy for example is a "Recent School" in one table but an "Early Lesser School" in another.[13] Cranleigh, Dover, Forest, Highgate, Hurstpierpoint, St. John's Leatherhead, and Warwick are "Early Leading Schools" while Christ's Hospital, Mill Hill, Perse, and Sedbergh are "Early Lesser Schools" and Exeter, Taunton, and Dean Close are "Early Peripheral Schools".[14] Few students of the public schools would be happy with these generalizations.

Dr. Mangan used his collapsed categories to support tentatively a small band of students of the Sudanese Political Service (SPS) such as Kirk-Greene who have speculated about that service's superiority over the other Imperial cadres. He thus entered an area of controversy somewhat removed from his own speciality, challenging the prevailing if conventional wisdom that the Indian services were the best in the world, a source of "awe and admiration".[15] In considering his use of Honey's ratings to analyze the SPS, a reaction is that no amount of trying will make Khartoum into Delhi.[16] The distinction between India and the Sudan is mirrored in their honours system. Indian officers received the Star of India that Prince Albert and Queen Victoria had taken pains to help design, and whose Grand Cross was a cameo of the Queen-Empress surrounded by diamonds and decorations. SPS members received the Colonial Office's St. Michael and St. George promising a prosaic *Auspicium Melioris Aevi* – A Pledge of Better Times.[17] It cost considerably less to make.

The *esprit de corps* of SPS historians is laudable, but not universally regarded as warranted.[18] The use of school categories when demonstrating the galactic qualities of the Sudanese service does raise questions about the schools of other Imperial cadres. If the men in the Indian Civil Service or Indian Political Service went to unknown schools and the SPS went to celebrated schools, inferences might be justified. Actually, all the Imperial bureaucrats were elitely educated in comparison with "average" Englishmen. No one has shown that the list of schools attended by men serving in different parts of the Empire offers large surprises, and the same schools appear in lists of schools attended by men in the ICS as in the SPS. The bottom line is that specific schools are not as terribly significant when discussing the Empire as is the uniform public school background. Potter in *India's Political Administrators* studied a larger sample of ICS officers than anyone else has so far. He concluded that it was the fact of going to a public school rather than any specific school that was crucial, and that the schools produced officers "in ones or twos, not in bunches".[19]

Prosopography

The Gurkhas Were Not the Guards

Preparatory schools, clubs, lodges, and regiments of the Imperial élite can all be categorized in considerable detail. It is true that there were distinctions between individual institutions. The Gurkhas were not the Guards. Yet some similarities in culture were remarkable. An interloper in London's clubland would find that the social conformity was confirmed by an impressive architectural conformity. A formula was early arrived upon as to what constituted a proper club house, with the result that one hardly needed to ask the porter where the various function rooms were, even if one had never been in the club before. Considerable erudition would be required to discern the allegedly awesome distinctions between them. The stories may not be apocryphal of someone sitting in a club for a morning without realizing that he was not in his own.

School reputations waxed and waned, but the famous schools are not so different from the less important when comparison is made with other kinds of schools. Arguments about their respective standings have no end. Did Tonbridge 'slip' in the 1930s and then 'bounce back'? Was Bootham the Rugby of Quakerism? Is it significant that Denstone had more boys enrolled in 1881 than Dover, Downside, King's Canterbury, Oundle, Radley, or Sedbergh? One begins to drown in comparisons. Thomas Hughes writes in *Tom Brown's Schooldays*, ". . . come now – would you, any of you, give a fig for a fellow who didn't believe in, and stand up for his own house and his own school? You know you wouldn't . . . If you ain't satisfied, go and write the history of your own houses in your own times, and say all you know for your own schools and houses, provided it's true, and I'll read it without abusing you."

The advice is well taken. There are limits to what can be squeezed from segregating the schools by finer and finer categories. Minor schools had every reason to toe the line of public school respectability for fear of being thought minor. A Provost of King's remarked about Dulwich, "Mine was one of the lesser middle class schools, and so all the more insistent on painful tasks and conventions."[20] The particular school or indeed the decade a man attended is interesting, but the continuities of the public school experience during the period from after the Crimean war to after World War II were remarkable.[21]

Prosopography is a waste of time if it is not directed: a definition of chemistry is applicable, that of converting abundant substances into useful substances. If the particulars are used to write what could be called 'particularistic history', the audience will be one's wife if one has one and a few admiring (?) colleagues. Particulars must be used to fashion an inclusive and meaningful account. A group's public school attendance comes into its own not in proving the social standing of one Imperial service over another, or of demonstrating distinctions between the services, but in the extraordinary opportunity to consider Imperial attitudes produced by education. There is more available on the attitudes to which the Imperial rulers were exposed in their youth than there would be for almost any comparable group. This presents a splendid chance to link education with policy-making. Why has more not been made of this opportunity? The situation is analogous to that prevailing in the natural sciences until recently, where the obsession with symmetry obscured the possibilities.[22] Historians of individual schools have been disappointingly limited in their vision.

An exception is Elizabeth College, Guernsey. What boys went to Elizabeth was painstakingly studied by its historian, V. G. Collenette. He was well aware that there was a public school 'product,' and unlike many compilers of school registers he saw his researches as leading to conclusions. He sought to create a composite picture: "The three volumes of the College Register are a rich and fascinating store of information about the Elizabethans since 1824. If we take the careers of every 100th boy in this register, we can compile a list which might fairly be said to be representative, and which might help to build up a picture of the sort of person that Elizabeth College had endeavoured to produce."[23]

Collenette's selection of every hundredth name produced forty-three biographies, of which seven spent part of their careers in India and of which at least another twenty had family connections with India. (There was an Old Elizabethan Society in India in 1925 with seventy-six members.) If his percentages were confirmed by the entire register, three hundred Elizabethans would have worked in India, and more than half of all OEs would have had family associations with the subcontinent. Other studies of the Indian adminstrators have produced similar results as far as family ties with the Imperial services and India.[24] It has been claimed without much overstatement that almost every English family could find relatives on its tree who had been in India. An example is Field Marshal Viscount Montgomery, whose maternal grandfather was Dean Farrar, author of the school novel *Eric, Or Little By Little*, but whose paternal grandfather was Sir Robert Montgomery, who saved the Punjab during the Mutiny.

Chaos

The usefulness of prosopography hinges more on theories of causality than has been acknowledged. Behaviour must be meaningful or else prosopography is useless, which echoes Wittgenstein's view that there is no such thing as a "private language". A language is a *social* ritual that requires interaction with others and assumes meaningfulness. Ideally a prosopographical study will uncover the ingredients of the social language of the group.

This is why the suggestion was made that the speculation about chaos offers opportunities. That 'irregularities' or what appears to be chaotic have a hidden coherence is relevant to hopes cherished about the results of prosopography. Having determined that a factor is common to the group – time spent at public schools, membership in clubs, or whatever – a logical question is whether this produced something, particularly whether it resulted in *denkkollectiv*, a school of thought or cognitive community. A community is immeasurably strengthened by ritual.[25]

The existence of a 'community of thought' sustained by ritual seems fairly certain in the case of the schools. The consequences included access to life's glittering prizes, literally and metaphorically. George Macdonald Fraser's rascally Flashman, Hughes' villain in *Tom Brown* that Fraser has resurrected for a ribald series, claims that "There's no question that a public school education is an advantage. It may not make you a scholar or a gentleman or a Christian, but it does teach you to survive and prosper – and one other invaluable thing: style."[26] Prosopography is especially valuable as a tool when investigating this 'old boyism' because the public school is a *permanent* rather than a *quondam* causal factor in lives. Old boyism is not a touch of flu. It resembles more the reredos permanently looming behind the (Imperial) altar.

Public schools, like Masonic lodges, were preoccupied with inculcating a lifelong appreciation of rituals. One result of prosopographical investigation, whether of old boys or admirals, is the uncovering of this ritualistic behaviour. It seeks what have been called after Rupert Sheldrake, *chreodes,* the canalized pathways of behaviour that are analogous to the linguist's phonemes and the semiologist and signist's cheremes. **Proponents of Sheldrake's theories of formative causation and morphic resonance could well contend that prosopography's hunt for commonalities resembles their own search for chreodes.** One can disagree with Sheldrake while still hoping to find commonalities and the pattern of which they are the building blocks. However, the attempt to find the influences of institutions on a group relates to Sheldrake's contention that past members of a species have a continued and cumulative influence that increases as the past number of the species grows. He compares the process with composite photography, in which pictures are produced by superimposing a number of images. The past TYPES combine in influence to increase the probability that such TYPES will occur again.[27]

Visible and Invisible

Uniqueness defeats the prosopographical exercise. Moreover, the prosopographical-causal approach relies on the argument that experiences can be neither *totally* private nor *totally* subjective.[28] Though the existence of different types of experience can be commonly appreciated and though empathy can be creatively employed in writing history, prosopography itself is not easy to apply to groups such as the British working class who lacked institutions with the archival self-consciousness of the public schools. Paul Scott underlined this in the *Raj Quartet* novels, where he explored tensions between an Indian old boy, Harry Kumar (Croomer) and Ronald Merrick, a British police officer who is painfully aware of not having gone to public school. In Imperial society it is Kumar rather than the Englishman who matters and upon whom "the historian's eye lovingly falls", *because he went to a public school.* It is Merrick, though English, who is "invisible".[29] The baubles by which old boys identified themselves thus take on particular importance.

This is not to maintain that the working class or the Empire's 'natives' lacked institutions with *denkkollectiv,* but that an extensive documentation of such affiliations flounders because of the paucity of surviving evidence. In contrast, the survival of so much material about old boys affords sport for those who enjoy sorting and straining data as if they were tea leaves. School registers mean that no curiosity about Harrovians in Haiti needs go unsatiated. There is a long deservedly neglected poem by an Old Etonian, James Stephen, entitled *The Old School List*.[30] A few verses will more than suffice to illustrate the preoccupations of old boy hagiography:

> *. . . a wild moraine of forgotten books,*
> *On the glacier of years gone by,*
> *As I plied my rake for order's sake,*
> *There was one that caught my eye:*
> *As I sat by the shelf till I lost myself*
> *And roamed in a crowded mist,*
> *And heard lost voices and saw lost looks,*
> *As I pored on an Old School List.*
>
> *What a jumble of names! there were some that I knew,*
> *As a brother is known: today*
> *Gone I know not where, nay I hardly care*
> *For their places are full: and, they –*
> *What climes they have ranged! how much they're changed!*
> *Time, place and pursuits assist*
> *In transforming them: stay where you are: adieu!*
> *You are all in the Old School List.*

Less effusively, Kenneth Boulding refers to the transmission of images by the archival process: "An effective transcript has a great effect in creating a public image, that is, in ensuring that the images of the various individuals who have access to the transcript are identical or nearly so."[31] The emphasis that schools placed on their own history indicates how seriously they took themselves, as well as the depth of their ideological and political resolve.

Rehearsing the Ju-Ju

Characteristic of *all* English public schools was their 'Empire-awareness'. James Morris refers to the imperial élite who ". . . were products of those curious institutions, the English public schools . . . whose friendships, slangs and values often lasted a man through life. These were the nurseries of Empire."[32] The Empire wanted old boys for its leaders and old boys desired congenial employment. Changes in recruitment to the public service that began in the 1850s were to the advantage of the schools. The division of the civil service into a higher and lower grades meant that there was a built-in hierarchicalism corresponding to the educational ladder, with the superior jobs going to old boys of the schools that produced "a sort of freemasonry among men which is not very easy to describe, but which everybody feels."[33]

Entrance requirements to the services were skewed towards the public schools, which were the only ones that could master the intricacies of the application procedures. Sir Arthur Godley (Lord Kilbracken), Permanent Undersecretary of State for India from 1883 to 1909 and a devoted Old Rugbeian, complained to Lord Curzon about the whole process: ". . . it is like Dr. Johnson's leg of mutton, ill-designed, ill-drawn and ill-amended."[34] Ill-designed the system might have been, but it was fitted admirably to the recruitment of public school products. Boys from the other backgrounds simply did not get into Imperial administration; Godley's system presumed a preparation at public school.

What was the end result of the dominance of a hundred or so schools in an Empire covering a quarter of the globe? One consequence was a unanimity in outlook, although the old boy product, did come in different sizes and shapes – despite the foregoing remarks about not becoming bogged down in distinctions. Tensions over the social standing of the schools did exist. The Indian Civil Service enjoyed boasting that its education had cost more than that of Army men. This provoked Terence Keyes, a Haileyburian who had been recruited to the Indian Political Service from the Army, to complain in 1921 to the Viceroy, Lord Reading: ". . . if the principle of paying according to expense of education is admitted, it would be necessary to adjust the pay of each civil and military officer alike according as he was educated at one of the cheaper schools or at Eton and Harrow."[35]

Regardless of arguments about the standing of individual schools, the homogeneous mannerisms of the old boys were a testimony to how, in the schools and the surrogates of the schools such as clubs, a "potent ju-ju" was learned.[36] A primary ingredient was ritualism and its totems, taboos, and ceremonialism: all were part of the tricks of governing. Because the schools influenced the development of institutions such as gentlemen's clubs, these too became rehearsal halls for the elaborate etiquette that enabled the British to keep an Empire with precious little military force. (In fact, the military attended public school and joined clubs with as much regularity as did the ICS.)

The culture of non-public schools, of myriad associations and movements, and eventually of Britain both at home and abroad, reflected the public school one. This is an emphasis on a position taken by Patrick Dunae. In *Gentlemen Emigrants* he states:

> The new fee-paying academies and boarding schools also adopted, or replicated, many of the rituals and traditions associated with the Ancient Foundation: corporal punishment, spartan dormitories, the monitorial or fagging system, school ties and uniforms, Old Boys' associations, and public school jargon. As a result, a wealthy merchant's son who attended, say, Haileybury, was not recognizably different from a landed gentleman's son at, say Harrow. Despite their different backgrounds, the youths spoke with the same accent, shared the same intellectual and recreational interests, and held similar attitudes in matters of politics and religion.[37]

In addition to seeing that it is the influence of the schools taken at large which is important, Dr. Dunae emphasizes their hortative nature, and the consequences for the Empire.

Excessive verbiage about ranking the schools, along with too much emphasis on their sports history, has side tracked the course set by Rupert Wilkinson in *The Prefects* when he sought out their wider social implications.[38] The subsequent loss of direction epitomizes the difference between what Mannheim called *Sinngemasse Zurechnung*, the approach which considers the whole system, and a tedious pursuit instead of *Faktizitatszurechnung*, a search for ideal types. (Future efforts at categorization would be more usefully done so by ideology rather than by social status. The ideology of individual schools was *sometimes* reflected in the careers of boys.)

Magic as Well as Reason

The question that Professor Honey's work raises is whether concentration on differences is as important as consideration of the public school influence taken as a whole. The answer that Rupert Wilkinson for one gave was that priority should go to the effects of the schools taken as a whole, while remembering that ". . . government survives by magic as well as by reason, by dignity as well as by its decisions."[39]

Neither social nor ideological differences because of the specific schools attended are so far detectable in the administrations of different colonies. Of course there have been no specific studies, such as of who in the Empire went to schools connected with merchant companies, or Woodard schools, or schools controlled by the Methodists or Roman Catholics. What is easily detectable is a ubiquitous pervasive public school style. The observant subtle distinctions both among schools and among clubs, but to the outsider the similarities are so pronounced that drawing the distinctions can seem pedantic. An architectural analogy seems apt. Some had a cornice or pediment and portico and others did not, but the purpose and result was the same.

Prosopography should avoid pseudo-scientific language creating differences that are subtle to the point of being non-existent. It is *interesting* to note that three Lord Chancellors went to Scottish public schools (Haldane to Edinburgh Academy, Simon to Fettes, and Kilmure to George Watson's), but *misleading* to assert that nearly 18% of Lord Chancellors from Halsbury through Hailsham went to Scottish public schools. Statistics about such small groups are dissembling. An example of how disastrous the statistical approach can be is Albert Armstrong's *Public School Power* (1988), which 'proves' remarkable assertions about Eton in British political life. Armstrong deduces by negative reasoning from Eton's statistical prominence in important posts that there is a conspiracy, *e.g.* that R. A. Butler failed to become Prime Minister because he went to Marlborough rather than Eton: "The Butler incident showed with terrible plainness the suppression of political ambition by Eton. Boys who went to any H.M.C. school other than the cabinet ranking schools were educationally disenfranchised and stood no chance in the Conservative party." Mr. Armstrong is convinced that Etonians, with a little help from other old boys ". . . destroyed the basic social structure of the country, which they themselves had created, and also they damaged the main political parties . . . wrecked the British work ethic, and separated science theory and practice. The matter is that simple." Really!

Patinas

There are numerous important denominators besides the public schools in the lives of Imperial administrators. Family connections between Imperial officers (which will be considered in the next chapter) are impressive, being extensive enough to suggest that Imperial historians should be members of the Society of Genealogists. Parenthetically, it can be argued that, although there was a dearth of aristocrats in the Imperial services, the families of overseas bureaucrats displayed not an upper middle class but upper class patina. When the middle class got overseas it acquired the perquisites of the upper class. This reinforces claims about the schools facilitating a comfortable blurring between the upper middle and upper classes.

Other forces were at work in the Empire, but its direction depended on the schoolboys who created an 'Imperial public school civilization'. (See *Craftsman's Road,* below, and *Emblems of the Royal Arch* from *Duncan's Masonic Ritual.*) This was a road that was travelled ritualistically, as Masonic guides emphasized. Having

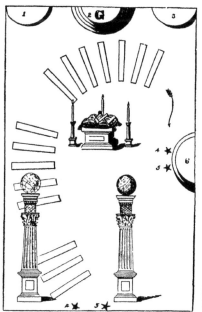 

Representation of the Craftsman's Road to the Middle Chamber of King Solomon's Temple.

Emblems of the Royal Arch Degree.

had the importance of etiquette and custom instilled, old boys were sensitive to what Sheldrake calls "the chreodes of the culture".

> On the present hypothesis, as children grow up they come under the influence of various social morphic fields and tune in to many of the chreodes of the culture, the learning of which is facilitated by morphic resonance . . . The social roles that people take up – the roles of school, children, secretaries, goalkeepers, mothers, bosses, workers, and so on – are shaped by morphic fields stabilized by morphic resonance with those who have played these roles before. Likewise, the patterns of relationship among the various social roles – for example between workers and bosses – are shaped by the morphic fields of the social unit, maintained by resonance from the group's own past and from other more or less similar groups.[40]

Virginia Woolf in her diary quoted the Countess of Cromer as saying, "You send a boy to school in order to make friends – the right sort." Prosopography sorts out *who* the right sort were. There has been much debate about whether the Imperial Hogen Mogens were dullards or eccentrics, drones or dedicated. They were a mixed lot, but the prosopographical survey of them will show that they were educated at English public schools – and were old school tie through and through.

The evidence of how significant this was seems overwhelming, but it still must be regarded warily.[41] Questions of whether school influence was *the* paramount influence in the lives of the Imperial rulers cannot be passed over easily. An argument of this book is that other institutions reflected and complemented the schools. A list of some

Public School Lodges.

of the school lodges from the 1930 *Public School Lodges' Yearbook* is an indication of this. (See *Public School Lodges*, page 86.) Whether old schoolism was the *principal* influence in some men's lives will be considered in succeeding pages. The proposition of *plenitude* when engaged in prosopography is important. Arthur Lovejoy urged that scholars keep in mind ". . . not only the thesis that the universe is a *plenum formarum* in which the range of conceivable diversity of *kinds* of living things is exhaustively exemplified, but also any other deductions from the assumption that no genuine potentiality of being can remain unfulfilled, that the extent and abundance of the creation must be as great as the capability of a 'perfect' and inexhaustible Source, and that the world is the better, the more things it contains."[42] No historical approach calls this diversity to mind more than prosopography, as will be seen.

NOTES – CHAPTER III

1. Grainger, *Patriotisms*, 125.

2. See Himmelfarb, *New History and the Old*, 112. Prosopography is subject to the criticism levelled at the exponents of historical *pointillisme, e.g.* that made about the work of the historian Theodore Zeldin that his explicitness was as impressionistic as the "old" history which he scorned. See *Ibid.*, 122-131. "Historical science presently hovers naked and trembling on the edge of quantification, with Clio in the huddled, hesitant posture of September Morn." Fischer, *Historians' Fallacies* , 104.

3. Michael Baigent, Richard Leigh, Henry Lincoln, *The Messianic Legacy*, Corgi, 1987, 223.

4. "Like a good schoolboy, I won't funk it. I'll come clean, honest, Sir. Reading this book was like reading an account of how many of the masters at my state grammar school would have liked it to have been . . . The minor schools were and are models for the grammar schools, and the grammar schools remain, despite comprehensivisation, models for much secondary education . . . **There are also issues to be explored around the social and historical construction of archival material – the fact that collections of letters in one place, within schools and other organizations, are more likely to be preserved, than those scattered in, say the houses of the sons' parents.** There are some powerful parallels here: *fathers/men/public sphere/organization/writing;* as against *mothers/women/private sphere/clienteles/speech."* Jeffrey Hearn, review of *Making a Man of Him, Gender and Education,* Vol. I, No. 1, 1989, 96-98. A much earlier and rarely noted prosopographical study of seventy-one working class boys is Arnold D. Freeman, *Boy Life and Labour: The Manufacture of Inefficiency,* P. S. King, 1914. He castigated the British educational system as a blind alley for the working class youth, and advocated compulsory continued education.

5. The sample can be *both* small and nonrepresentative. In the case of the America's Founding Fathers, perhaps their aides and underlings should be included because of *their* influence. Similarly, in the case of the English public schools, headmasters have received most of the attention and it is time that the net be thrown wider and include assistant masters – many of whom exerted great influence. The assistant masters who are remembered more today than many headmasters, provides an illustration. "In the world of pen collectors, little is gathered on the fascinating personalities behind the not-so-famous companies." Stephen Overbury, "Canada's Forgotten Pen Maker", *Journal of the Writing Equipment Society,* No. 24, 1989, 7. Prosopography can be disarmingly élitist in its choice of subject: "In a sense, there can never be one definitive singer, style of performance, or medium of expression fully capable of capturing the 'Ding an sich' of human existence. Editions of previously out-of-print diaries, authorized versus unauthorized 'celebiographies' of the rich and famous as well as oral autobiographies of the working class and the politically disenfranchised serve as symbolic rifts which have unlimited improvisational possibilities . . .". Wachter, "Biography of Works about Life-Writing", 316.

Another danger of prosopography is descent into **necromancy.** The historian who employs cliometrics to the school registers must beware of becoming a "self-proclaimed shaman" like the student of Westminster who quantifies the interests of members of Parliament. "He does everything, in short, except utilize the kind of sources, – constitutions, laws, judicial decisions, debates, commentaries, treatises – which might suggest a rationality and deliberation that were not self-serving . . .". Himmelfarb, *The New History and the Old*, 18-19.

6. Richard Ollard, *An English Education: A Perspective of Eton*, Collins, 1982, 12. "You must remember that it's not Clifton, and it's not Winchester, and it's no good you or anyone else trying to make it like that. It's a place for the Beta-query-plus boy." Lyman Thomas, headmaster of Repton, to Sir John Thorn when he was about to become head, qtd. John Thorn, *The Road to Winchester*, Weidenfeld and Nicolson, 72.

7. Mangan, *Games Ethic*, 75-76. The SPS had a total of about 400 members, so the exercise was reminscent of the academic who made assertions about behaviour and when asked for supporting records pointed to a mound of papers and then to a cage, remarking, "and there's the rat." See Fischer, *Historians Fallacies*, 109. The term *sui generis* is unknown in some circles. Everyone has an opinion. "In the Midlands the pecking order in the Sixties was clear: Rugby and Shrewsbury were more brainy places that Repton. Repton was higher in standard than Worksop or Trent College. And so on." Thorn, *Road to Winchester*, 90.

8. Bamford, *Rise of the Public Schools*, 25.

9. J. A. Mangan, "Male Models", *Times Higher Education Supplement*, 12 September 1988, 21.

10. See Bamford, *Rise of the Public Schools*, 25.

11. G. C. Turner, "Old Marlburians", in W. Lewis, *Marlborough College, 1843-1943*, OUP, 1943, 51-52. Westminster School's cricket and rowing ledgers have splendid references to fears of playing schools that were not public. Timothy J. L. Chandler, "Emergent Athleticism: Games in Two English Public Schools, 1800-60", *The International Journal of the History of Sport*, Vol. 5, No. 3, December 1988, 313, 318.

12. ". . . it is often argued that aggregatability of data is one of the chief virtues of operating in the scientific mode; each investigator 'stands on the shoulders' of his or her predecessors to make the next logical contributions. But where is this aggregatability in social and behavioural science? Where is the essential body of knowledge, systematically and patiently built up over decades of work? It is true that extensive literatures exist, but they are characterized at least as much by conflicting findings as by reinforcing ones." Egon G. Guba and Yvonna S. Lincoln, "Epistemological and Methodological Bases of Naturalistic Inquiry", *Educational Communication and Technology*, Vol. 30, No. 4, Winter 1982, 234. The difficulties have not stopped historians from attempting to create models, notably R. S. Neale's efforts to divide English social classes in the nineteenth century into five classes instead of the conventional three: an example of how an old question can be profitably reopened. R. S. Neale, *Class and Ideology in the Nineteenth Century*, Routledge & Kegan Paul, 1972, 15. Neale prosopographically examined the governors and executive councillors of the Australian colonies in 1788-1856. *Ibid.*, 97-120. He found that far more had attended grammar school or had a naval, military, or shipboard education than had attended public school. Considering the period and the nature of the Australian settlement, this is not surprising.

13. Mangan, *Games Ethic*, 77, 83. Glasgow Academy enjoyed some early success and eventually (Eton-Harrow fashion) it was coupled with Kelvinside. See *The Glasgow Academy: The First Hundred Years*, Blackie, Glasgow, 1946.

14. Mangan, *Games Ethic*, 77.

15. Maurice and Taya Zinkin, *Britain and India: Requiem for Empire*, Chatto & Windus, 1964, 56. In an attack on a well-regarded work of Robert O. Collins, *Land Beyond the Rivers: The Southern Sudan 1898-1918* (Yale University Press, 1971), Dr. Mangan accuses Collins of "surrealist indistinctness", remarking "How wide of the mark Collins is on occasion in his incautious generalizations . . .". Mangan, *Games Ethic*, 93-94.

16. *Cf.* Gawain Bell, *Shadows on the Sand: The Memoirs of Sir Gawain Bell*, C. Hurst, 1983, 14-15, 225-26. James Morris, *Pax Britannica: The Climax of an Empire*, Penguin, Harmondsworth, 1983, 184-87. *Cf.* Belhaven, *The Uneven Road*, 22. Lord Natwich, the homosexual peer in Alan Hollinghurst's *The Swimming Pool Library* (Penguin, Harmondsworth, 1988) is an alumnus of the SPS, and Old Wykehamist, *and* inveterate clubman. *The Swimming Pool Library* has innumerable references to the connections between the public schools, gentlemen's clubs, and homosexuality.

17. Morris, *Pax Britannica*, 508.

18. Regarding the Indian and Home Civil Services, ". . . the former demand so high a standard of intellect that it gave little chance to the average man, and entrance to the latter was also at that time ruled

almost entirely by competitive examination. To the undergraduate of good health and reasonable ability a Service which demanded less in the way of examinations . . . held a greater appeal." Sir Harold MacMichael, qtd. Michael S. Coray, "In the Beginning", Robert O. Collins and Francis M. Deng eds., *The British in the Sudan, 1898-1956: The Sweetness and the Sorrow,* Macmillan, 1984, 38. "We are too much at the mercy of the Sudan Civil Servant, who, with all his admirable qualities, has a rather limited and parochial public school outlook." Foreign Office memo qtd. Wm. Roger Louis, *The British Empire in the Middle East, 1945-1951,* Clarendon Press, Oxford, 1985, 702.

19. David C. Potter, *India's Political Administrators, 1919-1983,* Clarendon Press, Oxford, 1986, 68.

20. Simon Raven, *The Old School: A Study in the Oddities of the English Public School System,* Hamish Hamilton, 1986, 77. *Cf.* Reed, *Old School Ties,* 87.

21. Walford, *Life in Public Schools,* 205. See 209, 233, 248.

22. Gleick, *Chaos,* 116.

23. V. G. Collenette, *Elizabeth College, 1563-1963,* Guernsey Press, St. Peter Port (Guernsey), 1963, 45.

24. *E.g.* Robin Bidwell, "The Political Residents of Aden: Biographical Notes", R. B. Serjeant and R. L. Bidwell eds., *Arabian Studies* V, C. Hurst, 1979, 149-59. Also Roland Hunt and John Harrison, *The District Officer in India, 1930-1947,* Scolar Press, 1980, 22.

25. Baigent, *The Messianic Legacy,* 219. See Sheldrake, *Presence of the Past,* 22.

26. George Macdonald Fraser, *Flashman and the Redskins.* Pan, 1943, 148.

27. Sheldrake, *Presence of the Past,* 109.

28. The corollary is that it is the inability to secure the necessary information *because the documentation did not survive* that prevents analysis, **not** any inherent impossibility.

29. See Paul Scott, *A Division of the Spoils,* Granada, 1985 (1975), 369. *Cf.* 68, 115-16, 343, 355, 366. The way in which the distinctions were made visible is further discussed in the last volume of this trilogy, *Rituals of Empire.* The tokens had enormous social and political significance. See, *e.g.,* W. Mark Hamilton, "The 'New Navalism' and the British Navy League, 1865-1914", *Journal of The Society for Naval Research,* Vol. 64, 1978, 37-44.

30. Reproduced in Eric Parker, *Floreat: An Eton Anthology,* Nisbet, 1923, 319-20.

31. Boulding, *The Image,* 65.

32. James Morris, *Farewell the Trumpets: An Imperial Retreat,* Penguin, Harmondsworth, 1984, 27.

33. Robert Low, Chancellor of the Exchequer, qtd. E.J. Feuchtwanger, *Democracy and Empire: Britain 1865-1914,* Edward Arnold, 1985, 89.

34. Martin Moir, "A Study of the History & Organization of the Political and Secret Department of the East India Company, the Board of Control and Indian Office", PhD thesis, University of London, 1966, 42.

35. IOR: L/P&S/10/889, T. Keyes to Earl of Reading, 13 August 1921.

36. Morris, *Farewell the Trumpets,* 28.

37. Dunae, *Gentlemen Emigrants,* 53-54.

38. See also R. W. Wilkinson, "The Gentleman Ideal and the Maintenance of a Political Elite," *Sociology of Education,* Vol. 37, No. 1, Fall 1963, 9-10. *Cf.* M. L. Bush, *The English Aristocracy: A Comparative Synthesis,* Manchester University Press, 1984, 158-59, 162. Like anything when taken to extremes, the categorization of the schools can become bizarre. It resembles other excesses in categorization and classification, such as cladist taxonomy – which, according to Richard Dawkins has "gone right over the top." Richard Dawkins, *The Blind Watchmaker,* Penguin, Harmondsworth, 1988, (1986), 283. *There is a mean to be found between gross generalisms and nitpicking.* Discussing the problem of what level of explanation is appropriate, Dawkins takes as an example the steam locomotive: "Like Julian Huxley I should definitely not be impressed if the engineer said it was propelled by 'force locomotif'. And if he started boring on about the whole being greater than the sum of its parts, I would interrupt him: 'Never mind about that, tell me how it works'." *Ibid.,* 11. Dawkins continues: "For those who like '-ism' sorts of names, the aptest name for my approach to understanding how things work is probably 'hierarchical reductionism'. If you read trendy intellectual magazines, you may have noticed that 'reductionism' is one of those things, like sin, that is only mentioned by people who are against it. To call oneself a reductionist will sound, in some circles, a bit like admitting to eating babies. But just as nobody actually eats babies, so **nobody is really a reductionist** in any sense worth being against . . . The hierarchical reductionist, on the other hand, explains a complex entity at any particular level in the hierarchy of organization, in terms of

entities only one level down the hierarchy, entities which, themselves, are likely to be complex enough to need further reducing to their own component parts; and so on." *Ibid.*, 13.

If the subject is eventually explored more extensively by computer study of school registers, the social profile of the schools will probably be revealed as a pyramid: "If it is the élite character of the schools that counts, then we are looking in fact at a pyramid structure with little known, contemptuously named 'minor public schools' at the base, the also-rans in the middle and a few very grand ones at the top with Eton presiding over the whole edifice." Barbara Rogers, *Men Only: An Investigation Into Men's Organizations,* Pandora, 1988, 137. In *Decline and Fall,* Evelyn Waugh has a private education agency representative remark: "We class schools, you see, into four grades. Leading School, First-Rate School Good School, and School. Frankly, School is pretty bad." *Ibid.,* 138. An agonized acquaintance of the writer recalled how when being interviewed for his first job he apologized for his rather obscure school by suggesting that it was second-rate. "Not *second*-rate," was the deadly reply, *tenth*-rate." **The matter will be left with the parting observation that of course there were differences, but determining the intellectual ones seems a more interesting area of future work than further defining the social ones.** One Fellow of King's, ". . . was blessed with the empirical leanings of the true Rubgeian and persistent hankering to qualify and soften the stark commands of Thomas Arnold with the beguiling discourse of Matthew – another Rubgeian tendency . . .". Raven, *The Old School,* 83.

39. Armstrong, *Administrative Elites,* 208.

40. Sheldrake, *Presence of the Past,* 242-43.

41. See, importantly, Frode Svartdal, "The Covert Behaviour of Attributing", *Behaviorism,* Fall 1988, Vol. 16, No. 2 167-71. See also P. J. Rich, review of Christine Heward's *Making a Man of Him, British Journal of Educational Studies,* Vol. XXXVIII, No. 1, February 1990, 96-79.

42. Arthur O. Lovejoy, *The Great Chain of Being: A Study of the History of an Idea,* Harvard University Press, Cambridge (Massachusetts), 1978 (1936), 52.

CHAPTER IV

Possibilities

Probably only an infinitesimal fraction of all practising historians have any kind of theory of causation worthy of the dignity of that title. – Arthur Marwick, *The Nature of History,* 1970.

The rituals of religion perform the same service for the headmaster as the rituals of Versailles performed for the absolute monarchy of the 'ancien regime'. Why should I pretend otherwise. – John Rae, *Letters From School,* 1987.

Selectivity and simplification are essential to survival and intelligence. If in Mexico City street traffic, I give undue attention to air traffic and sidewalk vendors, my vehicles and I will not last long. – Steve J. Stern, *American Historical Review,* 1988.

Namier died in 1960 just after remarking that he had at last amassed enough material for his study of the parliamentarians. Hopefully there comes a time *before* one's demise when there are enough data and attention can turn to analysis. That still leaves the question as to which of the findings to emphasize.

A host of causes to be identified confront the prosopographer. This is the longest chapter of the book precisely because it tries to deal with the multiplicity of causes that clamour for recognition. There is no end to them. Valerie Fildes has emphasized mother-child bonding with her work on wet nursing. Patricia Clarke has stressed the place of the Imperial governess and the activities of the Female Middle Class Emigration Society. Aristotle's pupil Theophrastus was one of a long procession of students of lunar cycles, the effects of which have occupied not only eminent scientists such as Isaac Newton and Simon Laplace, but economists such as Simon Kuznets. Sherlock Holmes declared that a knowledge of at least seventy-five perfumes was essential to detection, and Peter and Jean Hansell's publications about dovecotes have shown their importance as a source of saltpetre for gunpowder.

As a tool, causality resembles a Swiss army knife with its innumerable blades rather than Occam's razor. Which causes are important? There is heavy traffic in history's rear-view mirror.[1] Amongst the mass of assembled material can be subtle predispositions rather than the glaringly obvious.[2] The decision as to what to emphasize will be circumscribed by reservations.[3] Besides those difficulties, there are those over where to begin and end. Everyone knows the rhyme:

For the want of a nail
The shoe was lost;
For want of a shoe
The horse was lost;
For want of a horse
The rider was lost:
For want of a rider
The battle was lost;
For want of a battle
The kingdom was lost;
And all for the want
Of a horse-shoe nail.

Dorothy Emmet allows that she *would* go as far as the loss of the horse, but "To extend it further seems not only harsh, but wildly implausible."[4] Her argument is that a single cause is being touted when there are other causes – if a pun is permitted – afoot. This is commonsensical but springs from an exasperation that matters must stop *somewhere.*

Selfish Genes

The suppositions made by historians in tackling causal problems would make a scientist blush, especially when their references to states of mind imply a knowledge of "mind" that no scientist would claim to have. Recent theories have stood conventional explanations on end. A case in point is Richard Dawkins's *The Selfish Gene* and *The Extended Phenotype,* which assert that organisms, including man, merely provide the causal vehicles for preserving genes. This confutes the conventional wisdom that the importance of genes is to provide information for the organism, and links the reasons for behaviour to the preservation of genes rather than to the preservation of individual organisms.[5]

As mentioned in Chapter II, Rupert Sheldrake incorporated Dawkins into a provocative hypothesis of morphic resonance. Sheldrake and others pursuing a holistic approach to knowledge are far outnumbered by those with a particularistic axe to grind, despite the difficulty that whatever emphasis is advocated is axiomatically at the expense of other explanations.[6] There are considerable personal satisfactions to single-minded approaches, and this contributes as to why there is no end to them.[7] The latitude at which one lives and hence the length of the day, the consumption of carbonhydrate-rich foods, and the body's secretion of a variety of substances have been suggested. Studies that show the harmful concentration of lead in the British diet have led to speculating ". . . whether the rulers of the world's greatest Empire might have made wiser decisions and preserved that incredible institution if their grey matter had not been clouded by this grey metal."[8] The same argument has been made more commonly in reference to the Romans. That people are

Possibilities

what they eat is not so much a truism as a causal hypothesis.

If pasta or pewter are not attractive as explanations, there are innumerable alternative possibilities. Considering Sidney Mintz's history of sugar, a reviewer acknowledged that: ". . . a single commodity can be used to pry open the history of an entire world of social relationships and human behaviour."[9] Tongue and taste have rivals in smells. There are those (such as Alain Corbin in *The Foul and the Fragrant: Odor and the French Social Imagination*) who assert that history is nasal. More 'disciplines' are born each day. Launching the Oxford University Press *Journal of Design History*, an enthusiast conceded that: "Design history is a relatively new field world-wide. There is still no clear agreement on what it encompasses nor is there yet a substantial literature that can command the respect of scholars in other fields." Nevertheless, subscribers were assured that ". . . a central goal is to recognize the ramifications – social, aesthetic, economic, technological, symbolic."[10]

Sifters and Selectors

Ampere's familiar attack on Ideologues, denying that there was such a thing as causality and claiming that there was only a **succession of images,** makes it evident that the ingredients making up the process called 'consciousness' have to be related to the way in which information is sifted subjectively. Historians are patently supposed to be sifters *par excellence*. Are they able subjectivists *par excellence?* A criticism of the burgeoning efforts of social historians is that their sieve is not fine enough, and that their lack of discrimination has introduced a subjectivism that is as biased as any previous historical school.[11]

Educational history may seem to be a particularistic enough pursuit, but its specialized permutations illustrate how endless is the proliferation of approaches. Although itself a speciality, it has subdivided.[12] The consequent increased choices of emphasis that now face educational historians are not in themselves bad, despite criticism that attention has been stolen from mainstream concerns. It is hard to imagine how the genii could be put back in the bottle or to argue that any of the 'new' historical studies should be relegated to their previous obscurity. What is necessary is to weigh the possible contributions of these new tools. Some will lend themselves more than others to a given situation. In estimating the influence of schooling on the Imperial mind, there are obvious competing causal contributors such as the family as an educator which should be discussed. Before endorsing the idea that the public school was pivotal, other contenders need to be examined.

The Family

Of the multitudinous causal factors in history, the family has been an obvious but strangely neglected one. It would be churlish not to acknowledge efforts to remedy this, particularly by Peter Laslett in *Household and Family in Past Time* (1972) and

93

Family Life and Illicit Love in Earlier Generations (1977), and by Emmanuel Todd in *The Explanation of Ideology* (1985). **Of course, increased sensitivity to gender and family in all aspects of educational history is also because of feminist scholarship.**[13]

A problem that family historians have recently focused on is whether the family has declined in influence. Simplistic explanations such as 'the rise of the individual' are not adequate explanations of the decline of the extended family and the creation of what Laurence Stone called the *Closed Domesticated Nuclear Family*. On the other hand, while there should be more consideration of family influence as an educational influence, it remains that in specific situations the family can be over-emphasized. Dr. F. Musgrove has put the case for the public schools as well as anyone: "The schools offered to meet these new social needs more effectively than the family. They developed a new exclusiveness that guarded the child from social promiscuity and contamination as effectively as the most jealous parental surveillance, and more effectively than the *nouveau riche* parent could manage."[14]

Contrary to the warm family circle that Thomas Hughes depicted in the first chapters of *Tom Brown*, the family attitudes that resulted in sending boys to boarding school struck observers as harsh and unnatural. The uprooting demanded a transfer of loyalty from the family to the school. Indeed, the public school boy learned to display a cynical attitude towards his family. E. M. Forster remarked in *Abinger Harvest* (1936) that it was not that an Englishman couldn't feel, but that he had been taught at public school that feeling was bad form. In the case of a number of other writers, the influence of the public school on English literature seems to have been more than that of the family. Admirers of P. G. Wodehouse have Dulwich rather than his parents to thank: "Dulwich College became the focus for emotions which, in children who have experienced a normal background, usually become attached to 'home'."[15]

The separation was a *rite de passage* as marked as a ritual of aboriginals or calamity of the wild. In the animal kingdom, surrogate parents are adopted by orphaned fledglings. A human may be accepted as mother by a monkey, and a kitten may be comfortable with a collie. The same process was part of British culture. Ejected from the family, boys accepted the school as a substitute.[16] Schoolmasters thought that the school did a better job than parents.[17] Parents lost their confidence in their ability, turning the child over to those who claimed to know better, who confidently acted in *loco parentis*, and who claimed to be more intelligent and more experienced than parents.[18] Alec Waugh remarked that schoolmasters regarded parents as a nuisance that periodically had to be appeased, and who could be left largely in the dark about school matters.[19]

Boarding is not an absolute requirement for the public school ethos. That St. Paul's and Dulwich are primarily day schools suggests that boarding is not *per se* the essential ingredient of the experience. Sir Henry Newbolt remarked that by being a 'domiciled' Cliftonian he had more of a feeling of never leaving the school than if he had been a boarder. Boarding contributed to the overall influence, but whether day boys or boarders, boys spent more time in school than at home. Not only did masters take the place of fathers, they extended their patriarchal oversight to parents.[20] As public schools became the *sine qua non* of the Establishment, this decline of parental influence accelerated – Nathaniel Woodard sought in founding his schools to remove children from the "noxious influence of home." Surrogacy was further enhanced in the case of parents living abroad. Most of those in Imperial service felt compelled to trundle their children off to boarding school at an early age. When one's father was the headmaster, the discomfort showed just how *patria familia* and sectarian the school was. Graham Greene's father was Charles Henry Greene, headmaster of Berkhamsted. Greene found that this made life miserable: "I was like the son of a quisling in a country under occupation."[21]

The period of high Empire was marked by families yielding children to the schools in what has been described as "mass hysteria".[22] This abandonment of children by parents took place early in life, for the nanny came into her own in the last half of the nineteenth century – as Kenneth Gaw has demonstrated in *Superior Servants*, his study of the Cantonese amahs, or as Jonathan Gathorne-Hardy has shown in *The Rise and Fall of the British Nanny*.[23] One cannot forget the amah or nanny factor, but strong as that influence might have been, it yielded to the prep and public schools.

The causal issue *viz-à-vis* the schools and family, as with many other aspects of the public school, is not that of competing influences, but of the dominance of one form of CULTURAL REPRODUCTION over others.[24] What is asserted is that for the Imperial ruling cadre, the school was what was of unmistakably paramount importance. The higher the family's status, the more anxious parents seemed to be to delegate responsibilities to a school. Winston Churchill said about Harrow that he would have rather been a bricklayer's apprentice: "I should have got to know my father, which would have been a joy to me."[25] Rather than the family or the regiment or the club competing with the school for influence, they reinforced school traditions. In the case of the family, fathers were old boys, and often several generations cherished connections with one school. Thus the family confirmed and transmitted the public school ethos, as did other Victorian institutions. Success at school was the fond parental expectation: ". . . there seems little point in trying to make Captain of Soccer when papa only understands rugby."[26]

Possibly *Rex atque sacerdos*

Religion is another causal influence which, like the family, would seem of the first order for prosopographical consideration. Here, too, there is a public school aspect that might be overlooked. Gathorne-Hardy turns from the nursery to the nave to observe that "From 1900 onwards the real religion of most British middle and upper-class men (followed dutifully by their wives) was their public school."[27] Not accidentally did Thomas Arnold serve Rugby as chaplain as well as headmaster. The Victorian headmaster was King, Prime Minster and Archbishop of Canterbury rolled into one.[28] One bishop claimed that Eton's spirit was akin to the Holy Spirit and filled him with ". . . an extraordinary feeling. It was almost as if everything was part of the school, or the school part of everything."[29]

Public school religion was a law unto itself, as Arnold Wilson, the British "Uncrowned King" of the Arabian Gulf and Iraq made clear in a letter to his father, the second headmaster of Clifton, Revd. James Wilson: "I do not want the School Chapel to become a church: there is a difference to my mind, though I cannot explain it."[30] School religion was frequently an Anglicanism comfortable with an increasingly secular society, seldom challenging an almost pagan school ritualism.[31] It was a cult of éliteness that had little to do with the Upper Room.[32] Often described as broad church, the public school chapel might better be understood as the mainstay of the lacrymose religious nostalgia that the Oxford Movement opposed. Cardinal Newman, it was said, tried to dam the tide while Arnold swelled the flood. Newman remarked: "The party grew . . . by the accession of Dr. Arnold's pupils, it was invested with an elevation of character which claimed the respect even of its opponents."[33]

The practitioners of school-*cum*-Imperial ritualism continually invoked Christianity, but this is unremarkable. The agents of ritualism of any sort invariably seek legitimacy through an appeal to whatever is to hand.[34] However, the part played by the schools in religious movements such as ritualism and the Oxford Movement is awaiting further study. An approach would be to research the leanings of school chaplains of the period, using indicators such as apostasy to Rome and membership in the Union of Modern Churchmen. Another opportunity for research is offered by the fact that, by bequest, schools inherited the right to present clergy to livings. Were livings that belonged to schools primarily awarded to old boys, as seems likely? Were the rights of presentation given over to clerical brokers to raise money? The right of **advowson,** the privilege of nominating the rector or vicar of a parish, was treated as a kind of real property and was bought and sold. There are a number of periodicals that could be analyzed that advertised sales of advowsons and next presentations as well as the exchange of benefices and placement of curates. These include *Church Preferment Gazette, Private Patrons' Gazette* (later *Church Patronage Gazette*), *Incumbent's Gazette,* and *Clerical Register.* The "simony press" served equally High and Low church clientèle.[35] Materials for a thorough examination of the schools' part in religious controversies are abundant, and it would seem unlikely the schools were without influence on those controversies.

To be kept in mind about connections between the schools, religion, and the Empire, is that the Church of England was never the Church of *Britain.* There were plenty of Imperialists whose allegiance was to kirk rather than parish, or nonconformists whose fidelity was to neither, and some were outright secularists. Joseph Chamberlain was as firm a Unitarian as he was an Imperialist. Members of the body politic were not all Anglicans. The need for an embracing religio-political ecumenenism meant that school and Imperial ritual was probably substituted for religion.

In the later part of the nineteenth century, the schools abandoned parish churches for their own chapels where they could worship without mixing with the larger Christian community. The change in physical location was accompanied by a change in religious practices. The school influence was emphasized by the confirmation of boys at school, frequently by an old boy bishop, rather than in their home parishes. **The subordination of religion to school ritual is illustrated by the extraordinary Eton custom of only the Sixth Form receiving the sacrament, and being compelled to do so.**[36]

The eucharist became a school ritual rather than a religious rite: "The school represented places of worship, with headmasters and their staff (frequently in holy orders in any case) representing the priests, uniforms and old school ties provided vestments, and the verse of the 'Eton Boating Song' or 'Forty Years On' serving as hymns."[37] Chapel at Eton was described as more "to celebrate a cult of Eton than to give thanks for the redemption of the world."[38] Moreover, at the very same time that the public schools were expanding and the number of their old boys entering the Imperial services was growing, the number of old boys going into the Church as a career was falling steeply. The percentage of laymen winning appointments as headmasters, as T. W. Bamford and others have shown, was constantly increasing.

Architecturally the chapel edifices emphasized school rather than Christian symbolism. Arnold Wilson objected when it was proposed to move the plaques in Clifton Chapel in order to achieve a 'religious' atmosphere: "To 'sky' the memorial brasses would be a crime. They were the source of inspiration not less strong than the long lists of names, dating from the 'sixties, some of which have since become famous, on the Honours Boards in Big School. They were a link between the Chapel and India and the Army and the Civil Service abroad."[39] In looking for religious influences in the Empire, the chapel buildings and the attitudes engendered suggest the possibility of an Imperial cult that was as much sustained by an ambitious public school, lodge, and government ritualism as by Christian theology – albeit sometimes eccentric. J. A. Mangan shrewdly remarks: "The fact is that a religious ideal has become confused with a secular reality."[40]

Headmasters who were Freemasons as well as priests bolstered this school-orientated religiosity. Masonic pageantry (which the boys could occasionally see in the chapel) was more colourful than "the average, dry Church of England conventional matins service", and Masonry was accused of being a counterfeit religion.[41] The old boys who became Freemasons did not have to venture out of their lodges for inspiration: "The mason adopts 'a peculiar system of morality, veiled in allegory, and illustrated by symbols' and vows not to reveal the secrets of the craft to outsiders . . . Masonry is founded on principles utterly different from the teaching at the heart of the Gospel."[42] The Masons awarded themselves clerical dignities, and dressed accordingly and gloriously: "A Great Prelate, when wearing a Cope, may wear a Mitre; *in no circumstances* may a Great Almoner or Deputy Great Almoner wear a Mitre; when officiating at a meeting of Great Priory of the Temple, the Great Prelate shall carry a Crozier."[43] Would a Masonic prelate with jewelled mitre be impressed by the vicar's simple ministrations? Yet paradoxically, he probably would be offended if the service on Sunday were as ritualistic as activities at lodge. Even a king looked more imposing than usual in his Masonic apron. (See photograph of *Edward VII*, page 98.)

97

Edward VII at a Masonic meeting.

Possibilities

Wanting to be Different

The attitudes of contemporaries can be a primary influence for a boy's course of action. Admiration for old school ties, literally and metaphorically, was not confined to adults. Children became well aware from each other of the significance of going to a public school, and were not always dragooned into going away – if autobiographical evidence is any indication. One Imperial mandarin wrote, "I longed to go away to boarding school . . . I had formed all sorts of fantasies of Reggie's and Walter's adventures [his brother and cousin] at school, and even if I was too young yet for *Tom Brown's Schooldays* or *Stalky and Co.*, my imagination was fed on exciting stories in Christmas annuals or the *Boys' Own Paper*, full of the fun and adventure of boarding school life."[44] Boys were anxious to "leave the nest" and acquire the status of attending prep and public school: "I opted for public school when I was twelve . . . I wanted to be different and, in my judgement, 'better' by going to a school with greater social prestige . . . adolescents expect and *want* a permanent separation."[45]

Public school literature includes plenty of references that argue for the fact that teenagers could be far more determined about going to the right school than their elders. They learned early how the land lay, primarily from their preparatory schools' preoccupation with entrance to public schools. Dr. Jean Barman of the Canadian Childhood History Project at the University of British Columbia has claimed that in Canada the educational model was often the English prep school rather than the public school, and that there has been a singular failure to recognize the preparatory school influence in the Empire.[46] (Evidencing an early and unusual interest in the study of causality in the preparatory school is a 1927 notice in the *New Statesman* advertising for a scientist to reside at Malting *[sic.]* House Preparatory School to investigate "apprehension of multiple and permissive causality which is painful to the human mind with its innate tendency to accept and manufacture explanations in terms of unitary and logical causality." What prompted this desire of a prep school to investigate causality, which would have been unusual even on a university level, is presently unknown but being pursued.[47])

Prep schools had their own rituals, but as they expanded in the later nineteenth century they took their lead from their elder brothers. They are important because they gave the first assist up the greasy pole of totemism, and the emphasis on ritual conformity began for most boys in the public school class with the celebrated prep 'crocodile' when children learned to march everywhere two by two: "It was no use blaming authority since the system had originated in the careful mind of Noah."[48]

Parents chose the prep schools as much for their public school affiliations as from their own merits.[49] They were the vestibule rather than the main salon, and their function remained a subsidiary one. Like the public school, the prep was crucial when the parents lived overseas. Vere Birdwood, of a sixth-generation Indian services family, emphasizes that: ". . . separation made us immensely independent, and to some extent independent of love. I think it probably hardened us. My brother, I remember, would pack his school trunk alone from about the age of eight."[50] The public school culture was reinforced by the preps, as it was by so many other institutions.

99

The 'Varsity

Another candidate in the causal contest is the varsity, but university was **not** a social requirement for the Imperial élite. The age limit for joining the Imperial services could preclude university. In the case of the Indian Political Service, the upper limit for entry was twenty-six years. A service such as the IPS had only a small number of men who had degrees. If a man went to university there wasn't time for him before the age of twenty-six to join the Indian Civil Service or Army, prerequisites for joining the IPS, and then go through the process of transfer to the IPS.

Those who attended university found that the atmosphere was influenced by the public schools, and that public school products had an easier time of it in college than anachronistically "someone from Eltham Green Comprehensive". Old boys were long adjusted to "being away from home, ancient traditions, occasionally having to wear odd clothes for ceremonies, bad food, freezing beds."[51] *Tom Brown's Schooldays* was appropriately followed by Hughes' *Tom Brown at Oxford.*

Leslie Stephens was "appalled" by Rugby's importance at Oxford.[52] The whole Oxford-Cambridge style owed much to schools, including the passion for sartorial identification in the form of scarves, caps and other glorious apparel. This TRANSFERENCE OF RITUALS from schools to universities is documented by Stuart Macintyre in his fascinating account of initiation ceremonies at the University of Melbourne's Ormond College (*Ormond College: Centenary Essays,* Melbourne University Press, 1984). Scotch College in Melbourne was regarded as the portico of Ormond, and it seems likely that such proximate developments at Scotch as the growth of ragging and the prefect system had an effect on Ormond. Another Australian example would be the consequences of the founding warden of St. George's College in The University of Western Australia being Percy Henn, who had previously enjoyed a distinguished career as headmaster of Guildford Grammar School. In the St. George's Chapel, the chaplain's chair is decorated with the arms of the college *and* of Guildford.

Schools Fathering Universities

Not uncommonly one of the Empire's new universities started life as what amounted to a public school, especially in India. Illustrating the schools' influence on universities overseas is the part played in Indian education by the devoted Rugbeian Thomas French (1825-1891), who after studying under Arnold established St. John's College in Agra and was its first principal in 1850-1859. (See contemporary photograph of *Thomas Valpy French,* page 101.) In old age, French quixotically went to Arabia, and promptly died in Muscat. St. John's and the other overseas public schools had an effect on the development of education in general, fathering universities in some cases.

Thomas Valpy French.

The public school influence on overseas universities was disseminated by men like French who in the course of their careers served in a number of Imperial outposts. Edward Stuart, a master at St. John's when French was head, became the education-conscious and school-founding Bishop of Waiapu in New Zealand, and then went to Isfahan in Persia – where, under his impetus, Stuart College became a leading Middle Eastern public school that produced a number of leaders for the incipient Persian universities. Besides its Rugby associations, St. John's cherished connections with Haileybury. These links were encouraged by Haileybury's headmaster, E. H. Bradby. French had a boy at Haileybury. So did his successor as head of St. John's, John Haythronthwaite, whose son was head boy. Haileybury kept up a connection with St. John's well into the twentieth century, donating money given in chapel collections. The long line of educationists that St. John's produced or nurtured is one of numerous examples of indirect links between the English schools and overseas tertiary education. Another excellent example is offered by Aligarh College near Delhi, whose influence is delineated in David Lelyveld's *Aligarh's First Generation* (Princeton University Press, 1978). (See rear endpaper.)

The periods when boys were at school and at university differed significantly as far as emotional development. Boys were more impressionable in their earlier years. With the majority of undergraduates coming from public schools, universities reflected the prior influence. The adoption of rowing colours neatly exemplifies this, the blue of Cambridge being the selection of a Mr. R. N. Phillips "because Mr. Phillips was an Etonian, and this was the Eton Blue."[53] *The Oxford Magazine* blamed the lack of social mixing at Oxford on the "Imperial provincialism of the English Public School man."[54] As the preparatory schools represented an interlude before public schools, the universities constituted only an interlude between school and Imperial careers. Henry Newbolt was right when he expressed the thought that Oxford offered "nothing to take the place of the ardent and imaginative loyalty of . . . public school."[55]

Crammers

The significance for prosopography of educational institutions other than the public schools cannot be left without mentioning the crammers. Prep schools have had a comprehensive general history written by Donald Leinster-Mackay, and the universities have had an abundance of histories. The crammer has not been so fortunate. Admittedly it was a less celebrated and less prestigious influence, but Imperial administrators could have sported its tie. Crammers were consistently employed for passing Sandhurst and ICS examinations, but work done at them is not conspicuous in archives. An exception are the papers written while he was cramming by David Lorimer, an IPS officer and Bahrain Political Agent. In 1895, at the age of 19, Lorimer wrote: "The present wretched school and examinations systems and their parasite, the still more wretched 'cramming system', are day by day destroying all true education, and worse still corrupting the public ideal of education."[56] Presumably, as he passed into the Army the next year, he got value for his money.

Crammers were considered a necessary evil because, although late nineteenth-century schools began a modern side and some had success with Army Entrance and Indian services' tests,[57] the crammers cynically prepared candidates for papers on which they only got twenty or thirty points out of a hundred *but which they were allowed to add to their total score.*[58] This is overlooked in accounts of the public schools and the crammers, and it is crucial. **A boy would sit papers in subjects he had never studied in school simply to grab a few more points, and this point-chasing led boys to leave school early to cram.**[59] *Blackwood's* (November 1861), with an oblique reference to Lord Palmerston, complained:

> *Your defense, my Lord Pam, of the system of CRAM,*
> *Is of all we have met with the best;*
> *Yet to cram, after all, if things rightly we call,*
> *Is to bolt what we cannot digest.*

Although usually short, cram courses could turn into considerably more than a six week proposition. Sir Evan Maconochie, author of *Life in the Indian Civil Service,* dedicated "To Undergraduates and School Boys of This Country", required two hard years after Sherborne "with Mr. Scoones in Garrick Street."[60] This he remembered rather fondly: "As for Mr. Scoones himself, there must be some still in the Services, and many others, who remember his mastery of his business, his robust common-sense, his shrewd estimate of our various capacities . . .".[61] Winston Churchill, having failed three times to get into Sandhurst, succeeded thanks to a crammer. For most, however, the crammers were a tiresome necessity and they produced no nostalgic "Old Crammers", and no armorial bearings or inscribed cuff-links.

The Military

Along with the family, religion, and the prep schools and universities, the military establishment interacted with, rather than competed with, the public schools as a centre of affection and influence. It displayed the same conventionalism, authoritarian submission, belief in stereotypes and preoccupation with prurience that marked the public schools. In fact, some influence seems to have been exercised by the schools or the military rather than the other way around.[62] Hughes' appraisal in *Tom Brown* of East, the prefect who leaves the school to join a regiment in India, is that "No fellow could handle boys better, and I suppose soldiers are very like boys." For many joining the military, like joining a club, was *de rigueur* after leaving public school.[63] However, most Imperial administrators first passed through either Sandhurst or some other military academy.

Sandhurst began by educating orphans and others of limited means, but became in the early nineteenth century no more than a public school.[64] It then further changed, becoming a military academy that took boys from the public schools at the same time as the dramatic expansion in the schools and Imperial services. One of the coincidences connected with the rise of the Empire that seems more than a coincidence. Prominent headmasters were involved in Sandhurst's reorganization, being called on, in 1857, to give their ideas. Among others, Moberly (Winchester), Elder (Charterhouse), Jelf (King's College School), Goodford (Eton), Goulburn (Rugby) and Scott (Westminster) offered advice.[65] Uppingham's Thring is significantly absent – he was averse to militarism. Equally opposed was Herbert Spencer, who in *Facts and Comments* (1902) scorned the presence of cadet corps in public schools.

Sandhurst already had Imperial connections, so circumstances were propitious for enhanced connections with the schools and the Imperial services. The Yolland Commission and the criticisms of the Council of Military Education resulted in Army classes in the schools and a dramatic increase in Sandhurst applications. Candidates were now expected to have completed public school. Like the preparatory schools,

Eton School drill, 1860.

103

Sandhurst followed the public school lead and was a conduit rather than primary influence. George Cottar, Kipling's hero in *The Brushwood Boy*, moved "inevitably" from public school to Sandhurst without giving up his "public-school mask".

A reason that Sandhurst lacked the signal influence of the public schools was the short length of its courses, which were further curtailed by military crises. By 1865 the course had been reduced from three years to one year, and during World War I it was six months or less.[66] Trevor Hearl, a student of military education, remarks "School is a world of its own; timeless. But professional colleges make their inmates look forward – the idea is to get out! Psychological fulfilment is in leaving for the real world."[67] Sandhurst was "unloved" and never inspired the sentimental literature that the schools did.[68]

What 'atmosphere' there was in the military academies was influenced strongly by the public schools. The commandant of Woolwich, F. M. Eardley-Wilmot, was styled 'the Military Arnold'.[69] The appointment of instructors at the academies with public school connections such as H. H. Hardy, who was Sandhurst's forceful director of studies after being headmaster of Cheltenham and Shrewsbury, confirmed the public school connections. (Hardy served under a Commandant, General Matthews, who had been a boy at Cheltenham when he was its head.)

Another military influence was the regiments. Public school old boys had a good preliminary knowledge of what went into regimental routine. Schooldays included liberal amounts of boot-polishing. (See *Eton Drill 1860*, page 103.) The symbolic accoutrements beloved by old boys were also provided by regimental societies, including blazer badges, buttons, and neckties. Nevertheless, regiments do not measure up to schools in the production of totems and talismans. In addition, despite their proud mess traditions the British and Indian regiments went through so many mergers that Haileybury's consolidations with other schools look minor in comparison.[70] The importance of schools was shown during World War I when recruitment specifically appealed to the public school tradition. (See *Public Schools Brigade Poster*, left.) The regiment appears to be a case, as with Sandhurst, of an institution which was influenced by the schools.

Imperial bureaucrats did not pursue military careers. Those entering the

UNIVERSITY & PUBLIC SCHOOLS BRIGADE

5000 MEN AT ONCE

The Old Public School and University Men's Committee makes an urgent appeal to their fellow Public School and University men to at once enlist in these battalions, thus upholding the glorious traditions of their Public Schools & Universities.

TERMS OF SERVICE.

Age on enlistment 19 to 35, ex-soldiers up to 45, and certain ex-non-commissioned officers up to 50. Height 5 ft. 3 in and upwards. Chest 34 in. at least. Must be medically fit.

General Service for the War.

Men enlisting for the duration of the War will be discharged with all convenient speed at the conclusion of the War

PAY AT ARMY RATES.

and all married men or widowers with children will be accepted, and will draw separation allowance under Army Conditions.

HOW TO JOIN.

Men wishing to join should apply at once personally, to the Public Schools & Universities Force, 66, Victoria Street, Westminster, London, S.W., or the nearest Recruiting Office of this Force.

GOD SAVE THE KING !

Public Schools Brigade Poster.

civil services from the Army deliberately turned their back on the prospect of military glory and may have joined to escape from the military. In fact, the regimental system was weakened by the practice of the Imperial services of drawing some of their best recruits from the military. The implication was that being in the ICS or IPS was in ways more desirable than being a regimental officer. (If military training were influenced by the public schools' élitism, then the educational system that the Army operated for soldiers might show that.[71] A valuable study could be and should be written about the public school influence on Britain's military rituals.)

Eton, Sugar, and Spice

By now it should be evident that the causal factors to be investigated are limited only by resourcefulness. The microbes that accompanied the Imperial magistrates had as much to say in demarcating boundaries as did Whitehall. Medical and ecological Imperialism are just beginning to be studied and appreciated. No prosopography has gone deeply into its subjects' medical histories. The tuck shop with its cream buns is as much part of the public school scene as the chapel. As for culinary causality, in *The Rise of the English Prep School*, Donald Leinster-Mackay quotes a Temple Grove old boy on that school's serving of pudding to reduce appetites before the meat course.[72] Could the status of schools be determined by whether the pudding came before or after the roast?

In 1918, Norman Lindsay produced his classic children's tale *The Magic Pudding*. The story was Lindsay's response to a dispute over whether children were more interested in mythological creatures such as fairies, or in food. It has never been out of print, and the adventures of the Society of Puddin' Owners have entertained generations of pudding fanciers. Lindsay provided a *Puddin'-Owners' Anthem*:

> *Hurrah for puddin'-owning,*
> *Hurrah for Friendship's hand,*
> *The puddin'-thieves are groaning*
> *To see our noble band.*

Regardless of the merit of puddings as a literary device, they can be related to the whole issue of school diet and to the strategies employed to keep the cost of school fare down. Michael Brander in *The Victorian Gentleman* supports the idea of pudding as an intentional appetite dampener, stating that boys in school were forced to down great helpings of *Yorkshire* pudding before the meat course.[73] Dr. Leinster-Mackay is silent on the actual variety of pudding served at schools such as Temple Grove, despite epicurean enthusiasms which have made him rather an authority on restaurants in Western Australia.

An aside such as Dr. Leinster-Mackay's remark about pudding can be taken up and shown to have manifold causal ramifications. The historiography of food could

The Headmaster of Rugby is reported to have said at the recent Conference on School Diet that "while adults should rise from the table hungry, children should reach a sense of repletion before rising." House-Master (with pride, to Parent): "Then with regard to food: we feed our boys to repletion five times a day, and our chef's puddings have no equal in any school in the kingdom."

become time-consuming, as there are those who assert that to discuss dishes without cooking them is sloppy scholarship. In discussing culinary bibliography, the *Annual Report* of the Library Company of Philadelphia solemnly remarks, "Current practitioners in the field address this problem by reassembling the materials and remodelling the process of creation so that the 'pudding' can be made again. Culinary historians, therefore, must sample a very wide variety of sources. They must not only find the recipe, but also explore the availability of ingredients, the utensils used in preparation, and the social implications of these things at the time they were used."[74] (Which writer on the English public schools – Dr. Mangan, Dr. Leinster-Mackay, or Dr. Wilkinson – would do best in the kitchen?)

Besides their filling properties, puddings have had ritualistic purposes. Christmas puddings are an obvious example of a pudding metaphor of considerable potency. Likewise there are special public school puddings. At Eton, the custom of *slunching the paddocks* commemorated the visit of Queen Elizabeth I when "she lunched" and hence "s'lunched". Generations of Collegians and Oppidans were provided with a coarse pudding to commemorate the event, and after a special dinner went to the Eton paddocks and threw pudding about. This was "Slunching the Paddocks", and the pudding was called "Slunch." This was not the only instance of puddings playing a part in school ritual; their usual rôle was to insure that the boys had enough to eat.[75]

A *Punch* cartoon about Rugby illustrates this. (See *Our Chef's Puddings*, page 106.) The effects of ample helpings were evident. Writing in *The Westminster Review* (March 1903), J. H. Vines concluded that an average Marlborough College boy of thirteen in 1901 was "four and a half pounds heavier and nine-tenths of an inch taller than his father (now aged forty-seven) was, supposing that the latter had been at Marlborough twenty-nine years ago."

Regarding the Imperial connotations of puddings, the ample figure that ever will come to mind is the Earl of Meath, who advocated the **Empire Pudding** cooked with ingredients painstakingly selected as symbolic of Imperial unity. Into the Earl's pudding went something from each possession and dominion. He promised that: "If the whole Empire confined itself, on Christmas Day, to the use, in its puddings, of Australian currants, that fact alone would go a long way to setting the new Australian dried fruit industry on its feet."[76] Meath tirelessly journeyed about the Empire, his portly form presiding over functions investing Empire Puddings with ceremonial as well as economic purposes. Perhaps related is an Indian Empire epigram that "We want lean and keen men on the Frontier, and fat and good-natured men in the States."[77]

Unless Dr. Leinster-Mackay carries his studies further, the correlations will remain unknown between the preparatory schools, consuming Empire Puddings, weight upon entering the Indian Civil Service (possibly previously put on by puddings at school) and the postings of Imperial bureaucrats. Just as Brian Gardner arranged his book *The Public Schools* (Hamish Hamilton, 1983) around the idea of the schools being categorized by founding dates, and found something of a common identity to those started in a particular era, it might be possible to arrange the schools by when during the meal the pudding was served – and what its ingredients were.

There are further observations that can be made about puddings and schools. The Pudding Purveyor of Haileybury, George James Coleman (See *The Pudding Purveyor of Haileybury*, page 108.) was a thirty stone testimonial to Haileybury's desserts. When Coleman died in 1865 his services as the College purveyor were recalled by Sir Monier Monier-Williams: ". . . a huge mass of flesh supported on massive legs like pillars – standing majestically at the further end of the Hall in an attitude of uncompromising solidity, and with a visage of imperturbable complacency, as if defying every one of us to say that the beef or mutton which we were eating was not of the very best quality and cooked in the most artistic manner. When the time came for the entrance of the puddings and sweets, Coleman always thought it part of his duty to serve us himself. Hence, a waiter followed him about with an immense tray, whilst the gigantic Purveyor sidled about with a kind of rolling gait from table to table, putting the dishes before us himself . . .".[78] Sir Monier Monier-Williams quotes the *Hertfordshire Mercury* obituary of the Pudding Purveyor: "Professors taught, but he fed the rulers of our Eastern Empire. They came and went, but he remained . . . Haileybury has given to India many great men, but there is a sense in which it gave to England one of the greatest men who ever trod its soil."[79]

The ultimate suggestion about the causal importance of school puddings, that they suppressed the libido, has been made by Dan Hofstadter: "But it was at dessert that

The Pudding Purveyor of Haileybury.

powder reigned supreme, in the form of warm, lumpily liquefied Bird's packet custard, which came in jugs and was carelessly doused on whatever was the 'pud' of the day – in this department a slightly rancid, freely perspiring suet pudding certainly took first prize . . . There is much to suggest that British school food was intended to fill a cautionary function. It warned the child off any incipient sensuality, especially of the gustatory sort . . .".[80] **Thus the pudding became a guarantee of British respectability.** When the last Wali of Swat died in 1987, his obituary in *Asian Affairs,* the journal of the Royal Society for Asian Affairs, recorded approvingly that "To the end, he remained a confirmed and unabashed Anglophile . . . His three-course meals were standard English fare starting with mulligatawny soup and ending with apple puddings."

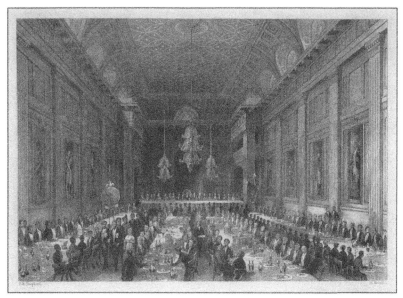

Dinner at Freemasons' Hall.

Regardless of the implications of puddings for sexuality, the way that they and other dishes were consumed did play a part in educating boys for the symbolic meals that were part of Imperial rule. Training in table manners was essential for the ceremonial dining that awaited in adult life. (See *Dinner at Freemasons' Hall,* above.) Public school table manners are fascinating and *Rituals of Empire* deals with house repasts, which were amazingly elaborate. The wife of John Martyn, the headmaster of Doon School in India, recalled that when he was a master at Harrow: "Everything was very formal, supervised by butlers of infinite superiority. One of them was not above telling the boys on occasion: 'Mind your manners, my lord. You are not at home now, you know.'"[81]

Causality was not absent from the table. Victorian and Edwardian dining at times had less to do with eating than with the display of power. The gastronomical side was often dismal, with a bias towards quantity rather than quality. In 1917 at a Calcutta luncheon, Edwin Montagu, the Secretary of State for India, thought the fare "warranted to kill anybody who ate it. Cooked on the European principle, the menu would have to be seen to be believed. Dish followed dish; meat followed meat. Well, well, abstinence secured my survival."[82] The proper rituals of consumption were more important than the food consumed.[83] Those who had not been trained in those rituals were at a considerable disadvantage. The dining rooms of the Empire required an etiquette that were as involved as that of conclaves of the Star of India or meetings of the Masonic lodges. (See *Garrick Dining Room,* page 110.) There can be several

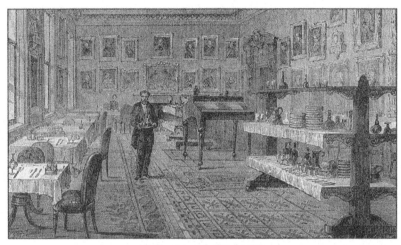

Dinning-room at the Garrick Club.

interpretations to John Mortimer's riposte that the masters at Eton were treated as country-house butlers.

Food does not have to have been cooked to have made a causal contribution. Staples such as water, liquor, potatoes and sugar have been seriously studied as causal factors. The potato and the Irish are permanently partners in the historiography of Ireland. Slavery and sugar are part of the Imperial story. Food acquired profound political and ritualistic significance in one culture or another, and can be a barometer of other developments: "It is possible to see in the British breakfast a link between the decay of taste which everywhere . . . accompanied the progress of the century and the quadruplings in the years dividing Waterloo and Sedan, of our national income."[84] Some ingenuity would be required to chart prosopographically the breakfast menus of Imperial leaders, but the day may come.

Self-evident Benefits

Oft suggested is that "The straight road to Waterloo and the crooked road to Wigan Pier began, after all, from the same place – the playing fields of Eton."[85] The observation is apt, but Wellington's famous remark about Waterloo and Eton, **the classic school causal comment,** was never made. What Wellington said was almost the opposite, a criticism of the influence of Eton. The route it took in becoming a touching tribute to the old school is a reflection of the power of Eton's image, and the convoluted origins of the quotation are themselves an indication of the complexity of causality. The Duke did go to Eton (1781-84), but he disliked the school and his returns to his old haunts were reluctant. On one occasion, in 1818, Wellington pointed out the garden of a house in which he had lived and remarked somewhat enigmatically that "I really believe I owe my spirit of enterprise to the tricks I used to play in the garden."

Montalembert visited Eton in 1855, and when he heard this story he passed it on as "C'est ici qu'a été gagne la bataille de Waterloo." This was translated into English by Sir Edward Creasy in his book *Eminent Etonians* as "There grows the stuff that won Waterloo." Finally, in 1889, the popular version of Waterloo being won on Eton's playing fields emerged in Sir William Fraser's *Words on Wellington*.[86] Cyril Alington appositely remarked, "Whether Waterloo was or was not won on the playing fields of Eton, Armageddon will certainly not be decided on the cinder track."[87]

The schools, as those who passed along Wellington's never made quotation believed, offered self-evident benefits. Along with the effects of the hidden curriculum with its introduction to the rituals of success, there were obvious benefits from better facilities, better teachers, and smaller classes. It was taken for granted that the public school was the best school, and that there should be one wherever there was an élite to be educated. Evidence of this belief crops up regularly in Imperial archives. When in 1941 it was proposed to establish a public school in Bahrain in the Arabian Gulf, the British Council's C. A. F. Dundas wrote to the Resident, Charles Prior: "I believe it is essential for sons of sheikhs and important people to be able to continue their education . . . until Bahrein *[sic]* becomes much more socialist in structure, the sons of notables (irrespective of their ability to pass examinations) will hold most of the positions of importance . . . I feel it is dangerous to run an educational system on purely selective lines, particularly in a Sheikhdom."[88] Besides demonstrating a firm conviction in élite education, the remarks by Dundas suggest that the aspirations of the British administrators for a native boy as well as for a British boy reflected the public schools. In England or overseas, of British stock or native, aspiring families impressed upon their children the importance of public schooling. An ambitious native establishment *wanted* an educational system on public school lines.

The Imperial influence of the schools was felt not only through British old boys but through the activities of all manner of people who were impressed by the doors public schools unlocked. The causal influence was not only the result of old boys or scouts or ambitious parents or the Imperial services, but the effect of a public school culture of postcards, boys' annuals, biscuit boxes, board games, jigsaws, sheet music, and lantern slides. (See *August Joys*, page 112.)

On the other hand, not everything was so obvious as magazines and biscuit boxes. The workings of the Imperial mind did not always accommodatingly display themselves. There are sceptics who have felt that some of the causes behind the Empire's splendid pageantry were dark and dishonourable in the extreme. The following pages consider a less reputable side of the schools, and of the Empire.

NO. 45, New Series.]   SATURDAY, AUGUST 10, 1912.   Price One Penny.
                                                                 [ALL RIGHTS RESERVED.]

August Joys.

112

NOTES – CHAPTER IV

1. Indeed, causality is so perplexing that authors desperately try to cut the Gordian knot by resurrecting Humean arguments against making casual connections. See David S. Hachen Jr., "The Delicate Balance: Technology and Control in Organizations", *British Journal of Sociology*, Vol. XXXIX, No. 3, September 1988, 337-57. A more reasonable approach is to encourage the frequent "re-mapping" of historical topics. See T. O. Lloyd, *The British Empire, 1558-1983*, OUP, 1984, vii. Also W. D. Rubinstein, "The Victorian Middle Classes: Wealth, Occupation, and Geography", Pat Thane and Anthony Sutcliffe eds., *Essays in Social History*, Clarendon Press, Oxford, 1986, 186, 205. Ecologists and lawyers sometimes seem more willing to take on the challenge of multiple causality than do historians. See *e.g.*, Bruce M. Rich. "The Multilateral Development Banks, Environmental Policy, and the United States", *Ecology Law Quarterly*, Vol. 12. No. 4, 681-745. His footnotes rival this author's.

2. Nor do *predispositions*, properties – or characteristics – **guarantee** ensuing events: the vase can be fragile but dropping it does not mean that it will break. Emmet, *Effectiveness of Causes*, 24.

3. See *Ibid.*, 54.

4. *Ibid.*, 44.

5. H. Hampe and S. R. Morgan, "Two Consequences of Richard Dawkins' View of Genes and Organisms", *Studies in History and Philosophy of Science*, Vol. 19, No. 1, March 1988, 119-38.

6. The Persian poet Jalaludin Rumi wrote, "What bread looks like depends upon whether you are hungry or not." qtd. Ornstein, *Multimind*, 104.

7. "The principal reason why India developed more slowly than almost any other country was simply lack of water." Arthur Lewis qtd., Tony Smith, *The Pattern of Imperialism: The United States, Great Britain, and the Late-industrializing World Since 1815*, OUP, 1981, 57. Perhaps.

8. John Emley, "When the Empire Struck Lead", *New Scientist*, 25 December 1986, 67. *Cf.* "Killer of Kings and Emperors", *The Listener*, 5 March 1987, 16.

9. J. H. Elliott, "Conspicuous Consumption", review of Sidney W. Mintz, *Sweetness and Power: The Place of Sugar in Modern History*, *The New York Review of Books*, Vol. XXXII, No. 16, 24 October 1985, 21. Another review of the same book touts sugar as a key to Imperial studies: "In its rich texture lies the vision of what sugar tells us about colonialism and about pre-industrial and industrializing England." Stanley J. Stein, "Sweetness and Power", *American Historical Review*, Vol. 91, No. 2, April 1986, 363.

10. Victor Margolin, "A Decade of Design History in the United States 1977-87", *Journal of Design History*, Vol. 1, No. 1, 67.

11. See Himmelfarb, *New History and the Old*, 17. Revisionism is continually being revised. See, *e.g.* Simon Szreter, "The Importance of Social Intervention in Britain's Mortality Decline c.1850-1914: a Re-interpretation of the Role of Public Health", *Social History of Medicine*, Vol. 2, No. 1, April 1988, 1-38.

12. This is not to say that new approaches do not yield useful insights, one of the intriguing in its implications being David Hamilton's idea of the "moral economy" of the classroom, the claim that "educational practice lies at the intersection of economic history and the history of ideas". David Hamilton, "Adam Smith and the Moral Economy of the Classroom System" *Journal of Curriculum Studies*, 1980, Vol. 12, No. 4, 282. The appearance of the blackboard and the idea of classrooms as an architectural unit are related by Hamilton to the decline of catechesis, "the ultimate victory of group-based pedagogies over the more individualized forms of teaching". *Ibid.*

13. See John Hagan, John Simpson, and A. R. Gillis, "Feminist Scholarship, Relational and Instrumental Control, and a Power-Control Theory of Gender and Delinquency", *British Journal of Sociology*, Vol. XXXIX, No. 3, September 1988, 301-36.

14. F. Musgrove, "Middle-class Families and Schools, 1780-1880: Interaction and Exchange of Function between Institutions", P. W. Musgrave ed., *Sociology, History and Education*, Methuen, 1970, 124. "By the 1870s and 1880s the family had abdicated from its front-line position in education." *Ibid.* ". . . whether or not they are enjoying intimate relationships, human beings need a sense of being part of a larger community than that constituted by the family". Anthony Storr, *The School of Genius*, Andre Deutsch, 1988, 13. A contrasting view is that social ideology is largely conditioned by family structure. Emmanuel Todd, *The Explanation of Ideology: Family Structures and Social Systems*, Basil Blackwell, 1985.

15. Storr, *School of Genius*, 118.

16. See Linda A. Pollock, *Forgotten Children: Parent-Child Relations from 1500 to 1900*. OUP 1985, 269-70. For the debate over the existence or non-existence of childhood as a concept through the centuries, see Robert Pattison, *The Child Figure in English Literature*, University of Georgia Press, Athens (Georgia), 1978, 64. Also see *The Parent as Prime Educator: Changing Patterns of Parenthood*, Fourth Western Hemisphere Seminar with the Cooperation of the Government of Peru, Bernard Van Leer Foundation, The Hague, 1987. Consider also Konrad Lorenz's geese imprinting experiments.

17. John Dancy, *The Public Schools and the Future*. Faber and Faber, 1963, 76-77.

18. Alec Waugh, *Public School Life: Boys, Parents, Masters*, W. Collins, 1927 (1922), 11-12.

19. *Ibid.*

20. J. D. McClure, "Preparation for Practical Life", A. C. Benson ed., *Cambridge Essays in Education*, OUP, 1918, 211. Boarding is being reconsidered in the state system. Two Kent schools, Cranbrook Grammar and Sir Roger Manwood's Grammar, have proposed to Kent County Council that they take boarders from overseas. "Beyond the Boarders", *Times Educational Supplement*, 9 February 1990, 1.

21. Graham Greene, *A Sort of Life*, qtd. Anthony Masters, *Literary Agents: The Agent as Spy*, Basil Blackwell, Oxford, 1987, 115.

22. Quigly, *Heirs of Tom Brown*, 5.

23. Gathorne-Hardy's 'nanny numeration' estimates about 93,000 nannies in 1861, rising to an awesome 200,000 nannies in the mid 1890s. Jonathan Gathorne-Hardy, *The Rise and Fall of the British Nanny*, Weidenfeld and Nicolson, 1985, 180-81. He estimates the number of nannies who lived between 1850 and 1939 at "between two and two and a quarter million". *Ibid.* He ponders if forced-feeding with tapioca left statesmen with food anxiety, and whether a sense of history was the relic of toilet training. *Cf.* Waugh, *Public School Life*, 154.

24. Daniel Goleman, "For Each Sibling, There Appears to Be a Different Family," *New York Times*, 28 July 1987, 13.

25. Winston S. Churchill, *My Early Life: A Roving Commission*, Collins, 1977 (1930), 30.

26. Rebecca Irvine, *A Girl's Guide to the English Public Schoolboy*, Severn House, 1985, 25-26. However, *cf.* Robert D. Hess and Judith V. Torney, *The Development of Political Attitudes in Children*, Adine, Chicago, 1967, esp. 101-10. The Victorian and Edwardian family considered public school to be a necessity, and indoctrinated children in this belief. **The public school dynasties of nonconformist families were notable.** See H. Derry Osborn, "Two Methodist Families", *Proceedings of the Wesley Historical Society*. Vol. XLVII, Part 1, February 1989, 15, 18. "Rupert, who although an independent child, was still strongly patriotic about such things as the school from which, one day, he would doubtless run away." Hollinghurst, *The Swimming Pool Library*, 59.

27. Jonathan Gathorne-Hardy, *The Old School Tie: The Phenomenon of the English Public School*, Viking Press, New York, 1978, 191. (See bibliography.) **"Ah – a sort of public school churchman."** Geoffrey Fisher, Archbishop of Canterbury, on John Thorn's explanation that he was only moderately "High Church". *Road to Winchester*, 74.

28. Paul Delaney, *The Neo-Pagans*, Macmillan, 1988, 4.

29. Rt. Revd. Simon Ward, qtd. Mortimer, "Training for Life in Prison", *The Sunday Times*, G2.

30. Arnold Wilson, *S. W. Persia: A Political Officer's Diary, 1907-1914*, OUP, 1941, 95.

31. See Matthew Arnold, *A French Eton*, in *Democratic Education, Collected Works on Education*, R. H. Super ed., University of Michigan Press, Ann Arbor, 1962, 320.

32. See and *Cf.* Abner Cohen, *The Politics of Elite Culture: Explorations in the Dramaturgy of Power in a Modern African Society*, University of California, Berkeley, 1981, 2.

33. Brian Simon, *The Two Nations and the Education Structure, 1780-1870*, Lawrence & Wishart, 1981, 284. See Cohen, *Politics of Elite Culture*. 2.

34. John D. Kelly, "From Holi to Diwali in Fiji: An Essay on Ritual and History", *Man*, Vol. 23, No. 1, March 1988, 54.

35. Josef L. Altholz, "The Simony Press", *Victorian Periodicals Review*, Vol. XXII, No. 1, Spring 1989, 16-18.

36. W. W. Vaughan, "Religion at School", A. C. Benson ed., *Cambridge Essays on Education*, OUP, 1918, 67.

37. Peter Parker, *The Old Lie: The Great War and the Public School Ethos*, Constable, 1987, 19.

38. Ollard, *An English Education*, 173. *Cf.* Kenneth Rose, *Curzon: A Most Superior Person*, Macmillan, 1985, 106. See Leinster-Mackay, *Educational World of Edward Thring*, 20.

39. Wilson, S. W. *Persia*, 172.

40. J. A. Mangan, "Social Darwinism and Upper-Class Education in Late Victorian and Early Edwardian England", J. A. Mangan, and James Walvin eds., *Manliness and Morality: Middle-class Masculinity in Britain and America, 1800-1940*, Manchester University Press, 1987, 140. See review of same by P. J. Rich, *History of Education Review*, Vol. 17, No. 1, 1988, 74-76. In correspondence, Dr. Mangan emphasizes his interest in Social Darwinism and the schools.

41. Rogers, *Men Only*. 212.

42. A. Michael Aves, letter to *The Times*, 14 March 1989, 17.

43. *Statutes of The Great Priory of the United Kingdom, Military and Masonic Orders of the Temple and of St. John of Jerusalem, Palestine, Rhodes and Malta of England and Wales and Its Provinces Overseas*, 1986, 61.

44. Jack Bazalgette, *The Captains and the King's Depart: Life in India 1928-46*, Amate Press, 1984, 3.

45. Colin Turnbull, *The Human Cycle*, Triad/Paladin, 1985, 96. "The West London pecking order went: Westminster, St. Paul's, Latymer, with the rest nowhere. And all that I knew by the age of twelve." *Road to Winchester*, 159.

46. Jean Barman, "The Preparatory School Abroad: From Britain to British Columbia", *History of Education*, 1986, Vol. 15, No. 1, 1-2. For the trauma as well as cultural significance of the school experience for younger boys see Anthony Trollope, *Dr. Wortle's School*, OUP, 1984 (1880), 20. Also George Orwell, "Such, Such Were the Joys", *George Orwell: Collected Works, Vol. II*, Secker & Warburg, 810. *Cf.* Donald Leinster-Mackay, *The Rise of the English Prep School*, Falmer Press, 1984, xiv, xv, 167-68, and *passim*.

47. qtd. Emmet, *Effectiveness of Causes*, 66.

48. Katheleen Betterton, qtd. J. F. Burnett ed., *Destiny Obscure: Autobiographies of Childhood, Education, and Family From the 1820s to the 1920s*, Penguin, Harmondsworth, 1984, 211. "The Anglicans had marched in crocodile to morning service. The few Dissenters had gone off to their Chapel in anarchy." Roy Fuller, *The Ruined Boys*, Andre Deutsch, 1959, 9.

49. *E.g.,* V. E. D. Haggard, *The Brewing Years: The Story of the Old Malthouse*, The Old Malthouse, Swanage, 1981, 17.

50. Charles Allen, ed., *Plain Tales from the Raj: Images of British India in the Twentieth Century*, Futura, 1986 (1975), 35-36.

51. Anton Gill, *How to be Oxbridge: A Bluffer's Handbook*, Grafton Books, 1985, 86. Oxford was a "boisterous repetition of Charterhouse". Graves, *Goodbye to All That*, Penguin, Harmondsworth, 1986 (1929), 36.

52. Richard Symonds, *Oxford and Empire: The Last Lost Cause?*, Macmillan, 20-21. See Timothy J. L. Chandler, "The Development of a Sporting Tradition at Oxbridge: 1800-1860", *Canadian Journal of History of Sport*, Vol. XIX, No. 2, December 1988, 1-29.

53. Gordon Ross, "Breathless Hush in the Close", Fraser ed., *World of the Public Schools*, 154.

54. Symonds, *Oxford and Empire*, 168.

55. *Ibid.*, 16.

56. IOR:MSS EUR D922, David Lorimer, "Modern Education", 9 February 1895. This is one of several essays in the India Office Records collection apparently written by Lorimer at a Crammer.

57. R. J. Montgomery, *Examinations: An Account of Their Evolution As Administrative Devices in England*, Longman, 1965, 31.

58. Michael Carritt, *A Mole in the Crown*, Central Books, 1985, 11-13.

59. Montgomery, *Examinations*, 31.

60. Evan Maconochie, *Life in the Indian Civil Service*, Chapman and Hall, 1926, 11-12.

61. *Ibid.*

62. Military values derived "*primarily* from those who choose to join the armed forces rather than from events (screening and/or socialization) that occur thereafter." Jerald G. Bachman, Lee Sigelman, Greg Diamond, "Self-Selection, Socialization, and Distinctive Military Values: Attitudes of High School Seniors", *Armed Forces & Society*, Vol. 13, No. 2, Winter 1987, 171.

63. ". . . the schools previewed regimental life itself. When one thinks of public school monasticism, hierarchy, and hardship, of barrackroom living and discipline, of teamwork rewarded by decoration, and of the reverence paid to community tradition – when one parades these factors together, it is not difficult to understand why public school gentlemen became military officers." Rupert Wilkinson, *The Prefects: British Leadership and the Public School Tradition*, OUP, 1964, 17.

64. It was a "second-rate public school". Brian Bond, *The Victorian Army and the Staff College, 1854-1914*, 172, 53, qtd. Trevor Hearl, "Military Education and the School Curriculum, 1800-1870", *History of Education*, Vol. 5, No. 3, 1976, 261.

65. *Ibid.*, 263.

66. Trevor Hearl to P.J. Rich, 17 January 1987.

67. *Ibid.*

68. *Ibid.*

69. T. Bland Strange, *Gunner Jingo's Jubilee*, Remington, 1893, 29.

70. D. T. D. Clarke, Curator, Colchester & Essex Museum, to P. J. Rich, 12 January 1987.

71. Articles in *The Journal of the Society for Army Historical Research* makes clear that "By the mid-nineteenth century, regimental schools had been established 'in every regiment of cavalry and battalion of infantry', and these were at the heart of the educational provision for the soldier." E. A. Smith, "Educating the Soldier in the Nineteenth Century", *The Journal of the Society for Army Historical Research*, Vol. LXV, No. 264, Winter 1987, 201. Establishment of the office of Inspector General of Army Schools (1846) and activities of the Council of Military Education (1860) and its successor (1870) the Director General of Military Education, demand more research. By 1870, there were 250 professional Army schoolmasters stationed in regimental schools. Purpose-built facilities for them were not unusual. What was the atmosphere of regimental schools? Smith comments: "In a period of rapid social change, there was a fear that the lower orders would no longer accept the place to which it had pleased God to call them. Education was, therefore, called in to inoculate them against the contagion of subversive doctrines, by stressing the importance of contentment with one's station in society and a sober and industrious life . . . educational provision for both the soldier and his child, in a form better described as indoctrination or social conditioning, would engender a feeling of subordination, subservience and respect for authority." *Ibid.*, 206. Inculcating social stability with unit libraries and Army sponsorship of approved books, may show that the public school influence was as responsible for instilling subservience through popular education as it was in making leaders. A dissertation is evidently in process on a related topic (1989): Elaine A. Smith, "The Corps of Army Schoolmasters, 1876-1920", Institute of Education, University of London.

72. Leinster-Mackay, *The Rise of the English Prep School*, 43, 50. *Cf.* R. F. S. Job, "A Test of Proposed Mechanisms Underlying the Interference Effect Produced by Noncontingent Food Presentations", *Learning and Motivation*, Vol. 20, No. 2, May 1989, 153-77.

73. Michael Brander, *The Victorian Gentleman*, Cremonesi, 1975, 47.

74. "The Larder Invaded", *Annual Report of the Library Company of Philadelphia for the Year 1986*. Library Company of Philadelphia, 1987, 19.

75. Parker, *Floreat*, 228, *cf.* 9-11, 46, 59, 61-65, 76-77, 175.

76. Trevor R. Reese, *The History of the Royal Commonwealth Society, 1863- 1963*, OUP, 1968, 156.

77. Coen, *Indian Political Service*, 37.

78. Monier Monier-Williams, *Memorial of Old Haileybury College*, Archibald Constable, 1894, 80.

79. *Ibid*, no. 2, 79-80.

80. *The New Yorker*, 25 April 1988, 97.

81. Mady Martin, *Martyn Sahib: The Story of John Martyn of The Doon School*, Dass Media, New Delhi, 1985, 32.

82. *Calcutta: 200 Years: A Tolygunge Club Perspective*, 2nd ed., n.a., Tollygunge Club, Calcutta, 1981, 124.

83. Albert Homas, *Wait & See*, Michael Joseph, 1944, 115. However, as is well known, fresh limes helped the Royal Navy to arrest scurvy and thus made a significant contribution to Imperial defence. See Martin Wainwright, "Henry Was A Scurvy Knave, After All", *The Guardian*, 10 September 1989, 21. Recipes, as opposed to the actual food, also have causal implications: "Even the root of *recipe* – The Latin recipere – implies and exchange, a giver and a receiver . . . a recipe needs a recommendation, a context, a

point, a reason to be . . . it can have a variety of relationships with its flame, on its bed." Susan J. Leonardi, "Recipes for Reading: Summer Pasta, Lobster à la Riseholme, and Key Lime Pie", *PMLA*, Vol. 104, No. 3, May 1989, 340.

84. Arnold Palmer, *Movable Feasts: Changes in English Eating Habits*, OUP, 1987 (K1952), 75.

85. Delaney, *Neo-pagans*, 6.

86. Paul Johnson. "Education of an Establishment", Fraser ed. *World of the Public School*, 14.

87. Qtd. Bruce Haley, *Healthy Body and Victorian Culture*, Harvard University Press, Cambridge (Massachusetts), 19878, 261. *Cf.* importantly J. A. Mangan, *Athleticism in the Victorian and Edwardian Public School: The Emergence and Consolidation of an Educational Ideology*, OUP, 1981, 195.

88. IOR:R/15/2/210. "Report on Mr. Dundas' Visit to the Persian Gulf from 19 February to 5 March, 1941", 55, 56. See P. J. Rich, "The Bahrain Public School Scheme, 1971", *Education Research and Perspectives*, Vol. 14, No. 2, December 1987, 76-84.

CHAPTER V

Psychohistory

The furtive fallacy is the erroneous idea that facts of special significance are dark and dirty things and that history itself is a story of causes mostly insidious and results mostly invidious. – David Hackett Fischer, *Historians' Fallacies*, 1970.

They may question whether a method devised for a patient on the couch – and which requires, even in that situation, great subtlety and skill to elicit truths – can be applied to someone not personally available for analysis. – Gertrude Himmelfarb, *The New History and the Old*, 1987.

There was a pretence that all this love was really the love of the classics, and that when it was pure it was a marvellous thing. The point is, of course, that the love of the classics wasn't pure in the least. – Jonathan Gathorne-Hardy, *The Old School Tie*, 1977.

The study of emotion may become one of the hot new topics in social history, a field already known for expanding the range of investigation. – Peter N. Stearns with Carol S. Stearns, "Emotionology: Clarifying the History of Emotions and Emotional Standards", 1985.

Heterosexuality does not loom large in English public school literature.[1] Sado-masochism does. Homosexuality, cabalisms and racism are recurrent. Despite this, and reminiscences about horrendous public school experiences notwithstanding, there has been no comprehensive examination of the psychological effects of the schools, let alone analysis of school psychological 'types'. The neglect contradicts the topic's self-evident interest, and reflects the immaturity of what is called "childhood history", and the uncertain status of **sociobiology, emotionology,** and **psychohistory.** Professor Peter Gay is one of the few historians who has undergone training as a psychoanalyst, but despite proseleytizing in books such as *Freud for Historians* he claims few converts. While it is well known that *historiai* is the Greek for inquiries, there is uncertainty about who is best able to make those inquiries. Is a feminist always the preferred choice for women's studies, or would fairness require a rabid male chauvinist? Is a gay historian as able as a straight historian to differentiate between affection, friendship, and passion?

Historians grudgingly use some sociological jargon such as 'nuclear family' and 'extended family' but employing 'emotionology', a late entrant, has so far had less appeal.[2] **Psychohistory** seems to have won more acceptance as a descriptive term.

Although proponents claim that its antecedents can be traced back to Vico and Dilthey, it came into its own in the late 1950s with Erik Erikson's *Young Man Luther* (1958) and Norman Brown's *Life Against Death* (1959). The field is divided into radical and conservative camps, respectively represented by the **Journal of Psychohistory** and the **Psychohistory Review** and their sponsors, the **International Psychohistorical Association** and the **Group for the Use of Psychohistory in History**. An apparent distinction between them is over the emphasis to be put on emotion as a causal factor, the radicals being more enthusiastic about its importance.[3]

While there has been comparatively little written in psychohistory, there is even less available about what could be called *prosopographical psychohistory*. There is no comprehensive prosopographical examination of the mental health of British civil servants, let alone Imperial civil servants – or any study linking mental states to schooldays. Despite such vacua, there is a temptation to generalize, because psychohistory has an enticing promise: "If childhood history – and psychohistory – mean anything, they mean reversing most of the causal arrows used by historians to date."[4] There would be more than schooldays to consider in a prosopographical psychohistory of the Imperial élite. Psychological abnormalities were also related to isolation and the lack of compatriot companionship at overseas posts. There is an analogy with prisoners, who ". . . invent obsessional rituals to mark the hours and give structure to the day."[5]

Nor is there any lack of innuendo about the anal and phallic traumas of a public school education. Terence Rattigan's play *Cause Célèbre* has two schoolboys in discussion:

> Tony: *I wonder what our parents think we do between thirteen and twenty-one.*
>
> Randolph: *What we do, I imagine . . . solo . . . they hope of course, but if it's the other – better with some nasty woman.*

Rattigan's own schooldays at Harrow, when Cyril Norwood was headmaster, seem to have figured in this and his other works.

The schools have been accused of encouraging *both* a flair for the cloak-and-dagger and for homosexuality, a combination which is singled out for comment by Len Deighton in his foreword to Anthony Masters' *Literary Agents: The Novelist as Spy*.[6] John Le Carré (David Cornwall) drew on schooldays at Sherborne, and on experiences as a master at Millfield and Eton, to create the "élite, class based-brotherhood" of agents in his spy fiction. His arch-hero, Smiley, is modelled on the Sherborne chaplain, Vivian Green.[7] School stories are full of the intrigue of strange cabals. (See *The Secret Societies of St. Frank's*, page 120, and *The Tubs*, page 121.)

Such speculations may be the work of novelists, but while psycho or boudoir history is approached with wariness, what appear to be economic, military or political influences can be such less honourable influences in disguise. The difficulty with either the pocketbook or glands has been that the backstage causes are apt to be the least documented and the most resistant to discovery. The most encouraging progress has been made by historians who despite difficulties have relied on documentary sources rather than gone off the deep end in conjecture. George Minois has studied

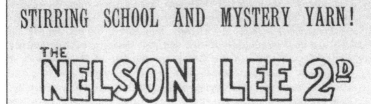

Roughly Nipper, Handforth, and Pitt were thrust into the tree tubs, after which the lids – each having a small hole to allow the head to pass through – were screwed down. The Removites were helpless – and the New Klux Klan could do their worst!

the confessors of the French kings, although understandably fewer secrets disclosed to them than with the relationship between priest and monarch. Virgia Berridge and Griffith Edwards have shown how opium became a factor in nineteenth-century society. (Its use was completely legal until 1868.)[x]

Not the least of the furtive factors concerns the **interplay** of political intrigue and sex. Guile, chance and stupidity are a part of this tarot and speculation about sexual politics is fraught with dangers. The historian can become so conspiracy-minded that instead of engaging a psychiatrist to help analyze data he should have gone to one for help with his own paranoia. The tawdry reasons behind events sometimes lack any but the most circumstantial of evidence,[y] but it would be wrong to ignore the psychohistorical aspect. History's darker glades are thickets that must be explored.

Money

In comparison with the more outrageous doubts cast by psychohistory, money seems almost an attractive explanation for conduct. Arguably it was Sandhurst's fees as much as anything that kept it a public school reserve, and actual Army service was influenced by initial and later expenses that an officer without private means would find hard to meet.[10] Where one served was influenced by money: "Either a light purse or an eager ambition might then be part of the reason for choosing the Indian rather than the British service."[11] In a curious way this too had its connection with the public schools: some men went to India because it was the best opportunity to save for the school fees of *their* children.[12] School expenses were a concern to those who took Imperial posts: ". . . the one thing that was never saved on was the children's education, because this was considered the greatest security of all."[13]

Some Imperial mandarins benefited financially from the position they had held, principally it seems when it came to employment after leaving the services – another area where prosopographical work would be rewarding.[14] Connections made as a government officer could prove useful especially after retirement. A minor *cause célèbre* is the case of the Persian Gulf Resident Lewis Pelly, who became a director of the British East Africa Company. The Company had a large trade with the Gulf, where Pelly had vigorously harassed slavers. He became embarrassingly embroiled in controversy when fellow members of the House of Commons accused him of hypocrisy for serving on the board of an enterprise that traded with slavers and indirectly employed slaves to portage its goods.

Imperial administrators were well paid by standards of the time, and perhaps that is why the records of the Empire appear to show them to be concerned with social and political issues rather than with personal finances. It may be that there will be surprises if a study is done of their bank records and directorships, but without discounting salary, pensions, and similar factors, finances do not appear to have been as influential as they might have been. The search for motivation must be more far reaching.[15] The schools are not simply a scheme for perpetuating capitalism. This is far from a Marxist position and contrasts with the views of those who have regarded public schools as a capitalist ploy: after all, Lord Camrose's Amalgamated Press published *The Financial Times* at the same time that it was publishing comics glorifying school life, and there were virtually no socialist comics for working-class boys to devour.

To confirm suspicions, a long-time headmaster of Westminster (the irrepressible John Rae) has discussed bribery:

> Implying that the headmaster takes bribes is a bit heavy . . . "No doubt my son would have been given a place if his father had had the foresight to offer the headmaster and his family a holiday in the Gulf?" I can't take you seriously. Why the Gulf? Perhaps you imagine that because the Arabs are buying up London they are buying their way into our independent schools as well . . . I have been offered much smaller inducements to take a boy into the school including, you will be pleased to know, a holiday in the Gulf. How did you get to hear about that? It was nicely phrased: "If you are able to help, headmaster, you will find that I am not ungrateful. The weather in the Gulf is delightful at this time of the year." . . . The Arabs may try the holiday-in-the-Gulf approach but the British are more subtle.[16]

Psychohistory

Rae stated that he **would** take a bribe: "It would have to be a bribe to the school and not to me. It would have to be substantial. And the boy concerned would have to be at least capable of holding his own in the classroom. If those conditions were met, I would sell a place if the price was [sic.] right."[17]

Natural Friendships

When Imperialism and the public schools are concerned there are more scandalous influences to consider than avarice. Oscar Browning was a master at Eton when Macnaghten was a boy there. (See *Vanity Fair's 'Oscar Browning'*, page 124.) What is one to make of the 2000 letters at King's College Cambridge written to Browning from assorted youths? His love-affairs were innumerable. His friendship with the young George Curzon was reciprocated, and they kept up a lifelong connection, with Browning visiting Curzon in India when he was Viceroy. Another master who was at Eton when Macnaghten was there, Johnson Cory (the author of the *Boating Song*) was no less an appreciator of male beauty.

In his *Memoirs*, John Addington Symonds claimed that every good-looking boy at Harrow was given a female name. It was Symonds' blackmail that forced Dr. Vaughan to depart quietly as headmaster of Harrow because of his affair with Alfred Pretor. Symonds ranged freely as a boy at Harrow, but then forced Vaughan's resignation for indiscretions that were not as grave as his own. *Memoirs* reveal that as an adult he took advantage of a friendship with a master at Clifton, Graham Dakyns, to 'cruise' the school and seduce a boy, who unfortunately from Symonds' viewpoint already loved even younger boys. These escapades were not Platonic. Symonds records of one tryst: "We lay covered from the cold in bed, tasting the honey of softly spoken words and the blossoms of lips pressed on lips." Browning's biographer, Ian Anstruther, calls him a **paedagogue** in search of the Holy Grail – but an unkinder view would be that he was a **paedophile** in search of satisfaction.

Observers would have to be blind to ignore the connections between homosexuality and the schools. Dr. John Rae admits "That many good teachers of both sexes are sublimated homosexuals no one would seriously question." He singles out Cory's conduct at Eton, and concedes that there are masters "whose homosexuality communicates an attitude to life and to relations between the sexes in particular, that I think is harmful. It is a subtle influence, all the more appealing to the brightest pupils because it is presented in intellectual terms."[18] One could disagree with Rae's remarks that the influence was subtle, either at school or afterwards. Lord Kitchener's long friendship with Captain O. A. G. Fitzgerald was well known and his rose garden was decorated with four pairs of naked bronze boys.

There were many facets to British homosexuality. George Ives, Laurence Housman, and other Victorian luminaries supported a secret homosexual society, the Order of Chaeronea. This had Masonic associations and took its name from the Battle of Chaeronea in 338 BC, when the 'Sacred Band' of Thebans were defeated by the Macedonian cavalry. The Greek connections appealed to members, and the order

Oscar Browning.

developed a symbolism involving the date 338 and silver rings engraved with the name of the battle. Laurence's brother A. E. Housman possibly was a member. Little is known about the society, and it deserves investigation. But prosopographers face considerable obstacles in uncovering what was *intra indignitatem.*

Fruitful Ground

Anthony Masters remarks, "If homosexuality [*sic.*] was to be implanted at an early age, no ground was more fruitful than the English public school."[19] As mentioned, a peculiar connection does seem to have existed between the worlds of espionage and public school homosexuality. An example is the case of Somerset Maugham, who combined his lingering memories of schoolboy friendships and his interest in the British secret services. In *The Moon and Sixpence* and *Cakes and Ale,* the narrator seems modelled after a real and beloved classmate at King's School, Canterbury. A boy with whom Maugham had a one-sided friendship figures prominently in *Of Human Bondage.*[20] The misadventures of Maugham and others in adult life suggest that some old boys ". . . were obeying a kind of sexual compulsion, a reaction to the celibate frustrations of the British public school."[21]

Was Imperial service a psychological catharsis? It would be exceptional if the colonies did not harbour men who were motivated by concealed impulses. The

Gordon and his "Kings".

125

atmosphere of the schools did little to suppress the primitive energies of adolescence, sports notwithstanding. Part of the blame put on the schools for distorting the sexuality of boys is attributed to the classical curriculum, *apropos* the Order of Chaeronea. Cory, who it will be recalled was at Eton while Melville Macnaghten was there, resurrected unexpurgated classics such as Plato's *Symposium*.[22] Boys were exposed to Horace's *Odes,* Juvenal's *Satires,* the poems of Catullus, and Virgil's eclogue about Corydon's love for Alexis.[23]

There was as little awareness of connections between Imperial careers and sexual impulses at the time as there was any self-consciousness about the homophile atmosphere of schools. In the main, Victorians did not entertain Freudian suspicions.[24] Only occasionally does the veil drop, such as with the reference by Hughes in *Tom Brown's Schooldays* to "pretty white-handed curly-headed boys, petted and pampered by some of the big fellows, who . . . did all they could to spoil them for . . . this world and the next."

However, enough evidence exists of questionable sexual pursuits carried on by Imperial administrators, to raise the question of whether their schooling did have an influence on their later sexual preference.[25] **An eye for adolescent pulchritude and an affection for youth was commended rather than condemned.** (See the popular Victorian engraving *Gordon and His Kings,* page 125.) This innocence about the implications of 'chapish' behaviour was characteristic of the Victorian public school. In *Sketchy Memories,* Macnaghten wrote about his Eton classmate J. E. C. Welldon "that a prettier girl has seldom stood before an altar". The future Harrow headmaster and bishop was a "fairy who . . . had begged permission to coy Bottom's amiable cheeks." Today such enthusiasms from the head of Scotland Yard would bring difficulties. James Barrie's adopted son wrote to him from Eton unabashedly about an affair with a young boy. "He is good looking, and because of that my tutor says I am so to speak in love with him, whereas it is just perfectly natural friendship."[26]

At the least, public schools encouraged a PETER PAN SYNDROME among Imperial leaders that expressed itself either as colossal innocence or self-duplicity. In the case of Baden-Powell, Frank Brodhead notes the scout leader's emphasis on "manliness" and being "chums in marriage": "From the age of eleven onwards, Baden-Powell lived in the exclusively male world of the Victorian public school and later in the barracks of colonial officers . . . B-P himself did not marry until after his mother's death in 1914, when he was 54. His wife was only half his age, and he named his first child after Peter Pan."[27]

The boy-loves of Imperial heroes are not a topic that can be raised with impunity. When Michael Rosenthal in *The Character Factory* voiced suspicions about B-P, because of his American background he was accused of exhibiting a "Boston harbour syndrome" about Imperialism. There are, however, ample examples of a strain of Uranian sexual nefariousness in the Empire's scandals: the boys maintained by administrators in the Punjab, General Sir Eyre Coote's forays to Christ's Hospital School for flogging-and-groping sessions, Sir Hector Macdonald's discovery in a Ceylon railway compartment with four Singhalese boys, Colonel Secretary Lewis Harcourt's affair with a thirteen-year-old Etonian, John Nicholson's amusements in

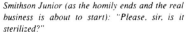
Smithson Junior (as the homily ends and the real business is about to start): "Please, sir, is it sterilized?"

Interviewing the Chief.

Wairistan, the White Cross League sodomites, William Cory's troubles at Eton, the Dublin Castle scandal of 1884, the Cleveland Street affairs on 1889-90, and the ordeal of Roger Casement.[28]

Contributing to such behaviour was the way that, as boys, the Imperial cadre had dreamed about adventures shared with exclusively male company. Illustrations of this abound in *The Magnet* and other school magazines. Hero worship was common in school and crushes were not always surreptitious. Anyone pursuing the subject will find that the eroticism described in school literature has its parallels in actual activities of the British abroad.

On the other hand, since prosopographical psychohistory is not even in its infancy, it must be employed cautiously.[29] A further example of the criticisms engendered by psychohistory's use is the furore over Martin Seymour-Smith's (1989) biography of Kipling, which claims that at United Service College he was excited by being caned, and that he later developed an inclination for young subalterns. Allegedly he was in love with a young American, Wolcott Balestier. Seymour-Smith thinks that Kipling's novel *Kim* has homosexual undertones. Kim is an adolescent flirt of "almost paedophilic attractiveness." Another of Seymour-Smith's speculations is that Cornell Price, Kipling's headmaster at United Service, may have shown him pornographic lines by Swinburne. For Seymour-Smith, the very lack of evidence shows that Kipling had a dark secret. A disbeliever writes, "Those linguistic signals which indicate that a biographer is leaving fact for fantasy – 'doubtless', 'undoubtedly', 'perhaps', 'if',

127

'must have been', 'may have', 'might have' – pepper the narrative."[30] This contretemps exemplifies the dangers to scavenging for skulduggery, but without turning *Kim* into camp it is possible to acknowledge that overseas Englishmen reacted against alien surroundings by taking refuge in memories and reliving the experiences of childhood.

Discussion of passion can arouse passion. In a rebuttal to a review in the *Times Literary Supplement,* Seymour-Smith replies: "Your reviewer of my Rudyard Kipling states that its thesis is that Kipling was a 'closet homosexual'. It is not. It is that Kipling had homosexual feelings, and that he soon suppressed them . . . I suppose he thinks that masturbation and 'homosexuality' at 'public schools' is a 'bathetic' invention of mine, as if I could ignore it when Kipling himself managed to put so much emphasis on it."[31] In any event, the Empire as well as the school was a place where illicit byways could be discreetly pursued, and was possessed of back alleys that were closed in England.

As strong a case can be made for a taste for flagellation as for homosexuality. (See *Punch's 'Is It Sterilized,'* page 127, and *Interviewing the Chief.)* The almost universal use of the rod supposedly had Imperial consequences:

> The fact that the rulers of Victorian Britain and her immense Empire came almost entirely from the public schools means that, among them, there must always have been a good, and probably a high, proportion of sado-masochists. It seems to me that it would be impossible to deny that this was the case. Every corner of the Empire must have had its flagellant administrators, and the Empire saw to it that these men should be allowed to

The Snake Charmer.

Horrible exhibition of the Egyptian Serpent Charmer.

continue behaving like so many public school prefects . . . For if dukes' sons could be birched in public at Eton on their naked buttocks, why should some young poacher, or sailor, some Indian or Negro, expect that he should escape the lash?[32]

Speculation as to 'Tartary's dark glades' of adolescence affecting adult conduct has produced hypotheses. They remain hypotheses.[33] After all, loneliness may have been as much a factor in promoting homosexuality as sexual appetite. Nonetheless, the fact remains that placing hundreds of boys between the ages of twelve and nineteen in close proximity without any chance of normal female company could lead to what Alec Waugh coyly called in *Public School Life* (1922), "uncomfortable complications". Not surprisingly, as he noted, an unnatural system could have unnatural results.

A case for school-contracted sexual aberrations having Imperial manifestations is strengthened by the way that Imperial images became suffused with eroticism. This theme has been emphasized by the distinguished scholar Edward Said's use of the celebrated J. L. Gérôme painting *The Snake Charmer* as the cover illustration of his magisterial *Orientalism*.[34] Gérôme encapsulates Western imperialism's erotic view of the 'natives' – a naked boy entwined by a snake "performs" in an exotic setting. (See page 128.) Admittedly notions of the bizarre lasciviousness of the East were hardly novel. This is well illustrated by an anticipatory 1827 London penny print *Horrible Exhibition of the Egyptian Serpent Charmer.* (See above.)

From the beginnings of Western imperialism, the psychological relationships between the ruler and the ruled produced an outpouring of speculation which – in the fashion of Dr. Syntax – doted on the picturesque.[35] The public schools contributed to a general outlook which Professor Said has tellingly described as *Orientalism.*

The structure of the Empire favoured an inequality in sexual relationships similar to what existed between older and younger boys at school. Administrative outposts resembled public school houses, and the relationships with the natives resembled the prefect-fag relationship.[36] Still, historians are obligated to show "a decent diffidence in drawing conclusions about the thoughts and motives of the dead."[37] After recounting an exchange of kisses between a boy and Edward Thring, headmaster of Uppingham, Dr. Leinster-Mackay enjoins *Honi soit qui mal y pense!*[38] He has a point. Historians are susceptible to allegations of the 'unseen hand'. After all, their calling is rewarded for successful detective work. John Mack complained about the lack of restraint of Lawrence of Arabia's biographers, but ruefully admitted that he had carried on with his own snooping into Lawrence's school experiences.[39]

To end this brief review of a complicated subject, it can be emphasised that in discussion of the public schools and Empire the associations between the schools, sexuality and power must be mentioned. Hyam goes so far as to suggest that: "Sexual relationships soldered together the invisible bonds of empire."[40] However, there was another relationship that would be a strong candidate when the forging of "invisible bonds" is mentioned, cabalism.

Clandestine Causality and Cabalism

An unappreciated consequence of attending public school may have been a lifetime dabbling in CABALISM and the clandestine. This is not only a matter of causes whose existence are deliberately concealed, but of the instilling of an appetite for the clandestine, a revelling in it – encouraged by the arcane ritualism of the public school. The outright love of secrecy is rarely mentioned as a causal factor, but schoolboy novels gloat over secrets. Secrets *per se* were an important part of school life, an assertion of adolescent autonomy that when 'grown up' became an assertion of adult autorchy. Freemasonry above all was:

> . . . the supreme example of the archetypal cabal during the eighteenth and nineteenth centuries. Not only did Freemasonry function as a cabal to outsiders. Within the craft's own ranks, the hierarchy – especially when it culminated in 'unknown superiors' formed a **cabal inside a cabal,** an enigmatic pyramid whose apex was swathed in shadows . . . The archetype of the cabal plays a particularly important rôle in contemporary Western society . . . Above all, a cabal is organised, is secret and is at very least believed to be powerful. **Whether it is powerful or not is ultimately beside the point. It can become powerful simply by virtue of people's belief in its power.**[41]

A distinctive feature of a culture is its symbolism, and therefore secret manipulation of its symbols can be a powerful causal force.[42] Few historians have been convinced enough of this to devote their efforts to 'secret history' as such, and the field has been left to those who possibly overstate the dangers of reporting on oath-bound clandestine societies in order to glamorize their debunking efforts. John Lawrence in a hebetudinous consideration *Freemasonry – A Religion?* (1987) sets a suitable sombre tone: "On several occasions I have spoken to men who have lived in fear of revealing masonic secrets though they have genuinely felt uneasy at the direction the knowledge was taking them. When they realized that I already knew what they were talking about, and they weren't betraying any secrets, the grave-clothes were loosened and with a sense of relief they settled down to talk with me." Lawrence regards the whole business as dubious, remarking that the mystery surrounding Masonry "is far worse than the schoolboy pacts of secrecy which many of us engaged in because what is being demanded is a blanket assurance and commitment that everything learnt within the lodge will be kept secret, whether it be good or bad."[43]

This seems to be an overly dark view of the movement which, after all, usually includes the local establishment. Admittedly the passwords and handshakes make heavy going for the academic who is accustomed to getting information in the library rather than from informants, but the influence of secret organizations does run through history, exemplified by the circle around Louis XV of France and the Chevalier d'Eon that became known as the *Secret du Roi*. Analyzing those activities, Jonathan Dull concluded that such cabals were characterized by "a mind set prone to wish fulfilment", were doctrinaire, depended on the establishment to preserve a general ignorance of their functions, and used governments for their own purposes.[44] In

the case of the schools, which enjoyed close relationships with Masonic lodges and with the élite clubs which (at least in novels) provided the setting for skulduggery, it is not difficult to imagine affairs of state being decided in shadowy corridors by men who were at school together.

The code that protected the conversations of the club and lodge from being discussed with the uninitiated made membership attractive. The passwords exchanged between old boys at reunions displayed a Masonic quality. The public school ethos seems to confirm the observation which Ivan Illich makes in *De-Schooling Society* that "Schools are designed on the assumption that there is a secret to everything in life; that the quality of life depends on knowing that secret."[45] Those who lacked the secret could only wonder at the nature of the esoteric knowledge that schools and lodges conferred, and envy the chosen. (See *Are You a Mason?,* page 131.) The British intelligence services were public school preserves. Malcolm Muggeridge remarks that "Secrecy is as essential to Intelligence as vestments and incense to a mass, or darkness to a spiritual seance, and must at all costs be maintained, quite irrespective of whether or not it serves any purpose."[46] The old boys had a thorough indoctrination in mumbo-jumbo although there were no formal courses in it. The schools luxuriated

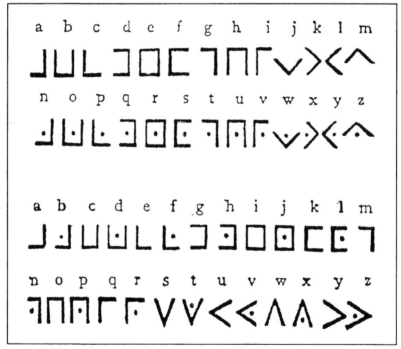

The Royal Arch Cipher.

in the arcane. Macnaughten points out in his reminiscences: ". . . when 'absence' was called, we had to be present; a third of a year was called a half."

The schools besides this esoteric language of their own were closely identified with the **ultimate passwords,** those of Freemasonry. Freemasonry, like spying and the gentlemen's clubs, was in its heyday largely a public school affair. Initiates not only learned an esoteria of recognition signs but a secret cipher. (See *Royal Arch Cipher,* page 132.)

Freemasonry

Among the most baffling of causal factors in the Empire is Freemasonry. It is not a single organization but a bewildering number of sometimes competing bodies with singular names that make confusing historical claims. (See *The Structure of Freemasonry,* page 134.) The controversy over its influence has continued unabated for hundreds of years and is still creating strife. The summer of 1989 was enlivened by a full scale row in the Church of Scotland when the Church's general assembly directed congregants who were Masons to "reconsider their position". The fraternity's hold on adherents has led to charges that it is "a kind of adultery" that comes before family commitments.[47] Recently the lodge involvement of the British police and judiciary has been the centre of press attention, but the criticism apparently has helped to promote recruitment and solidarity.

In Victorian and Edwardian times society was less questioning of the propriety of Masonic influence. Royalty freely gave its patronage and, as illustrated, even King Edward VII looked more imposing when he had put on his Masonic apron. How *really* influential Masonry was then and is today is arguable:

> People do not like the idea of cosy little élite clubs. But . . . the CIA, KGB and MI5 are the true secret societies of today. It would be interesting to know whether they have in turn absorbed masonic thoughts. Although masonic influence appears to have receded in America, it is still thriving in France and Italy. People are justified in being worried. Masonry isn't yet a toothless wolf.[48]

Despite recent tabloid interest the significance of Freemasonry (as befits an organization believing in secrecy) remains elusive. It has been described with exasperation as **a quasi-religious ritual performed semi-naked,**[49] but this hardly seems an adequate description of its attractions. The latest but surely not the last explanation to be offered is that of David Stevenson, Reader in History at the University of Aberdeen, who suggests that the Masons preserve the ancient world's "art of memory", a mnemonic technique classified by Cicero as an attribute of Prudence, one of the Four Cardinal Virtues. Students were instructed to study a complex building, memorising the layout and features. When trying to study, they were asked to imagine themselves to be walking through the building, and in each

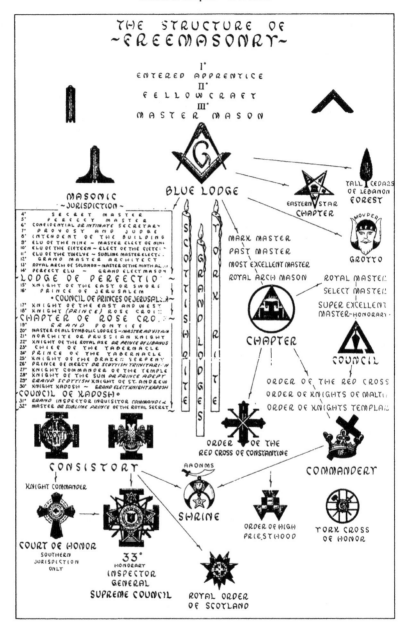

location to fix an image of what they wished to recall. Some Masonic lodges were conceived in this tradition as temples of memory, places whose symbols invoked an imaginary building that was full of secrets. That is part of the motivation behind the intense Masonic interest in the allegedly coded philosophic meanings of buildings such as Roslin Chapel in Scotland, with its mysterious carvings.[50]

Dr. Stevenson asserts that Masonry was partly a reaction to Protestantism, by providing a substitute for banished rituals. He explains that there were elements of juvenile horseplay in rites of passage whose "psychological appeal is indicated by their survival today in initiatory practices in many trades, schools, universities and other groups", and he discusses the Scottish practice of "brothering" when boys were welcomed to a household or guild.[51] The young seeker of life's secrets is commonplace in nineteenth-century depictions of Masonic ceremonies. (See *The Initiate,* and *The Candidate,* page 136.)

The earliest connections between Freemasonry and the public schools are obscure, but by the end of the nineteenth century specifically school lodges fed an appetite for secret ritual.[52] These old boy lodges are strange even in such a strange movement, for the Masonic comradery in sharing esoteric totems was further complicated by the introduction of those relating to the school.

Double Entendres

Len Deighton offers a *double entendre* about the British secret services, writing that it was their "particular charm" they were staffed by products of "our most illustrious public schools . . . This gives their adventures a tone that is convivial if not to say gay."[53] There is little reference in the vast public school literature to the inculcation of this love of cabalism, but there is considerable *Masonic* literature about public school Freemasonry. Similarly, there is virtually no reference in studies of Imperialism to Freemasonry's part in the Empire,[54] but there is plenty of *Masonic* literature about Imperial Freemasonry.

It is unnecessary to add that much of this literature is supposedly secret, protected by fearsome Masonic oaths. These have not been enough to prevent recent exposés in England, fuelled by Stephen Knight's best-selling diatribe *The Brotherhood* and furthered by Martin Short's successful sequel, *Inside the Brotherhood.* Exposing lodgery is profitable. Reviewing Short's book, Alan Rusbridger remarks in the *Times Literary Supplement:*

> Freemasonry and paranoia are inseparable. Any study of freemasonry is also a study in paranoia and can itself be dismissed as paranoiac . . . It is reasonable to argue that an enterprise crippled by lack of conclusive material is best not attempted. It is also reasonable to argue that the obsessive secrecy that Freemasons impose on themselves is not a proper excuse for impeding diligent and well-intentioned reporting, however flawed.[55]

The Empire, at least fictionally, was full of old boy spies whose cover was an innocuous civil post. One of John Buchan's (Lord Tweedsmuir) memorable characters is Victor Head, officially ADC to a general who conveniently goes on leave for a year, enabling Head to carry out "research amongst the native population", *e.g.* espionage. This echoes the concealment as "ethnological studies" of the secret activities in *Kim* of Colonel Creighton, who is **both** a Mason and spy.

The search for the ingredients of the school phenomenon has gone on without appreciating that the schools' love of secrecy and the ultra secrecy of public school Freemasonry complemented each other, constituting an overlooked joker in the old boy tarot. The covertness of Masonry makes difficulties for

The Initiate.

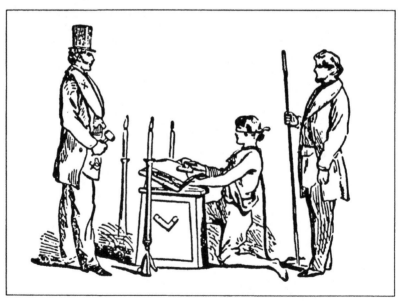

The Candidate.

136

prosopographers, as do all quiet secretive influences. J. I. M. Stewart is right that "the most famous clue in the Holmes corpus is that afforded by the dog that did nothing in the night-time."[56]

Difficulties abound, but historians cannot afford to overlook the Masonic ingredient, which manifests itself in surprising ways. A pertinent case is the rise of the world-wide Mormon movement, ostensibly a revealed religion. Mormonism has an enormous debt to Freemasonry. The religion's prophet, Joseph Smith, began his career in the late 1820s at a time when Freemasonry was the subject of "delirious hatred":

> Masonry was being denounced everywhere as a threat to free government, a secret cabal insidiously working into the key positions of state in order to regulate the whole machinery of the Republic. So it happened that Joseph Smith was writing the Book of Mormon in the thick of a political crusade that gave backwoods New York, hitherto politically stagnant and socially déclassé, a certain prestige and glory. And he quickly introduced into the book the theme of the Gadianton band, a secret society whose oaths for fraternal protection were bald parallels of Masonic oaths, and whose avowed aim was the overthrow of the democratic Nephite government. "And it came to pass that they did have their signs," he wrote, "yea, their secret signs, and their secret words; and this that they might distinguish a brother who had entered into the covenant . . ."[57]

The Masons have aroused some of the same suspicions as the 'deep cover' old boys who worked as secret agents. Glamourized by writers such as Buchan and Kipling, ultimately the old boy spies attracted another kind of notoriety and produced a genre of scandalous press stories and sensationalist books about 'public school traitors'. (One is tempted to add that they were usually both school and Cambridge University traitors.) There was a journalistic pleasure in ripping the veil from The Honourable Schoolboy, and in speculating about "fifth man" connections that might date to adolescence.

Ritual, The Omnipresent Ingredient

Ritual is a helpmate to secrecy, whether of the schoolboy or adult variety. Ostensibly its purpose is to keep out the cowans and evesdroppers, but it gathers momentum and becomes a causal influence quite apart from any intrigue it abets. The Freemasons are an example of the seductiveness. Imperial administration is another.

As Correlli Barnett described in clever Ascot fashion, the Imperial ethos as a case of "romanticism out of emotion by idealism".[58] He could have added that it was "sired by secrecy and backed by ritualism". Again and again one is reminded how ritualism was a significant part of education and of the Imperial expertise, as an old boy of Timaru in New Zealand indicated:

> Perhaps one of the strongest influences in my young life was . . .
> traditional pageant and due ceremony . . . I believe that ceremony and
> pageantry of true quality play an important part in our lives . . . The great
> corporate feeling of pride and joy in our School worked their subtle magic
> in me.[59]

Much furtive history puts the reader into a causal conundrum of "Heads I win, tails you lose." The secrecy of secret societies means that there is no way to gainsay allegations that they have a causal influence. Typically, in Stanley Devo's unfortunately best selling *The Cosmic Conspiracy* (whose nine printings are a testimony to the public's credulity) the claim is made that the Illuminati are at work under cover in France, England, and America, and that the Russian Society of the Green Glove and the Chinese Society of the Green Dragon are functioning. Short of tracing down and exposing these weird organizations, there seems no way to substantiate or disprove his addle-brained speculations.

Fortunately for this consideration of causal influences, the public school and Masonic influences may have been weird but were not always subtle. The schools exerted obvious pressure on boys. Graham Greene recalled how his time at Berkhamsted reminded him of being a foreigner in a savage country, and how on several occasions he attempted suicide.[60] **The pent-up emotions of adolescence were ultimately discharged in eccentric ways: mad dogs and Englishmen, out in the noonday sun.** The results were not always something to be proud about. If the sun seldom set on the Empire, it is equally true that sometimes the sky was blood red when it did set.

The effects of the schools, good and bad, were reinforced by organizations that might initially appear to have had only a tangential relationship to the old boy cult. The Masons are an instance. Another outstanding example of this, and of the perpetuation of perpetual adolescence by the Imperial élite, was the gentlemen's club which will be discussed in the next two chapters. In clubland the school tradition was not only maintained but nurtured. Jan Morris has written with her usual aptitude:

> Britishness was Authority: the style was the Empire. It was taken to
> allegorical extremes in the institution of the Club, a subtly potent factor in
> the British imperial system. The gentlemen's club, its membership strictly
> limited, had been exported from London to every part of the Empire, and in
> cities like Sydney, Toronto, or Cape Town had flowered into societies
> almost as grand, and just as rich, as its originals in Pall Mall and St.
> James's. But as a means of political as against social dominance it found
> more obvious meaning in the Asian and African possessions of the Crown
> . . . Soon we have a Scotch in our hands, and are surrounded by comfortable
> knick-knacks *[Again, the knick-knacks!]* of our class and kind, like stuffed
> trout, framed cricket scores, or the remarkable cravat habitually worn by
> A.S. Mortimer of Oedange . . . 'Harry!' comes a voice from the door.
> 'Heavens, my dear chap, how splendid to see you! Donald, you remember
> Harry Gribble don't you, lower Sixth the year before us?'[61]

School was *the* experience in the lives of Imperial leaders, becoming in a sense their religion. It was the *causa causars* of Imperialism. Proving this though is not easy. Hume's skepticism about understanding the conjunctions of human activity remains well founded.[62] It has been easier for writers to refer rather generally to the influence of the old boy network than to be specific about the chains that bound the old boys and Empire.[63] **One aspect of the problem that is neglected is how the chains were reforged repeatedly during life by other institutions.** Because school was so essential to their emotional make-up, when the old boys were separated from England and thousands of miles from *alma mater,* they found particular reassurance and solace in the club, where the old school seemed slightly less far away. Sometimes they could attend a Masonic lodge at the club in company with other old boys, the ultimate ritualistic orgy. Any time that Freemasonry combined with the old school nostalgia and the club, the elixir was overpowering.[64] The club as a unique asylum for old boys and old boy Freemasons is the next topic to be considered.

NOTES – CHAPTER V

1. See Eve Kosofsky Sedgwick, *Between Men.* Colombia University Press, 1985, New York, 176, 177, 180-200. Robert Graves flatly stated: "In English preparatory and public schools romance is necessarily homosexual. The opposite sex is despised and treated as something obscene. Many boys never recover from this perversion." *Goodbye to All That,* 23. The subject is one on which attitudes have changed drastically since the Victorian and Edwardian era. To modern observers, Disraeli's portrayal of Millbank's affection for Coningsby seems more than a panegyric about Eton friendships. The schools have had their share of writers who have been homosexual. Old boys of artistic and literary importance who are considered to have had homosexual sympathies include J. R. Ackerley (Rossall), C. R. Ashbee (Wellington, W. H. Auden (Gresham's), Benjamin Britten (Gresham's), Samuel Butler (Shrewsbury), Goldsworth Dickinson (Charterhouse), Menlove Edwards (Fettes), E. M. Forster (Tonbridge), Duncan Grant (St. Paul's), Edward Marsh (Westminster), Harold Munro (Radley), 'Saki' Harold Munro (Bedford Grammar), Siegfried Sassoon (Marlborough), Ronald Storrs (Charterhouse), and Ernest Thesiger (Marlborough). Michael Elliman and Frederick Rolls, *The Pink Plaque Guide to London,* GMP, 1986, *passim.*

2. Peter N. Stearns with Carol Z. Stearns, "Emotionology: Clarifying the History of Emotions and Emotional Standards", *American Historical Review,* Vol. 90, No. 4, October 1985, 813. "Historical study of emotions has the added attraction of linking social history to social and psychological theories that have largely been ignored in favor of more conventional sociological models of stratification and mobility. The history of emotion may help historians overcome, at least in part, a key weakness of psychohistory – the failure to deal persuasively with groups in the past." *Ibid.,* 815. See Karen Taylor, "Disciplining The History of Childhood." *The Journal of Psychohistory,* Vol. 16, No. 2, Fall 1988, 189. Peter N. Stearns, "Social History Update: Sociology of Emotion", *Journal of Social History,* Vol. 22, No. 3, 592-99. There is now an International Society for Research in Emotion. Emotionology prospers!

3. Henry Lawton, *The Psychohistorian's Handbook,* Psychohistory Press, New York, 1988, 5-31, 186-87, 198. See the issue of *The Journal of Psychohistory* devoted to child rearing, Vol. 17, No. 1, Summer 1989, *passim.* "Childhood history has just begun. A few dozen good studies may not seem much to show for two decades of work, when compared, for instance, to the tens of thousands of excellent books and articles produced by feminist historians during the same time period . . .". Lloyd DeMause, "On Writing Childhood History", *Journal of Psychohistory,* Vol. 16, No. 2, Fall 1988, 162. (DeMause is a principal advocate of the more aggressive school of psychohistory.) See Stearns, "Emotionology", 814-15, 819, 827. Also Mildred Dickemann, "Human Sociobiology: The First Decade", *New Scientist,* 10 October 1985, 38-42. A well argued defence of psychohistory is Peter Loewenberg, *Decoding the Past: The Psychohistorical Approach,*

139

University of California Press, Chicago, 1985 (1969). See also Richard L. Schoenwald, "Norman O. Brown and the Legacy of Freud", *The Psychohistory Review*, Vol. 18, No. 1, Fall, 1989, 81-88.

4. DeMause, "On Writing Childhood History", 162. *Cf.* Rainier Dieterich, "Psychology of Personality, Psychodiagnosis and Psychotherapy", *Education*, Vol. 39, 83- 102.

5. Storr, *School of Genius*, 44. "Many independent schools are badly run and are more like refugee camps than educational establishments, a former public school headmaster [John Rae] said yesterday." *The Times*, 30 September 1989, 4.

6. Masters, *Literary Agents*, vii. See Simon Shepherd, "Gay Sex Spy Orgy: The State's need for Queers", Simon Shepherd and Mick Wallis eds., *Coming on Strong*, Unwin Hyman, 1989, 213-230.

7. Masters, *Literary Agents*, 234-36, 239, 252. "One day in the mid-sixties, Sir Roger Hollis (Director General MI5) made a bizarre appearance in Cornwall's life . . . Answering a knock at the door, he found Hollis . . . (who) announced that he was collecting money for the nearby Cathedral School." *Ibid.*, 255.

8. Georges Minois, *Les Confesseur du Roi: Les Directeurs de conscience sous la Monarchie Francaise*, Fayard, Paris, 1988. Virginia Berridge and Griffith Edwards, *Opium and the People: Opiate Use in Nineteenth-Century England*. Yale University Press, 1987. Philip Abrams, "Notes on the Difficulty of Studying the State", *Journal of Historical Sociology*, Vol. 1, No. 1, March 1988, 63. *Cf.* Andrew Mution, "After the Acts", *Times Literary Supplement*, 16 November 1989, 1230.

9. See George Monger, "The Seamier Side of Childlore", *FLS Children's Folklore Newsletter*, No. 3, March 1989, 1-7. Consider, *e.g.*, Ruth Harris, "Melodrama, Hysteria and Feminine Crimes of Passion in the Fin-de-Siecle", *History Workshop*, No. 25, Spring 1988, 31-63. "Although no causal connection can be drawn between the commentary surrounding violent women on the one hand and the wide, but still minority, movement for the emancipation of women on the other, criminological discourse was inflected by the very real fears which 'feminisme' aroused, anxieties which perhaps explain the pervasive fascination with womanly violence." *Ibid.*, 58-59.

10. "The Social Exclusiveness of Sandhurst", Extract from the Report of the Select Committee on Sandhurst Royal Military College, Evidence, *Parliamentary Papers 1854-5*, Vol. XII, qtd. W. L. Guttsman ed., *The English Ruling Class*, Weidenfeld & Nicolson, 1969, 227. See T. A. Heathcote, *The Indian Army: The Garrison of British Imperial India, 1822-1922*, David & Charles, 1974, 135-36. Also Anthony Bruce, *The Purchase System in the British Army, 1660-1871*, Royal Historical Society, 1980, 144-58.

11. Philip Mason, *A Matter of Honour: An Account of the Indian Army, Its Officers and Men*, Jonathan Cape, 1974, 374. *Cf.* Allen, *Plain Tales*, 98.

12. The payment of school fees for their children continues to be a reason why men go overseas, and has certainly been an impetus for British expatriates to serve in the Arabian Gulf in recent years.

13. Allen, *Plain Tales*, 216.

14. For the involvement of British Political Residents of the Arabian Gulf in banking, see Geoffrey Jones, "Banking in the Gulf Before 1960", R. I. Lawless ed., *The Gulf in the Early 20th Century: Foreign Institutions and Local Responses*, Occasional Paper Series No. 31, Centre for Middle Eastern and Islamic Studies, University of Durham, 1986, 9-11.

15. See Wilkinson, *The Prefects*, x.

16. John Rae, *Letters From School*, Fontana/Collins, 1988, 119, 121.

17. *Ibid.*, 23.

18. *Ibid.*, 150.

19. *Literary Agents*, 37. *Cf.* Eric Presland, "Power and Consent", Warren Middleton ed., *The Betrayal of Youth*, CL Publications, n.d., 67-68. Also 'Y', *The Autobiography of an Englishman*, Paul Elek, 1975, 24-39. Norman Sherry's biography of Graham Greene has much to say about public schools and sex at Berkhamsted, where Greene's father was headmaster. Norman Sherry, *The Life of Graham Greene, Volume One: 1904-1939*, Jonathan Cape, 1989, 38, 43, 45, 88, 107.

20. Masters, *Literary Agents* 36-37.

21. Wilfrid Blunt, *Slow on the Feather: Further Autobiography, 1938-1959*, Michael Russell, 1986, 69-70, also 90-91, 112. See Morris, *Pax Britannica*, 119. Rebecca Irvine remarks that the public schoolboy has ". . . problems with 99.8% of the female race. As if that weren't enough they labour under the convenient delusion that it is the girls who are odd." *Girl's Guide*, 7. Another argument that can be made is that the imagery was heterosexual: **Britannia was the mistress**. Sheldrake has used this image in *The Guardian*

article quoted in the preface.

22. See Jeffrey Richards, "'Passing the Love of Women': Manly Love and Victorian Society", Mangan and Walvin eds., *Manliness and Morality*, 92-122, esp. 100-101. *Cf.* James Lee-Milne, *The Enigmatic Edwardians: The Life of Reginald, 2nd Viscount Esher*, Sidgwick & Jackson, 1986, 8-18, 21-22.

23. See Bernard Knox, "Subversive Activities", review of Louis Crompton's, *Byron and Greek Love: Homophobia in Nineteenth-Century England*," *New York Review of Books*, 19 December 1985, 3-7. *Cf.* Fernando Gonzales-Reigosa and Howard Kaminsky, "Greek Homosexuality, Greek Narcissism, Greek Culture: The Invention of Apollo", *The Psychohistory Review*, Vol. 17, No. 2. Winter 1989, 149-82.

24. In fairness, Freud was as concerned with the conflict between a variety of competing forces as he was with the centrality of sexual satisfaction. See Erich Fromm, *Beyond the Chains of Illusion: My Encounter with Marx and Freud*, Abacus, 1986 (1962), 37. Consider Ernest Gellner, "Incestuous Initiation", *Times Literary Supplement*, 24 January 1986, 79-80.

25. There are serious obstacles to archival research in this area because of government regulations. For example, personal records are not released by the British Army even when the individual is dead: the permission of descendants must be obtained.

26. Nico Davies to J. M. Barrie, 23 March 1919, qtd. Birkin, *J. M. Barrie*, 281. Another example is Richard Graves' troubled romance with Peter Johnstone at Charterhouse. When Johnstone was charged with propositioning a corporal in a regiment stationed near the school, Graves wrote, "It would be easy to think of him as dead." Richard Perceval Graves, *Robert Graves: The Assault Heroic, 1895-1926*, Macmillan, 1987, 177.

27. Brodhead, "Social Imperialism", 289 n. 27. Martin Fagg, "Scout's Honour", *Times Educational Supplement*, 20 October 1989, 30.

28. Ronald Hyam, "Empire and Sexual Opportunity", *Journal of Imperial and Commonwealth History*. Vol. XIV, No. 2, June 1986, 34-89. See Timothy d'Arch Smith, "The 'Wrenians'", Warren Middleton ed., *Betrayal of Youth*, C.L. Publications, 246-53. Also Neil Bartlett, *Who Was That Man?*, Serpent's Tail, 1988, *passim*.

29. Ruth Benedict, *Patterns of Culture*, Routledge & Keegan Paul, 1961, 200. *Cf.* David E. Stannard, *Shrinking History: On Freud and the Failure of Psychohistory*, OUP, 1980. John D'Emilio, "Not a Simple Matter: Gay History and Gay Historians", *The Journal of American History*, Vol. 76, No. 3, September 1989, 435-42.

30. T. J. Binyon, "Kipling and Sex: A Just-Not-So Story", *The Sunday Times* 19 February 1989.

31. Martin Seymour-Smith, letter, *Times Literary Supplement*, February 24 - 2 March 1989, 195. See the reply by the reviewer, David Trotter, TLS, 10-16 March 1989, 249. *Cf.* Craig Raine's review in *Punch* 10 February 1989, 249. The review is in *TLS*, 3-9 February 1989, 99-100. It is highly quotable: "His thesis is that Kipling was a closet homosexual . . . Homosexuality becomes the key to all mythologies." Needless to add that "many academics are far from happy about the evidence for this new interpretation . . .". *The Sunday Times* 5 February 1989, A3. See and consider E. W. Evans, *The British Yoke: Reflections on the Colonial Empire*, William Hodge, 1949, 168. Christopher S. Hill, "Causal Necessitation, Moral Responsibility, and Frankfurth-Nozick Counterexamples", *Behaviorism*, Fall 1988, Vol. 16, No. 2, 129-35.

32. Ian Gibson, *The English Vice: Beating, Sex and Shame in Victorian England and After*, Duckworth, 1978, 313. "By the first decade of the twentieth century it could no longer be doubted by open-minded people that there was a connection between flagellation applied to the buttocks and sexual excitement; that the deviation could take a passive ('masochistic') or active ('sadistic') form or be a combination of both ('sado-masochistic'); and that the children, especially boys, thus punished were liable to experience sexual problems and impotence later in life." *Ibid.*, 45. See A. L. Rowse, *Homosexuals in History: A Study of Ambivalence in Society, Literature and the Arts*, Weidenfeld and Nicolson, 1977. *Cf.* Ollard, *An English Education*, 27, 121-35. Also Sir Arthur Conan Doyle, *Memories and Adventures*, OUP, 1989 [1924], 16.

33. See Morris, *Pax Britannica*, 119. Also Sari J. Nasir, *The Arabs and the English*, 2nd ed., Longman, 1979, 32. Moreover, psychology and psychoanalysis are in flux. See *e.g.* Jack Danielian, "Karen Horner and Heinz Kohut: Theory and Repeat of History", *The American Journal of Psychoanalysis*, Vol. 48, No. 1, Spring 1988, 6-24.

34. The cover of *Orientalism*, Penguin, Harmondsworth, 1978. The original is in the Sterling and Francine Clark Art Institute, Williamstown, Massachusetts. The painting was the property of Elizabeth

Scriben Clark when it was exhibited at the Metropolitan Museum in New York between November 1897 and April 1898. It is discussed in Linda Nochlin, "On 'Orientalism' in 19th-Century Painting", *Art in America*, May 1983, 119-31, 187-89.

35. Francis Steepmuller, ed. and trans., *Flaubert in Egypt: A Sensibility on Tour*, Little Brown, Boston (Massachusetts), 1973, 198-99. Hunt and Harrison, *District Officer*, 149. *Cf.* Rana Kabbani, *Europe's Myths of Orient*, Macmillan, 1986, 5-6, 87. See Plate 6, John Faed, "Bedouin Exchanging a Slave for Armour", c.1857, and Plate 9, John Frederick Lewis, *"The Hareem"*, c.1850, *Ibid.*

36. Hyam, "Empire and Sexual Opportunity". Hunt and Harrison, *District Officer*, 137.

37. Katharine Tidrick, *Heart-beguiling Araby*, OUP, 1981, 2.

38. Leinster-Mackay, *The Educational World of Edward Thring*, 15.

39. John E. Mack, "T. E. Lawrence and the Uses of Psychology in the Biography of Historical Figures", L. Carl Brown, and Norman Itzkowitz eds., *Psychological Dimensions of Near Eastern Studies*, Darwin Press, Princeton (New Jersey), 1977, 51.

40. "Empire and Sexual Opportunity", 75.

41. Baigent, *Messianic Legacy*, 230-31. See S. H. Flitner and Renate Valtin, "'I Won't Tell Anyone': On the Development of the Concept of the Secret in Schoolchildren", *Education*, Vol. 35, 1987, 46-59.

42. See Jonathan Unger, "The Making and Breaking of the Chinese Secret Society", *Journal of Contemporary Asia*, Vol. 5, 1976, 89-98. See J. E. Goldthorpe, *An Introduction to Sociology*, 3rd ed., OUP, 1985, 194.

43. John Lawrence, *Freemasonry – A Religion?*, Kingsway, Eastbourne, 1987, 68. A notable exception to the lack of serious historical consideration of clandestine influences is H. V. F. Winstone's *The Illicit Adventure: The Story of Political and Military Intelligence in the Middle East from 1898 to 1926*, Jonathan Cape, 1982. On reading Winstone's *magnum opus* it is hard to avoid concluding that there was a troupe of old boy *bon viveurs* who roamed about on hush-hush missions – between spells of doing acrostics in the "padded armchairs of the United Service Club". Note Winstone's confusion over "services".

44. Jonathan R. Dull, "The Iran-Contra Scandal and the 'Secret du Roi'," *Society for Historians of American Foreign Relations Newsletter*, Vol. 19, No. 4, December 1988, 1-13. Not a dull article!

45. Qtd. with an interesting commentary in Eric Midwinter, *Schools in Society: The Evolution of English Education*, Batsford, 1980, 44. See on the *freemasonry* of the old boys reunions, John Bainbridge, "Days at Eton", *Gourmet*, February 1989, 126.

46. In *The Infernal Grove*, qtd. Masters, *Literary Agents*, 93.

47. Martin Short, "The Wives' Tales", *The Observer*, 18 March 1989, 37-38.

48. Roger Clarke, "Beware Falling Masonry", *Sunday Times Books*, 23 April 1989, 611. See "Freemasonry 'Flourishes in Met'", *The Guardian* 27 February 1989. *Principles of Policing*, a handbook given to Metropolitan Police, warns that "The discerning officer will probably consider it wise to forgo the prospect of pleasure and social advantage in freemasonry so as to enjoy the unreserved regard of all around him. One who is already a freemason would also be wise to ponder whether he should continue as a freemason."

49. Jocelyn Targett, "Brother can you spare a favour?", *The Weekend Guardian*, March 25-26 1989. Note the conversion by the Masons of disused churches into lodge halls. Described by N. B. Cryer, *Masonic Halls of England: The South*, Lewis Masonic, 1989, Shepperton, 9, 74.

50. Roslin has a number of curious architectural details which suggest Masonic connections.

51. Stevenson, *Origins of Freemasonry*, 156-57.

52. The respectability of historians considering clandestine organisations is enhanced by Adam Schaff, who dealt with Freemasonry as a factor in the French Revolution. He dismisses writers such as Barruel who saw the upheaval as a Masonic conspiracy, but agrees with Louis Blanc that the issue is genuine: "Thus, while one should not subscribe in the least to Barruel's primitive conception, one should not go to the other extreme which would lead to a negation of facts. If it is true, as Louis Blanc maintained, that the greatest figures of the Revolution were Freemasons, then one cannot simply dismiss the role of this organization in the origin and development of the Revolution. In any case, **this is an issue worthy of serious study . . .**". Schaff, *History & Truth*, 7-8.

53. Masters, *Literary Agents*, 37.

54. Apparently considerable influence was exerted through discussions of government policy at lodge

meetings. See *e.g.* Edward Farley Oaten, *My Memories of India*, Suba/Gangulied, Jenks Prakajham, Patna (India), 1884, 96.

55. Alan Rusbridger, "Matter for Paranoia", *Times Literary Supplement*, 21-27 April 1989, 421. "Masonic revenge killing has a long if hysterical history – victims are said to have included Mozart, and Roberto Calvi under Blackfriars Bridge in 1982. It doesn't take an overtly creative imagination to suspect that anyone who prints the 'facts' could be in for trouble." Targett, "Brother can you spare a favour?", *The Guardian*.

56. J. I. M. Stewart, *Myself and Michael Innes: A Memoir*, Victor Gollancz, 1987, 175. See J. H. Hexter, *The History Primer*, Allen Lane, 1971, 394.

57. Fawn M. Brodie, *No Man Knows My History: The Life of Joseph Smith, The Mormon Prophet*, 2nd ed. rev., Alfred A. Knopf, New York, 1986, 65. "There is good evidence that Joseph Smith was familiar with Masonic literature . . . Professor J. H. Adamson of the University of Utah has analyzed in detail Smith's use of the Masonic legends . . . Joseph Smith's adaptation of these myths will be obvious to any student of the *Book of Mormon* and the history of its writing." *Ibid.*, 66. "There is no doubt that Joseph's primary interest in Masonry lay in its ritual." *Ibid.*, 280. "After being expelled from the Garden of Eden, the actors representing Adam and Eve donned tiny white aprons which were exactly like the Masonic aprons except that they were painted with green fig leaves. Then followed instruction in certain grips, passwords, and 'keys'. Each man was given a secret name by which he was to be known in the kingdom of heaven. It may seem surprising that Joseph should have incorporated so much Masonry into the endowment ceremony in the very weeks when all his leading men were being inducted into the Masonic lodge. They would have been blind indeed not to see the parallelism between the costuming, grips, passwords, keys, and oaths. Joseph made free use of other Masonic symbols – the beehive, the all-seeing eye, the two clasped hands, and the point within the circle . . . Joseph taught his men simply that the Masonic ritual was a corruption of the ancient ritual of Solomon, and that his own was a restoration of the true Hebraic endowment." *Ibid.* 281-82. "The Masons, annoyed at rumors of corruption of the Masonic ritual in the Mormon lodges . . . were determined to revoke the dispensations and declare all the Mormon lodges clandestine." *Ibid.*, 367. When being assassinated, Smith gave the Masonic sign of distress. *Ibid.*, 393-94. Mormon rites continue to resemble the Masonic ones. *Ibid.*, 400. In 1990, however, there was a major revision of them.

58. Barnett, *Audit of War*, 12. Barnett seems fond of stud analogies: "Thus a century of cross-breeding between the aesthetic and moral strains in romanticism had made the 'enlightened' British Establishment of the 1940's . . .". *Ibid.* 17.

59. Norman H. Whatman, "Fifty-Four Years On", *The Timaruvian*, 1985, 7. I am grateful to Professor John Hattie for pointing out that New Zealand state schools are public school in *ethos*, an example of how a school's finances and catchment area do not always determine whether it is a public school. It will be interesting to see whether the current devolution of authority in New Zealand to local governors will affect this.

60. Norman Sherry, "The Tortured Schoolboy", *The Sunday Times*, 2 April 1989, C1-C2.

61. Jan Morris, *The Spectacle of Empire*, Faber and Faber, 1982, 199-200. "Whatever they were, though, whatever their pretensions, the clubs of Empire had this in common: that they made the Right People feel more important, and made the Wrong People feel small." *Ibid.*, 200.

62. Peat, *Synchronicity*, 41.

63. *Ibid.*, 45.

64. *Freemasonry produces an ultra sensitivity to ritualistic matters.* Whatever else the movement is – political plot or social fraternity of charitable society – it is a supreme teacher of the idea that "things are not what they seem", of **allegory** and **metaphor.** "Freemasony is a system of morality developed and inculcated by the science of symbolism. Veiled in allegory, lodge teachings are taught by the use of symbols." L. James Rongstad, *How to Respond to The Lodge*, Concordia, 1977, 11. Arthur Craddock, who is a distinguished English Freemason, suggested to this author than non public-school men joined Masonry to "make up" for what they lacked in their education, *i.e.* that Masonry offered instruction in "ritual poise" similar to that of the public schools. Arthur Craddock interview with P. J. Rich, London, 4 September 1989.

CHAPTER VI

Places

One of the best places to find out how the English think is a London club. – Idries Shah, *The Natives Are Restless*, 1988.

We were telling people they could become Christian, send their sons to Eton and Sandhurst, wear a topper at Ascot . . . but you couldn't actually join the club. – Gavin Lyall, *The Wrong Side of the Sky*, 1961.

So he lunches and dines and lunches, till the sands of the hourglass have run out, and the moment comes for him to enter that great club of which all humanity must perforce become members. – Ralph Nevill, *London Clubs*, 1919.

At the height of the clubs' influence, a fond father would put his son's name in the candidate book at the same time that he entered him for the old school. Consideration of causality's *modus operandi* can suggest, and prosopography can reveal, curious ramifications to club memberships. The Empire's administrators belonged to an extraordinary number. (See *Royal Bombay Yacht Club*, below and *United Service Club Lucknow*, page 145.) They were schools for learning the Imperial social order.

Royal Bombay Yacht Club.

Chutter Munzil, United Service Club, Lucknow, India.

How **reciprocal,** to use a term of which more will be said anon, were the relationships between the schools and the clubs? Public school old boys had a head start on club membership if they went up to university and joined a club such as Oxford's Vincent or Gridiron, or the Pitt at Cambridge – to which Salman Rushdie belonged along with several other Old Rugbeians. Later, headmasters and fellow old boys smoothed admission to the clubs of St. James's. A *meisterwerk* about the public schools will have to consider the clubs as an instance of how the schools' relevance to Imperialism was enhanced by the ways other institutions were infused with the schools' mores.

While the connections between schools and clubs illustrate the diffusion of English public school influence, they have been as little noted as has been the connection with that other surrogate for reality, the public school lodge: "For the institution which is well known to be central to the whole British establishment, the men's clubs are striking for their absence from any of the normal sources of information; books by independent observers, analyses of their influence and how they work."[1] Yet the association seemed obvious enough for authorities on social nuances such as Sir Charles Petrie to claim that the school influence was self-apparent in the elaborate club rituals, and to remark pointedly "The influence of the Public Schools was also to be noticed in the taboos which had been evolved . . .".[2]

Like the public schools, gentlemen's clubs had an importance for the English that they never had in other countries. Sir Arthur Bryant wrote: "Hitler, who never entered one of these ancient temples, had already – though he knew it not – met his doom in them . . . the enduring atmosphere of normality within was far more powerful than the temporary atmosphere without."[3] In fact, Parliament was defined as "an exclusive club with only 635 members" and described as resounding to "the boisterous banter of the boys' toilets at school."[4] The many comparisons of Westminster with clubs and

145

schools are not surprising – if the public school was so pivotal in determining mores, its reverberations should be detectable in other institutions. So they were.

There was a parallel expansion in membership of Masonic lodges, public schools, the gentlemen's clubs, and Empire. Clubs in London such as the Oriental, the East India, the Calcutta, the Madras, and the Bombay reflected in their very names the Imperial expansiveness. They helped to sustain its social structure. The Empire depended on rulers who "cleaved to others to constitute a fraternity who, belonging to the same club, wore the same mask, had the same manners, the same heavy volition."[5] In the last part of the nineteenth century, one hundred new clubs were founded in London alone. The membership of London clubs grew from only 1200 members at the start of the century to a startling 200,000 at the end.[6]

Pasque Rosee's Coffee House

The argument is **not** that clubs exclusively owed their characteristics to the schools. The antecedents of the clubs, like the antecedents of the schools and lodges, were

Haymarket Tennis Club.

146

Tattersall's.

diverse and pre-nineteenth century – in the case of the clubs the roots can be found in institutions such as coffee houses and the convivial Haymarket tennis and billiards establishments. (See *Haymarket Tennis Club*, page 146.) as well as turf organizations (See *Tattersall's*, above.) A little extravagantly and prematurely, David Stevenson claims that in the seventeenth century, "Organized religion had disappeared, organized voluntary social institutions, Royal Society and masonic lodge, in which the ideal of friendship could be practised, had taken its place."[7]

The remark would be more accurate if made about the nineteenth century, but admittedly there is a mythology about the early links between English clubs and the British overseas in the 'First Empire'. The common story is that the gentlemen's club was the idea of a seventeenth-century English merchant adventurer who became addicted to coffee in the Middle East, returning to England with a supply and with a Turkish friend, Pasque Rosee. In 1652, Pasque Rosee's Coffee House in St. Michael's Alley in the Cornhill opened. Before the century's end there were five hundred coffee houses in London. Three London clubs exist who trace their existence to that period: Brooke's, Boodle's and White's.[8] The coffee-house appears not only in club pedigrees and in Masonry's family tree, but in that of other voluntary societies: "It was the spread of coffee-houses in England from the 1650s, and the simultaneous tendency for at least some alehouses to be upgraded to provide better facilities and appeal to more respectable clients than in the past, which provided the most widespread opportunities for the emergence of publicly visible (as opposed to secret) new institutions."[9] There was a bluecoat school in Calcutta in the 1730s whose building also housed a Masonic lodge.[10] Overseas associations between schools, lodges, and clubs do go back to the eighteenth century.

Club life began to spread as soon as the British acquired the first or old Empire and can be dated at least to 1727, when Benjamin Franklin and his friends established the Junto in Philadelphia. While it was later that clubs became a widespread if informal ingredient of Imperial government, a rudimentary structure was in place at an early date. Men's clubs are not a recent phenomenon, and just as some schools bogusly claim King Alfred as a founder and the Freemasons fancy that King Solomon was one of their grand masters, the clubs claimed antecedents (as did some schools) in the *sodalitas* leaders of Rome: "For men, clubs are close to a racial inheritance."[11] However, regardless of these alleged earlier influences, it was in the Victorian era that clubs came to display the impact of the schools and began to reinforce the school 'spirit'. Eton's "Pop", remarks Macnaghten in *Sketches,* ". . . was something like a club, and something like a *very* select House of Commons!" Those who had enjoyed membership in school clubs such as Pop sought to perpetuate the warm glow. (Not surprisingly, Macnaghten was a long-time member of the Garrick.)

Learned Societies and Piacula

Little appreciated is how much the learned societies and lodges which flourished in the nineteenth century resembled clubs in atmosphere. (This is explored in an Imperial context in the next chapter.) There was in fact a Royal Societies Club for those who belonged to the increasing number of learned societies in London: "The cult of friendship provided some of the impetus behind the craze for the new voluntary social institutions . . . and helped give the craze justification by linking it with emerging philosophical beliefs: sociability in formal societies or informal groups could be seen as an important part of religious practice, *agape* in action, to a greater or lesser extent forming a substitute for public worship in congregations . . .".[12] The clubs and learned societies became as much a social necessity as going to a good school.

Entrance was a solemn affair, and the posting of the candidate's name and subsequent balloting with ivory balls was highly ritualistic. The supposed establishment of fraternity by such expiating piacula was similar to the balloting rites of the burgeoning Masonic movement: ". . . the social bond provided by membership of a masonic lodge provided a substitute bond to that of organized religion, with strong ethical overtones and ritual to replace, or more than replace, that present in protestant public religion."[13] Lodges, clubs, and learned societies had a great deal of ceremony in common. Prize day was not confined to schools. (See *Society of Arts Distributing its Premiums,* page 149.)

The Society of Arts distributing its premiums.

The Masons, clubmen and academicians enjoyed the pleasures of the banquet table, which on occasion assumed aspects of religious communion. Masons proceeded to invent table rituals in profusion and even had a ritual involving Maundy Thursday when they ate at a cruciform table. Learned societies and Masonic temples in England and overseas could be comfortable and clublike, with reading rooms and dining facilities. Membership in the clubs, the lodges and societies such as the Royal Colonial Institute

> . . . was evidence of the highest respectability. In 1892 some 10 percent of the resident fellows were members of such distinguished London clubs as the Carlton, Oriental, Athenaeum, United Service, and Conservative. Nearly a third of the governing board belonged to the peerage or to royalty, and maintained a residential club to provide a convenient meeting ground . . . And just before the outbreak of World War I it set up a masonic lodge for the purpose of enhancing ties of empire."[14]

Archetypal clubmen and typical old boys have much in common, and the Imperial élite achieve an amazing homogeneity by virtue of being uniformly **both** club members and old boys.[15] Headmasters went to considerable efforts to recommend boys for club membership when they left school,[16] which has been called the "conveyor-belt effect."[17] Yet the club, lodge, and society memberships have been as much or more overlooked in prosopographical studies as have been school affiliations.[18] This is all the more an omission because of the portentous implications of belonging. In Victorian and Edwardian society, BELONGING became itself an ideology. The club, with the public school, was integral in a self-conscious insistence upon the value of membership as an end in itself. However, there were practical consequences as well to club membership. In the case of residential clubs, membership made it possible for a man to be 'in society' without having his own establishment, and thus (in at least a small way) may have encouraged late marriage.[19]

The parallels between school and club life are many. Just as some public schools took over the mansions of the aristocracy, so did clubs. This was symbolic of how these institutions helped in the marriage of the aristocracy and middle class. On occasion, the club provided an opportunity to acquire the social standing lost through non-attendance at a public school. Allegedly in search of the status he lacked by not having attended a proper public school the Arabian explorer, Wilfrid Blunt, founded the Crabbett Club, whose success can be gauged by the fact that the members included both Lord Curzon and Oscar Wilde.

The clubs offered a sounding-board for opinion and a rich source of information. Those who frequented them knew the 'inside story' of what was going on.[20] Membership carried manifold intellectual and political connotations. Darwin prevaricated about proposing Huxley for the Athenaeum because of his iconoclasm. The Royal Geographical was Lord Lugard's chosen battleground for his attack on government by chartered companies.[21] The clubs were far more than places to read the newspaper and like the schools they espoused elaborate rituals which were transported to the outposts of the Empire.

Respositories of Ritual

Clubs *deliberately* became rehearsal halls of ritual. The founders of the Ootacamund Club in India's Nilgiri Hills prided themselves in following a code incorporating "ritual and seemliness."[22] And rituals in a way *were* the Empire.[23] The clubs were the guild for the old boy practitioners of Imperial ritualism, and helped guarantee that similar rituals would be observed in Alberta and Ceylon.[24]

Equally significant to what is argued here about relative influence is that clubs normally cannot be considered as important in a man's life as school. The bulk of the evidence indicates that they reinforced the affections of schooldays. The Crabbett was described as having a fifth-form atmosphere: at an 1891 club function attended by Curzon and Wilde there was 'skinny-dipping'. Wilde wrote, "There is a great deal of the schoolboy in all Englishmen, that is what makes them so lovable. When they came out they . . . began playing lawn tennis, just as they were, stark naked, the future rulers of England."[25] Elements of the fifth-form can be found in most Victorian clubs. (George Fraser on the other hand likens club life to an American Indian sweatbath initiation: "I felt almost as though I'd been elected to the Apache Club – which in other respects proved to be about as civilised as White's, with fewer bores than the Reform, and a kitchen slightly better than the Athenaeum's."[26])

In recognition of their association with the schools, clubs were the preferred venue for old boy functions. After a meeting at the Mussoorie Club in India, an Old Haileyburian wrote: "When five O.H.s meet anywhere there is obviously only one thing to be done, celebrate the occasion with an O.H. Dinner."[27] Being 'clubbable' became synonymous with being an old boy.[28] It is not coincidental that Thomas Hughes, the author of *Tom Brown's Schooldays,* was a Savile Club founding member in 1868 along with G. C. Bell, the long-time headmaster of Marlborough.[29] The club, with its conventions about who could sit in which chair and which clubs were of equal status, pleasantly reminded old boys of school. In the dining-room of one, the senior members sat at what was appropriately called The Prefects' Table.[30] Club members included the public school hierarchy: the governors, headmasters, prominent assistant masters, and important old boys. The general meeting of the Travellers' Club had to be postponed in 1877 to avoid clashing with the Eton and Harrow cricket match.

It was in the clubs that the educational establishment balanced accounts with other sectors of the establishment. The philosopher the late A. J. Ayer relates how, when his efforts to get a Jewish boy into Eton were frustrated, he carefully decided on the Travellers' Club as the proper place to confront the Provost, Sir Claude Elliott. There Sir Claude told him that Jews were "not clever in the right way . . . for instance, you couldn't expect them to play the Wall Game." Ayer took the matter to Macmillan, then Prime Minister, and the rule debarring foreign boys from sitting the Eton scholarship examination was reversed. The boy got his scholarship.[31]

Ayer's choice of The Travellers' is instructive. The setting suggested shared values and the need for gentlemen to sort out problems without a fuss. No doubt others used their clubs in a similar fashion. Frank Ernest Hill in *Man-Made Culture: The Educational Activities of Men's Clubs* asserted that not enough attention had been given to the discussion of educational issues that went on in clubs, particularly since the major clubs had prominent educators as members.[32] Lord Edward Cecil mentioned the considerable values of fraternisation in his club in Cairo, where "the schoolmaster of the Public Instruction exchanges remarks with the Scots Guards ensign."[33] Clubs were not the emporia of ideology that the schools were, but this does not detract from their significance. One can endorse the historian of White's: "The importance of White's is not to be measured merely by its importance *qua* club; it is part of the social history of England."[34] As meeting places, clubs were a 'behind the scenes' factor in deciding preferment for headmasterships and other educational patronage.[35] School registers, for the convenience of users, listed club addresses and details.[36]

The clubs reinforced the *real politik* of Imperialism, yet from all accounts they were a place where adults carried on as adolescents.[37] This is not a contradiction in terms. It confirms the thesis about the school atmosphere of the Empire. The resemblance between the clubs and the schools was not surprising, since clubs employed totems and taboos reminiscent of schools. Club customs were as contrived and Imperial as 'those of the public schools'.[38] The imposing edifices provided a proper setting for pageantry. Typical was a lavish banquet hosted by the Constitutional Club in 1909 honouring "The proprietors and editors of newspapers in the Britains beyond the Seas." A toast was to "The Pro-Consuls" and the responder was Lord Curzon.[39] Imperial celebrations in London were the occasion for decorating the clubs and conferring honorary membership on visitors.[40] The other side of this ceremonial coin was that in many colonies the governor was the titular head of one or more clubs. Every governor of Trinidad and Tobago from 1886 to 1960 was President of the Trinidad Union Club.[41] Thus the dignitary who presided over the Imperial rituals presided as well over those of his club.

He might preside as well over Masonic rituals at his club. Club ritualism was enhanced by special connections with Freemasonry. The association between the clubs and the Craft was a long one. One of the Garrick's treasures was its actor-founder's Masonic gavel, used by the Prince of Wales (himself a prominent Freemason) at the club's 1931 centenary dinner. A treatise could be written about the Imperial interest in gavels made from symbolic trees, beams of ships, the joists of houses, and the tusks of favourite or fearsome animals. (See *Masonic Gavels,* below, from William Sanderson's *Two Hundred Years of Freemasonry.*)

Lodges, including the public school ones, held their ceremonies in rooms purpose-built into the clubs for Masonic rituals. At White's, Masonic ritual classes were conducted in the basement. The Devonshire's handsome lodge room hosted over a hundred meetings yearly, including those of the prestigious *Arlington* lodge, which was limited solely to Devonshire members. Initiations were held upstairs over the Tavern building at the MCC. The National Liberal had an elaborate suite for Masonic meetings. Several of the school lodges met at the Royal Automobile Club. The

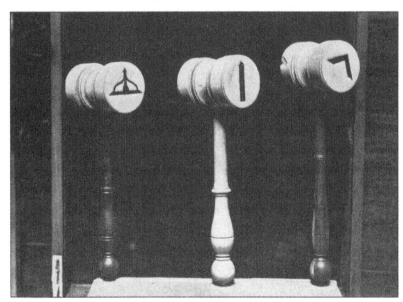

Masonic Gavels.

Savage and Eccentric had their own lodges for members, and the selective *Argonauts* and *Hatchlands* lodges met at the City of London Club. A number of lodges met at the Hurlingham.[42] A visitor to London clubs in the 1990s will still find locked closets holding lodge paraphernalia for the evening's business.

Club Distinctions

Professor John Honey's social ratings of schools pale before those of clubs. Club membership, like Masonic membership, became part of the honours system. When the editor of the *Daily Express*, R. D. Blumenfeld, was offered a knighthood, he asked for and got membership in the Carlton instead. Election to the Athenaeum was regarded as "the next best thing to a Fellowship of All Souls", and rather more convenient, as being nearer the hub of things.[43] The Athenaeum was a Holy of Holies, membership in which conferred the distinction of an order. George Fraser in *Flashman and the Dragon* describes the Emperor of China as ". . . remote as a god, sublime not in omniscience but in ignorance, lost to the world. He might as well be in the Athenaeum."[44] (See *Hall of the Athenaeum*, below.) The status conferred by individual clubs was as precisely defined as the status of Imperial decorations.[45] The perceived differences between clubs contributed to the founding by Victorians in search of well upholstered Elysiums of still more clubs. The existing ones always

The Hall of the Athenaeum

seemed to fall short of Utopia. The Carlton was reputed to be like a Duke's house "with the Duke dead upstairs", while the conversation at White's was considered so deadly that men were supposed to fall asleep both while listening and talking.[46]

Despite the fact that they faced each other, nobody ever confused the constituencies of the Athenaeum and United Service. The clubs' social standing was not determined by their buildings. A club without a building that was of considerable behind-the-scenes significance was the dining club of Indian Political Service members that met in London, the Political Dinner Club. It enabled those home on leave to catch up on what was going on in the India Office. Some clubs gypsied from one member's estate to another. The Crabbett used Wilfrid Blunt's country place and was an offshoot of another wanderer, the Wagger, which had met at Wilton, Lord Pembroke's estate in Wiltshire.[47] **The club weekend circuit at country houses is an unstudied combination of two of the bastions from which the establishment exercised the reins of power.**

There were and are small clubs without buildings that tied together the public school leadership, meeting usually in a London club. An example was the "UU" (suspected to stand for "United Ushers", and dating from the 1870s) that met for dinner and the reading of a paper by one of the members: ". . . it included some of the most influential figures in the public school world and by this token was an important recruiting ground for future heads."[48] Older than the 'UU' was the 'Nobody's Friends', which included headmasters. It still exists, meeting at the Archbishop of Canterbury's Lambeth Palace. A majority of public school headmasters belonged to one or another of the prestigious but buildingless clubs that ". . . in a characteristically English way created an inner, charmed circle and made those who [sic.] we excluded suspect that it was here that the effective decisions were taken."[49]

First Eleven

Regardless of edifices or lack thereof, each club found a place and purpose in the social hierarchy.[50] An authority tellingly used schoolboy jargon to describe this: "The United Service and the Athenaeum were by any calculation in the first eleven . . .".[51] A man's memberships told something about him just as his school did, especially if he belonged to several, and his presence could indicate his moods as accurately as a thermometer would his health. Curzon would start the day in the Athenaeum or Constitutional library, lunch at White's, drop by the Beefsteak for some comradery, and have his nightcap at the Bachelors'.[52]

To belong to several took a healthy purse. J. B. Atkins recalled his "sad retrenchment" when for a lack of money he had to leave the Savile and the Royal Cruising, keeping up only the Travellers' and the Royal Yacht Squadron.[53] Curzon did have the means and could choose from his clubs to match his disposition. The Bachelors', which he frequented when in high spirits, was one (the Bath was the other) that Wodehouse based his Drones' Club on: "The Bachelors' lacked the serious political overtones of the Carlton and the Reform, and even the theatrical raffishness of the Garrick, yet was not as unpredictable as the Travellers', a favourite haunt of Victorian explorers."[54] Appropriately because of his keen interest in clubs, after Curzon's death his house at Carlton House Terrace became the most Wodehousean of all clubs, the Savage.[55]

Houses of the Same School

Associations with schools and colleges contributed to the development of club rituals: at the United University, members were served their food on either dark or light blue plates according to whether they went to Oxford or Cambridge. The Oxford and Cambridge, while it did not have different coloured plates, had its annual membership list alternatively bound in Cambridge and Oxford blue.[56] The University and the Oxford and Cambridge merging caused a member to explain, "Actually, it is rather like two houses of the same public school."[57] In fact, the Army and Navy for years was run by Lady Helen Barlow, who was a house Dame at Eton College before becoming the Club's secretary.[58] Thus old boys of her Eton house enjoyed her continuing ministrations in their mature years, and (according to at least one member) the same dismal food. When the new assistant club secretary introduces herself in Richard Gordon's novel *A Gentlemen's Club,* a member remarks, **"Haven't been matron of a boys' school, I suppose . . . That would help enormously."**[59]

The club with some of the strongest school connections was – as might be expected – the Public Schools. Its merger with the East India, a club specifically founded for the Indian services, appropriately links the Indian services and the schools. Eighteen public school headmasters attended its inaugural meeting and many during its history served as honorary vice-presidents. At its inception, the Public Schools was limited to old boys of Bedford, Beaumont, Charterhouse, Cheltenham, Clifton, Eton, Fettes, Glenalmond, Haileybury, Harrow, Loretto, Malvern, Marlborough, Radley, Repton, Rossall, Rugby, Sherborne, Shrewsbury, Tonbridge, Uppingham, Wellington, Westminster, and Winchester. This caused controversy amongst old boys of other schools such as St. Paul's and Dulwich, and eventually the list was greatly increased.[60]

With eighty per cent of its members on active service and over eight hundred of them killed in World War I, the Public Schools went into voluntary liquidation and reopened in 1920. It soon regained popularity. There were public school clubs elsewhere in the Empire. The London club was affiliated with clubs in Australia, New Zealand, Rhodesia, and South Africa, and became the favourite location for dinners of old boys of colonial schools. Its most distinctive decoration was a collection of shields displaying the arms of its members' schools.

The United Services and The United Service

Some clubs had stronger associations than others with the Imperial services. Foremost was the East India, with its lobby adorned with elephants' tusks.[61] Apocryphally it started as a hostel for East India Company officers on leave, and it adopted the East

India Company badge for its own. Many directors of the company were involved in its affairs over the years. The formal name was the East India United *Services* Club, referring to the covenanted services of India. This has led to confusion with the United *Service* Club, and since the two clubs at one point nearly amalgamated, the confusion could have been even more.

Almost renamed the Clive or the Imperial Services Club, eventually the East India by merger became "The East India, Devonshire, Sports and Public Schools Club", which Lejeune called "a name like an archaeological inspection pit, revealing successive layers of Clubland ruins."[62] The East India was not for *all* India hands. The Club worried about the status of applicants in the Public Works, Telegraph, and Education service. The concern over status illustrates the clubs' place in the Imperial power structure. For example, despite its aspirations, the East India did not compete successfully with the United Service. Its members were what would be called middle-management, while Indian Army officers of high rank joined the United Service.

By the 1880s the United Service no longer boasted such an exalted standing, and in 1893 it was reduced to taking members who were only Army captains or Navy lieutenants. Before that it was said that nothing had disturbed its quiet except the "eccentricities of senility".[63] In the early twentieth century the United Service declined further in prestige, but the East India had not risen far on the totem pole. Arnold Wilson, the celebrated Arabian Gulf Resident quoted several times in these pages, welcomed his election to the Athenaeum in 1929, ". . . where he was able to come into contact with a rather wider spectrum of the world of learning and affairs than had been possible at the East India and United Services *[sic.]* Clubs."[64] The suggestion was that he found the East India "slightly philistine".[65]

Evidently there are as many difficulties to be encountered in determining the social status of individual clubs as in speculating about the status of individual schools. The history of the United Service shows this. It was nicknamed the "Senior" but was not known as an intellectual beehive. The club's historian defended this by referring to the public schools: "The fact is that the average English schoolboy is not intellectual, but very practical. He does not care to follow the meanderings of *hic haec* and *hoc* because they do not seem to lead anywhere that he wants to go . . . But put him out in the world to command and control men and get a job done, the more dangerous the better, he will be interested and will tackle it thoroughly and solidly, bringing to it perseverance and practical common sense."[66]

While the United Service was prestigious enough to recruit exclusively from the senior ranks, it was expected that on reaching field rank an officer would become a candidate, and if elected that he would resign from his other club if he could not afford both.[67] One reason the club declined was because men became fond of their original club and simply did not apply. The 'Senior' gradually became just a good club,[68] and experienced clubmen felt that its members ". . . had an exaggerated idea of their own importance and of the value of exclusiveness to the reputation of the Club."[69] This contributed to the painfulness when it was necessary as a financial necessity to increase the Senior's membership.[70] A new member in 1893 wrote:

The first thing that struck me was the attitude of the Club staff. They evidently thought that the dignity of the Club had been lowered by our admission, and looked on us very coldly. The hall porter, my friend of later years, Bailey, could scarcely bring himself to give me my letters or answer a question. A young captain, when he first came to the Club, went upstairs and was immediately pursued by a boy who said that the hall porter wished to speak to him. That dignitary said, "I don't think you are a member of this club, sir." "Oh, yes I am," said he and gave his name. Bailey apologised, explaining "We have never seen a member run upstairs before, sir."[71]

By 1900-1909 the United Service did not have a waiting list. It had become popular with officers who as subalterns had not joined a London club and as they advanced in seniority felt the need of one. Three Indian Army Officers were prominent: Lt.-Col. C. F. Massy, who became chairman of the club committee; Col. P. W. Bannerman, chairman of the finance committee; and Col. C. H. T. Marshall, an active committee member.[72] This author's initial research indicates that the Indian Political Service representation is largely post-1900 at a time when the membership was expanding from 1600 to 2000 and bedrooms and enlarged common rooms were constructed. (Not **all** the evidence points to a decline in prestige in this period – the club's private dining-room became a favourite place for Cabinet dinner parties.[73])

The disappearance of the Empire was accompanied by a rash of closings and consolidations in clubland. Some, like Arthur's, had already disappeared, others now succumbed. (See *Arthur's and Brooks,* page 158.) In 1974, after a long struggle, the Senior merged with the Naval and Military Club (the "In and Out"). Appropriately, the Seniors' club house at 116 Pall Mall is now occupied by the Institute of Directors, which has taken considerable care in preserving the building. The earliest part, constructed between 1826 and 1828 to the plans of John Nash, has been restored. The massive chandelier in the Main Hall, given by George IV to commemorate the Battle of Waterloo, is in place. Numerous portraits from United Service days can be viewed. The original furniture remains.

The fortunes of the Senior are well documented, as are those of other London clubs. Overseas clubs are not so easy to research, but will be discussed in the next chapter. Officers had numerous postings during their careers and joined a club at their new post and resigned from the one at the previous post.[74] Thus the overseas clubs were *caravanserary.* **Causally and prosopographically speaking, the most significant clubs are those that the Imperial leadership joined in England, as the expressed preference for one over another represents more of an ideological statement than joining a club overseas.** But for all the fun to be had from cataloguing the distinction between clubs, they remain minor compared with the yawning gulf between club men and the great unwashed.

Arthur's Club (top) and Brooks.

Implications of Power

The United Service or the East India were not the only clubs whose membership supposedly conveyed implications about status and power. The Carlton was "the Tory party's canteen",[75] and in their time, Arthur's and Brook's were equally political. One curious indication of the clubs' political rôle was that letters on club stationery had a totemistic authority lacking in letters on ordinary paper.[76] Another aspect was how honorary memberships, conferred on the diplomatic corps, added to the clubs' influence.[77] So did the appointment of platoons of patrons, vice-patrons, honorary presidents and vice-presidents. A club's expanding influence was not always welcomed. When the United Service began, the Earl of St. Vincent warned that it ". . . wears an unconstitutional aspect, and cannot fail to attract the attention of Parliament."[78] Lord St. Vincent anticipated in his suspicions those generations of English novelists who found the club the perfect setting for foul play (à la Christie's *The Mysterious Affair at Styles*) and chicanery, "where men of the world discuss the world's secrets in 'the *argot* of the Upper Fourth Remove'."[79]

Changes in a club's stature provide a bell-wether of other changes.[80] The history of the United Service in admitting junior Indian Army officers (long after its refusal in the nineteenth century to accept East India Company army officers[81]) indicates the improved social stature of the Indian services after the Mutiny. Another example of a club's history as a social barometer is that of the Oriental, which was allegedly started because of the United Service diffidence towards Indian officers.[82] It therefore could be supposed to have been socially inferior to the United Service. The founding of the East India allegedly represented a response to the frostiness of the United Service and the commonness of the Oriental, which had opened its doors to those in 'trade'.

Unhappily, a problem with prosopographically evaluating what individual club membership meant, as with evaluating the significance of attending individual public schools, is that clubs like schools had their ups and downs. When the East India started it did not succeed in attracting the high-ranking officers who were in the Oriental, and it is questionable whether the East India ever became more prestigious than the Oriental. The muddle over status illustrates the difficulties with interpreting prosopographical data involving clubs.

What **is** evident is that many military officers belonged to the East India and United Service but did **not** belong, in appreciable numbers, to the Oriental. Authorities can be quoted both to the popularity of the Oriental's curry and to the canard that it was a hospital with a smell of curry powder and members who resembled guinea-pigs.[83] After World War I the Oriental had more luck than previously in recruiting high-ranking Indian services' members. Of necessity, the club changed course again with Indian independence, realizing that: "It would not be very long before there would be no more 'K.C.S.I.s' and 'C.I.E.s' to green the Club's committee list."[84] The characterizing of the United Service as a club for top officers, the Oriental as commercial, and the East India as middle management, will remain tentative until analysis explains the anomalies.

Neither the United Service nor the East India were ever the government annexes

159

that the Guards or Cavalry were,[85] but they and similar clubs were informally part of the government structure. An example of how symbolic imagination and the gathering together of powerful figures were combined was the short-lived Ark Club, organized by Edith, Marchioness of Londonderry, and meeting sometimes at Mount Stewart in County Down and sometimes at Londonderry House overlooking Hyde Park:

> Each member of the Ark Club was given the name of a bird, a beast or a magical character which in many cases was a rhyme on their name or began with the same letter as their Christian or surname. Presiding over the club was Lady Londonderry herself, Circe the Sorceress, and among the original members were her husband, Charley the Cheetah . . . Winston Churchill as a warlock, Neville Chamberlain as a devil, and Edward Carson as an eagle . . . Nancy the Gnat and Billy the Goat – Nancy and Waldorf Astor – Mairi the Midge, Lady Londonderry's daughter, Lady Mairi Bury . . . Lord Hailsham as Quintin the Hog.[86]

The blending of an adolescent ritualism with the hierarcicalism of power was evident as well in clubs overseas where, since there were no political parties to provide a forum and there were less of the comforting daily rituals that sustained Victorian and Edwardian life in Britain, the clubs took up the slack.[87] Aspects of them were as strange as those of the Ark, but as will be seen a good deal of sober policy-making and schooling in Imperial etiquette, went on within their walls.[88] It's easy to turn around the comment that "public schools are for children and teenagers what gentlemen's clubs are for adults", and remark that clubs are the public schools of adults.[89] They were so for the Raj, as will be seen.

NOTES – CHAPTER VI

1. Rogers, *Men Only*, 167. See Charles Petrie, *Scenes of Edwardian Life*, Severn House, 1975 (1965), 39. Arthur Ponsonby, *The Decline of Aristocracy*. T. Fisher Unwin, 1912, 77-78. Ponsonby identified 109 "Principal Clubs" in London in 1912: 44 with a subscription of £10 and over and twenty-five with an entrance subscription of £30 and over. He maintained that clubs demonstrated the English superiority over the Continent: "With us the café has never succeeded." *Ibid*. The tradition of a gentleman belonging to several, with each membership revealed something about his personality, continued into the post World War II era. R. A. Butler belonged to the Carlton, Farmers', Beefsteak, and Grillon's. Sir Arthur Bryant belonged to the Athenaeum, Beefsteak, Grillon's, Pratt's, Royal Automobile, Saintsbury, and MCC.

2. Petrie, *Edwardian Life*, 45. See 43-44. Also Philip G. Cambray, *Club Days and Ways: The Story of The Constitutional Club, London: 1883-1962*, Constitutional Club, 1963, 5-6. Malcolm I. Thomas, *The Brisbane Club*, Jacaranda Press, Milton (Queensland), 1980, 2, 18. Warren Perry, *The Naval and Military Club, Melbourne: A History of its First Hundred Years, 1881- 1981*. Lothian, Melbourne, 1981, xxxi. Clubs were very influential politically. Percy Colson, *White's: 1693-1950*, William Heinemann, 1951, 57. The identification of some West End clubs with the Conservative Party went so far as the Chief Whip taking an interest in their fortunes. In 1877, the Whip, Sir William Hart Dyke, arranged for applicants on the overlong waiting list of the Carlton Club to join the St. Stephen's. Charles Petrie, *The Carlton Club*. Eyre & Spottiswoode, 1955, 115. Most London clubs with political sympathies eventually became apolitical. After the Carlton opened in 1832, White's "reverted to its old and agreeable neutrality, welcoming new members

for their clubbable qualities not their opinions." Coulson, *White's*, 66. Nevertheless: "When government largely consists of a closely knit fraternity who have shared each other's thoughts and habits since boyhood, minor political problems can be solved in the lobby of the Commons or the smoking-room of a club . . .". Kenneth Rose, *Curzon: A Most Superior Person*, Macmillan, 1985, 350.

3. Qtd. Street, *Arthur Bryant*, 196. The atmosphere of the masters' common room at a public school aimed at resembling that of a club, and some were built with that in mind. At Charterhouse the masters had their own building with its distinctly club atmosphere. Hearnden, *Red Robert*, 81.

4. Andersen, *The Power and the Word*, 266. For the invasion by women of traditional men's clubs, see Kate Saunders, "Running Circles Round Men", *The Sunday Times*, 25 February, 1990, GI.

5. Grainger, *Patriotisms*, 137.

6. Ralph Nevill, *London Clubs: Their History & Treasures*, Chatto & Windus, 1919, 156-57. *N.B.* the growth at the same time of working men's clubs to sustain working class culture. Werner Glinga, *Legacy of Empire*, Manchester University Press, 1988, 111-115.

7. David Stevenson, *The Origins of Freemasonry: Scotland's Century, 1590-1710*, CUP, 1988, 185. See Bernard Williams' discussion of the "communitarian" stance in "The Need to be Sceptical", *Times Literary Supplement*, 22 February 1990, 163.

8. Colson, *White's*, 14-15. Robert J. Allen, *The Clubs of Augustan London*, Harvard University Press, Cambridge (Massachusetts), 1933, 13-14.

9. Stevenson, *Origins of Freemasonry*, 187.

10. Walter K. Firminger, *The Second Lodge of Bengal in the Old Times, Being a History of the Early Days of Lodge Industry and Perseverance No. 109 of England*, Thacker, Spink, Calcutta, 1911, 9-10.

11. Frank Ernest Hill, *Man-Made Culture: The Educational Activities of Men's Clubs*, American Association for Adult Education, New York, 1938, 8. Hill thought that the interest in education that characterized the nineteenth-century clubs could be revived as an answer to sagging contemporary enthusiasm. *Ibid.*, 147. A more controversial solution has been to admit women. *The Economist*, 9 May 1987, 38.

12. Stevenson, *Origins of Freemasonry*, 186.

13. *Ibid.*

14. L. H. Gann, and Peter Duignan, *The Rulers of British Africa, 1870-1914*, Croom Helm, 1978, 26-27.

15. See Sirdar Ikbal Ali Shah, *The Golden East*, John Long, 1931, 268.

16. Grainger, *Patriotisms*, 168, 176.

17. *Ibid.*, 169.

18. Petrie, *Edwardian Life*, 39.

19. Leonore Davidoff, *The Best Circles: Social Etiquette and the Season*, Cresset, 1986 (1973), 24.

20. This remains true, even in countries where the formal ties with Britain have been cut. For example, in the Arab shaikhdom of Qatar, the entire cabinet, diplomatic corps, and business leadership frequent the Doha Club.

21. Gann and Duignan, *Rulers of British Africa*, 27.

22. Trevor Fishlock, *India File*, John Murray, 1983, 176.

23. Morris, *Spectacle of Empire*, 199.

24. Patrick A. Dunae, *Gentlemen Emigrants: From the British Public Schools to the Canadian Frontier*, Douglas & McIntyre, 1981, 227. See 232-33.

25. Elizabeth Longford, *A Pilgrimage of Passion: The Life of Wilfrid Scawen Blunt*, Alfred Knopf, New York, 1980, 292.

26. George McDonald Fraser, *Flashman and the Redskins*, Fontana/Collins, 1985, 163.

27. Qtd. L. S. Milford, *Haileybury College: Past and Present*, T. Fisher Unwin, 1909, 311. See the account of Old Paulians in India in Hubert Arthur Sams, *Pauline and Old Pauline, 1888-1931*, priv. ptd. (CUP), 1933, 77-97.

28. Tim Heald, *Networks: Who We Know and How We Use Them*, Hodder and Stoughton, 1985, 29. *Cf.* Edward C. Mack, *Public Schools and British Opinion Since 1860*, Columbia University Press, 1941, 401. An interesting variation on this theme was the "approved" hotels of the public school Alpine Sports Club. Presumably the clientéle were 'clubbable'. See *e.g. Public Schools Alpine Sports Club Year Book 1930*.

29. This was in 1868. A. D. Hall, *The Savile Club, 1868 to 1923*, Committee of the Club, 1923, 8, 10-11,

17. Other Savileans included Kipling, Leslie Stephens, and E. M. Forster.

30. Charles Graves, *Leather Armchairs*, Cassell, 1963, 49.

31. A. J. Ayer, *More of My Life*, OUP, 1985, 196, 97. John Thorn recollects being interviewed for the headmastership of Repton at the United Universities. *Road to Winchester*, 71. And he describes headmasters' meetings with Labour Party leaders over educational policy. *Ibid.*, 93.

33. Lord David Cecil, *The Leisure of an Egyptian Official*, Century Publishing, 1984 (1921), 89, see 116.

34. Colson, *White's* 135.

35. See Robert Heussler, *Yesterday's Rulers: The Making of the British Colonial Service*, Syracuse University Press, 1982, 71.

36. See *Wellington College Register, January 1859-December 1948*, 7th ed., Butler and Tanner, 1948, xcv. *The Rugby School Register for August 1842 to January 1874* (rev. and ed. by A. T. Mitchell, A. J. Lawrence pub., Rugby, 1902) shows the clubs of those boys who entered in September 1869 with James Crawford, the Acting Gulf Resident in 1893: Crawford belonged to the East India. Three of his compatriots belonged to the Junior Carlton and three to the Naval and Military. One each belonged to the Oxford and Cambridge, Oriental, Army and Navy, Junior Conservative, Wellington, and Junior Constitutional.

37. See J. B. Atkins, *Incidents and Reflections*, Christophers, 1947, 240. For an account of Clubland's conservatism from a staff viewpoint: Anthony O'Connor, *Clubland: the Wrong Side of the Right People*, Brian & O'Keefe, 1976.

38. The Partabgarh Luncheon Club, the idea of the Maharajah of that ilk, had a tie resembling the MCC's. The Political Agent in Mewar sported it at matches. Trench, *Viceroy's Agent*, 334. "Some years ago the late Mr. Norman Forbes walked into the Garrick wearing round his neck a striking confection of pink and grey. 'What's that tie?' asked a fellow member, applying to it an uncomplimentary epithet. 'It is the Garrick Club tie', he replied on the spur of the moment and it was thereupon mini-officially adopted." Bernard Darwin, *British Clubs*, William Collins, 1943, 47.

39. Cambray, *Club Days and Ways*, 42. See Petrie, *The Carlton Club*, 190-91. "The Club's frontage twinkled with multicoloured lights to welcome HRH The Prince of Wales . . .". *The Madras Gymkhana Club, From Polo to Rubiks Cube: 100 Years 1884-1983*, 11. The snobbery of Imperial ritualism had its club counterpart: ". . . taboos which continued to exist until the twenties of the the present century. The new member was, for example, warned that he would be well-advised not to sit in the window of the smoking-room until he had been elected for at least two years, and he must eschew the tables near the fire in the coffee-room until he was a Privy Councillor or at least an Under-Secretary. On the other hand, to sit at one of the tables along the wall was a confession of failure. They were called Brook Street, 'because no one knew the people who lived there'." Petrie, *The Carlton Club*, 190. "I had been to the Savage as a guest two or three times, but when I first entered the old Club in the Adelphi to do my 'month's probation'. I felt very like a new boy at a public school . . .". Percy V. Bradshaw, *'Brother Savages and Guests': A History of the Savage Club, 1857-1957*, W. H. Allen, 1958, 81.

40. Petrie, *The Carlton Club*, 127-30. The Carlton's dinner for Colonial Premiers in 1900 was so large (1600 guests) that it took place in the Albert Hall, where 4500 pounds of beef, 2500 quails, 1400 bottles of champagne, 1500 bottles of hock, 300 bottles of brandy, 300 of Chartreuse, 500 of Crême de Menthe, and 200 bottles of whisky were consumed. *Ibid.*, 157. See Cambray, *Club Days and Ways*, 66. Such ceremonial required impressive dining and catering facilities. "The megalomania accompanying the expanding Empire made the official architecture in the cities more and more pompous. The premises of the Royal Automobile Club could be taken for a state residence, for instance." Glinga, *Legacy of Empire*, 7.

41. *Trinidad Union Club Rule Book*, Trinidad, 1984, 2.

42. See Graves, *Leather Armchairs*, 55, 3, 18, 115. Also Denys M. Forrest, *Foursome in St. James: The Story of the East India, Devonshire, Sports and Public Schools Club, East India Club*, 1982, 170. *Cf.* Lejeune, *Gentlemen's Clubs*, 107. *Cf. Masonic Year Book for 1986-7*, United Grand Lodge of England, 1986, 200-73, 633-8. There is a distinction between a lodge confined to club members and a lodge meeting at a club and to which club members belonged. The latter were more numerous. Not all club lodges met in their own club. The Royal Aero met at the Junior Carlton.

43. John Marlowe, *Late Victorian*, Cresset Press, 1967, 288.

44. George MacDonald Fraser, *Flashman and the Dragon*, Fontana, 1986, 198. At its heart was ". . . the huge mahogany-cum-leather shell of the club's library . . . In various corners two or three rather ancient

members were sunk deep in their tall armchairs, in various stages of newspaper-induced reverie." Joseph Brodsky, "Isaiah Berlin at Eighty", *New York Review of Books*, 17 August 1989.

45. See Colson, *White's*, 119.

46. Richard Hough, *The Ace of Clubs: A History of the Garrick*, Andre Deutsch, 1986, 13-14. See T. S. Louch, *The First Fifty Years: The History of the Weld Club (1871-1921)*, Perth, 1964, 79. (Governor Frederick Weld, after whom The Weld Club in Perth (Western Australia) is named, went to Stonyhurst, a school founded by his grandfather. *Ibid.*, 1.

47. Rose, *Curzon*, 148. Wilfrid Blunt, the Crabbett's doyen, presided in flowing Arab robes at oriental banquets of whole roasted kid. *Ibid.*, 149-51.

48. Hearnden, *Red Robert*, 72-73.

49. Heald, *Networks*, 195. An excellent account of two such clubs, *The Trimmers* and *The Clywedos* is in J. M. Stewart's *Changes and Chances: Memories of Shrewsbury and other places*, Abbey Press, Abingdon Upon Thames, 1971, 30-32, 70-73.

50. "A few stand pre-eminent, of assured rank and universally accepted high tone." Arthur Griffiths, *Clubs and Clubmen*, Hutchinson, 1907, 2. **An ingenious comparison can be made by examining the rateable value of clubhouses.** Petrie shows that in 1878 the Carlton clubhouse was rated at three times that of the Athenaeum and six times that of the Guards. Petrie, *The Carlton Club*, 113.

51. J. M. Scott, *The Book of Pall Mall*, Heinemann, 1965, 104.

52. Rose, *Curzon*, 146-47,

53. Atkins, *Incidents and Reflections*, 238. Atkins was the honorary librarian of the Travellers' and of the Royal Yacht Squadron, and discusses the pleasures of being such. About the Travellers' he writes: "To have more control than anyone else for some years over this enchanting room was a piece of good fortune . . .". *Ibid.*, 241.

54. Angela Lambert, *Unquiet Souls: The Indian Summer of the British Aristocracy, 1880-1918*, Macmillan, 1984, 6.

55. Graves, *Armchairs*, 79. Another house on the same street, No. 21-23, became the Curzon House Club, a gambling asylum specializing in *chemin-de-fer.*

56. *Ibid.*, 50, 40.

57. *Ibid.*, 50.

58. *Ibid.*, 66.

59. Richard Gordon, *A Gentlemen's Club*, Muller, 1988, 10.

60. Graves, *Armchairs*, 66. Doubts were expressed about the eligibility of Bromsgrove, St. Albans, Hereford Cathedral and University College schools. Forrest, *Foursome in St. James*, 99. Graves states that there was an earlier public school club in London, established in 1863, adding that it disappeared by 1867 and that nothing is known about its entrance requirements. *Ibid.*, 100. However in *Tom Brown's Universe*, Honey reproduces a letter from the Captain of the Westminster eleven to his Shrewsbury counterpart indicating that for games Westminster recognized as public schools the list of the Committee of the Public Schools Club. An advertisement from *The Times* for 1865 indicates that the club was located at 17 St. James's Place and that "Gentlemen who have been educated at Charterhouse, Eton, Harrow, Westminster and Winchester are alone eligible . . ." J. R. de S. Honey, *Tom Brown's Universe: The Development of the Public School in the 19th Century*, Millington, 1977, 240-41. The letter is also in the *Fleming Report.*

61. Graves, *Armchairs*, 76.

62. Lejeune, *Gentlemen's Clubs*, 113, qtd. Forrest, *Foursome in St. James*, 51.

63. *The United Service Club and Its Founder*, by "L.S.", United Service Club, 1930, 22-23.

64. Marlowe, *Late Victorian*, 287. *Services* is his error.

65. *Ibid.*

66. Louis C. Jackson, *History of the United Service Club*, United Service Club, 1937, 29.

67. *Ibid.*, 122.

68. *Ibid.*, 74.

69. *Ibid.*, 92.

70. *Ibid.*, 95.

71. *Ibid.*, 97.

72. *Ibid.*, 110.

73. *Ibid.*, 116-17.

74. ". . . those eligible for membership – which meant all Europeans of good standing . . .". Robert Jackson, *Thirty Seconds at Quetta: The Story of an Earthquake*, Evans Brothers, 1960, 16.

75. Heald, *Networks*, 187.

76. Captain Peter Wright was expelled for writing to Lord Gladstone on Bath paper. Graves, *Armchairs*, 129. Lejeune, *Gentlemen's Clubs*, 47. Another scandal was caused by an anonymous letter on the Junior Carlton letterhead attacking Stafford Cripps when he was Chancellor of the Exchequer. Graves, *Armchairs*, 98. When John Thorn was headmaster of Repton, the Governors received a highly critical letter that he expected would get an abrupt answer. The Chairman however cautioned, **"But we must be careful. I see he writes from the St. James Club."** Thorn, *Road to Winchester*, 103. A letter to the Prime Minister on Union Club paper in 1882 prompted inquiries by the Director of Criminal Investigation. R. C. Rome, *The Union Club: An Illustrated Descriptive Record of the Oldest Members' Club in London, founded circa 1799*, B. T. Batsford, 1948, 55. "The use of Club writing paper for letters to *The Times* on any political theme has often been raised and it has invariably been the Committee's opinion that the practice is undesirable. Long, long ago, when the Club was still in King Street, the need arose for the Committee to inform a member 'that their attention having been directed to some recent letters addressed by you to the newspapers, they venture to request that further communications to the newspapers upon your private affairs, shall be made in such a matter as that the name of the Garrick Club may not be introduced.'" Hough, *Ace of Clubs*, 50. Related to this was the forbidden publication of conversations held at the club. The novelist Edmund Yates was expelled from the Garrick for commenting on W. M. Thackeray's conversations there. Charles Dickens unsuccessfully intervened. See Edmund Yates, "Memoirs of a man of the world", *Harper's Franklin Square Library*, 14 November 1887, 3-10.

77. Rome, *Union Club*, 29, 31

78. Jackson, *United Service Club*, 5. "St. Vincent had been in his day a super-martinet, and it is conceivable that his real objection was to the idea of senior officers meeting their juniors on the easy terms of a club." *Ibid.* However, the Prime Minister, Lord Liverpool, also considered its establishment "a most ill-advised measure". *Ibid.*, 6. Young officers could join The Junior United Service Club, started in 1827. See R. H. Firth, *The Junior: A History of the Junior United Service Club*, Junior United Service Club, 1929, esp. 4, 82, 105.

79. Lejeune, *Gentlemen's Clubs*, 10-11.

80. S. G. Checkland, *The Rise of Industrial Society in England, 1815-1885*, Longmans, Green, 1964, 293, qtd. Armstrong, *Administrative Elite*, 208. Also Morris, *Pax Britannica*, 395.

81. East India Company officers were blackballed when they applied to the Junior United Service Club in 1831. Denys Forrest, *The Oriental: Life Story of a West End Club*, B. T. Batsford, 1968, 23. In any event, the early United Service was only for the well-placed, as shown by the fact that there was no reduction in fees for those abroad such as other clubs offered. Jackson, *United Service Club*, 23-33, 43.

82. Forrest, *The Oriental*, 150. Of 817 elected between 1934 and 1952, 439 were or had been resident in India. However, Forrest provides no breakdown as to what numbers were in the ICS.

83. Graves, *Armchairs*, 43.

84. Forrest, *The Oriental*, 76. The question of amalgamating the Oriental and East India arose, but the social gulf was too vast. *Ibid.*, 79.

85. In a version of part of this chapter published as the booklet *Clubs of the British Residents and Agents of the Arabian Gulf*, Perth (Western Australia), 1987, the statement was made that officers were expected to join the Guards and Cavalry, and that the Cavalry Club had more Royal visits per annum than other London Clubs put together because so many regiments headed by royalty had their dinners there. (See Graves, *Armchairs*, 126.). This produced a spirited exchange of letters with retired IPS officers and the relatives of officers. One criticism was that it was a matter of *economy* rather than snobbery to join: "Nearly every cavalry officer joined the Cavalry Club not because of its royal and aristocratic connections, which is news to me – I never saw royalty in the Club and would not know an aristocrat if I saw one – but because during one's first two years in a cavalry regiment, British or Indian, one could join it without paying an entrance fee. Nor was I ever expected to join the Guards or Cavalry Club! The part about the Cavalry Club and mention of my dear father has given me much amusement . . . It is *hopelessly inaccurate* and entirely misleading, although I don't deny that my father was once a member . . . Usually the annual susbscription is

the deciding factor plus entry fee for any young officer; I believe my father despite his 'aristocratic associations' was pretty impecunious and I can't imagine him riding up to the main entrance on his own charger ten minutes before one of the many (?) Royal visits!!" Col. R. C. Gabriel to P. J. Rich, 7 October 1987.

86. Margaret Willes, "The Animals Went In, Two By Two . . .", *National Trust Magazine*, No. 56, Spring 1989, 27-28.

87. See Emile A. Nakhleh, *Bahrain: Political Development in a Modernizing Society*, D. C. Heath, Lexington (Massachusetts), 1976, 41, 49-50, 57.

88. See, *e.g.* Oaten, *Memories of India*, 6, 10, 122.

89. Glinga, *Legacy of Empire*, 22. "The public schools represent the first 'compulsory' club in the life of a gentleman." *Ibid.*

CHAPTER VII

Privileges

In their desire to establish some common meeting-ground our upper classes have shown that they know how to look after themselves, as the palaces of Pall Mall and St. James's will testify. – Arthur Ponsonby, *The Decline of Aristocracy*, 1912.

He is intensely loyal to any institution with which he happens to be connected, such as the British Empire or the M.C.C., because loyalty to School and House is one of the fundamental virtues of the public school boy. – Lewis Baumer, *The Lighter Side of School Life*, 1914.

. . . (Imperialism) was taken to allegorical extremes in the institution of the Club, a subtly potent factor in the British Imperial system. – Jan Morris, *The Spectacle of Empire*, 1982.

The Empire's clubs, much influenced by the public schools, enforced caste, comforted the homesick, and perpetuated the Imperial privileges. The London club often provided the starting point for Imperial adventures.[1] Jules Verne's Phileas Fogg started out on his *Eighty Days Around The World* from the Reform, and many other Imperial paladins set out and returned to a St. James's bolt-hole.[2] Kinglake frequented the Travellers' and Athenaeum. Samuel Baker was a habitué of the Wyndham, the Athenaeum, and the Marlborough. Edward Palmer was "a much beloved and most excellent Savilian."[3] It was in the Athenaeum that Burton translated the *Arabian Nights*.[4]

The Imperial manifestations of St. James's have been described distrustfully as "English Edens" that minimised interest in social improvement, providing an escape from the local realities to "white men's caves" to which the British withdrew to meet a "ritual need".[5] The architecture of clubhouses confirms this. In the anonymous *Letters of an Indian Judge to an English Gentlewoman* (1934), the author described the Gymkhana Club in Bombay: "The lavatories for the gentlemen there, are much more splendid than the High Courts, in their wealth of marble, their magnificence of window. Surely something is out of perspective somewhere, when the lavatories become more magnificent than the High Courts!"[6] (See *Bombay Gymkhana Club*, page 167.) The Empire's clubs did not promote fraternization by the mandarins with their subjects. (See *Nice Work, If You Can Get It*, page 168.)

Bombay Gymkhana Club.

Club architecture and landscaping resisted assimilation. In Cairo, hollyhocks growing at the Gezira Sporting defied the Middle Eastern climate.[7] As the Bombay Gymkhana illustrates, there were ornate Imperial clubs that looked like schools. Imperial club architecture favoured Cotswold and Tudor, and was suggestive of public schools. Buildings "seemed to represent gentle, pastoral, particularly English values – like the cricket pavilions of school."[8] A characteristic of Imperial club architecture was the verandah, which did strikingly suggest those of public school pavilions "Forty years on" – particularly when populated with blazered old boys nursing their Pimm's.

In contrast with colonial clubs which resembled pavilions, the clubs of St. James's were "vast, colonnaded, galleried" affairs that resembled the buildings that the bureaucracy erected in adjacent Whitehall for the India Office and other ministries. In the Reform Club, Sir Charles Barry incorporated "not one Roman *palazzo*, but three". Macaulay enthused that it was "A building worthy of Michelangelo!"[9] The contrast between these fortresses and humbler clubhouses is intriguing. It is almost an acknowledgement that London is the main schoolhouse of the Empire and that the Imperial outposts are, like the school pavilions, more modest places for the old boys to observe a match.

The siting of clubs and public schools was of considerable significance, especially in hill stations where elevation assured status. At Simla, the Viceroy had the choicest peak. The hill stations were to the fore in inculcating and exemplifying the Imperial style. The clubs in such locations were "pinnacles of power", but they had other Imperial functions. One was to regulate the drinking and control the alcoholism that developed when officers sequestered themselves in their bungalows. The club ". . . was the usual site for drinking and socializing, considered a more appropriate location than isolated private houses. As drinking was frequently a problem among bored colonial officers, it was felt that the club's public situation might provide greater social censure and thereby encourage temperance."[10]

Privileges

In overseas clubs, as at home, the affairs of the Empire were often decided. In Cairo, the Turf Club occupied the old building of the British Agency, and it has been suggested that the kind of business transacted had not changed with the change in ownership. In any case, clubs were *par excellence* where public school and other loyalties were refreshed. As might be expected, there was a close association of overseas clubs with Freemasonry.[11] Often the club's lodge constituted an inner coterie of the leading members.[12] The consecrating officer for the lodge of the Gymkhana in Bombay was also the District Grand Master **and** the president of the club.[13] Thus the élite learned its rituals at school, rehearsed them in the clubs and lodges, and then put them in good use in running the colonies.

Ritual's Bastion

Club rituals made no more concession to climate or local custom than did the public schools established overseas. In 1937 at the Waltair Club in the Indian port of Visakhapatnam:

> No Member would be seen on the Club premises after 6.00 p.m. unless he was dressed in "Fish and Chips" (Evening Dress) which in summer was "Red Sea Kit, White shirt long sleeves, black bow, white long pants, and

Savages and Schoolboys.

169

Submission.

black cummerbund with black evening shoes and black socks" . . . The call for drink was "Koi Hai" and when the bearer appeared the order was "Pucho".[14]

Besides the social privileges enjoyed Imperial administrators had practical need of a club.[15] When they went on leave the club back 'home' in England was their centre. When they were abroad it was their agent for forwarding mail. When they arrived in a post, the club provided introductions and for the exchange of information.[16] The Club was a school of social ritual for the Imperial adminstrators, furnishing similar instruction to that which they had received at school – continuing the rehearsal of ritual. The public school boy's idea of an an encounter with local society could be more a fantasy of capitation or submission than understanding. (See *Savages and Schoolboys*, page 169, and *Submission*, above. *The Gem*, 21 April, 1934.) The esoteric nuances and their resemblances to school customs are worth study.

Reciprocity

An aspect of club life with decided implications for the dissemination of the Imperial idiom was reciprocity, whereby members had the use of fraternal clubs when they travelled.[17] The relationships between clubs recall the earlier discussion of Dr. Honey and Dr. Mangan, determining the social standing of schools by games fixtures. In one fictional account of a protypical London club: "The Albany was continually refreshed and educated by 'reciprocal clubs' all round the world. The Opossum Club in Sydney sent members who surprised us by not wearing corks dangling from their hats and drinking beer out of tins. We learned much about the 'Third World' from members of the Palm Tree Club in Lagos, who neither performed black magic in the bar, nor ordered human flesh in the coffee room. Members of the Champs-Elysees Club displayed traditional French politeness by inventing excuses to avoid eating the club food."[18]

Reciprocity bound together clubdom.[19] The East India affiliated with the Union in Alexandria. The Bengal Club in Calcutta affiliated with Hong Kong and Shanghai clubs. The Sports Club in London (which eventually merged with the East India) was nicknamed the "Spotted Dog" because of its close affiliation with the Selangor in Kuala Lumpur, which itself received the nickname because of its pseudo-Elizabethan timbered building. During World War II the Athenaeum in Melbourne sent food parcels to its reciprocal affiliate, the Devonshire. Similarly the National in Toronto despatched **puddings,** a fact which might be added to the pudding evidence discussed in Chapter IV. (There is no information about whether these were savoury or sweet puddings, and since it was Christmas-time, they may have been plum puddings.)

As an alternative to reciprocity, some clubs simply conferred honorary membership for a limited period of months.[20] Whether reciprocal or honorary, these memberships extended to visitors were another aspect of club influence.[21] The East India eventually forged reciprocal arrangements with eighty-four clubs, including seventeen in Australia alone.[22] By comparing reciprocal lists of clubs throughout the Empire it is possible to re-establish the relative social status of clubs and arrive at an understanding of the networks that flourished[23] at various times. If a town were populous enough to maintain several clubs, distinctions inevitably emerged.[24] In Penang in Malaysia, the *tuan besars* (big masters) belonged to the Penang Club, founded in 1858. The *tuan kechils* (small masters) belonged to the Penang Cricket Club. In Kuala Lumpur the tuan besars were in the Lake Club and the tuan kechils joined the Selangor. But the Selangor was special – tuan besars belonged as well. A hierarchical system also operated in Singapore, where the less senior were in the Tanglin and the senior men joined the Singapore Club.

Studying reciprocal arrangements is a way to appreciate these distinctions, but it would be as mistaken to draw hasty conclusions about social standing based on reciprocity as it would be to rely on games fixtures to determine a school's status.[25] A number of factors influenced reciprocity. For example, the Caledonian in London deliberately did not affiliate with the New in Edinburgh nor the Western in Glasgow – not because of a lack of social rapport but because the Caledonian would have lost money on Scots who would have been able to use the New's reciprocal privileges rather than pay to join the Caledonian.[26]

Oasis of Exclusiveness

The club was so much part of the Imperial culture that Olaf Caroe, who was secretary of the Foreign Department of the Indian Government, felt reminded of the Athenaeum whenever he visited the Hyderabad Residency.[27] The connections extended to the reading matter available in the clubs. In the Union Club ("patterned after the bastions of Pall Mall") in Victoria, British Columbia, the ex-India colonels kept track of events through the Allahabad *Pioneer Mail* and the *Lahore Civilian and Military Gazette.*[28] The Empire's clubs were careful to keep abreast of those in Britain, and this was particularly evident when it came to pursuits such as rowing and golf. The appearance of school rowing clubs was complemented by the founding of rowing clubs overseas. As for golf, St. Andrew's in Scotland has an archive of letters waiting to be explored from the secretaries of outposts such as the Aden Golf Club, where a silver golf ball was presented to the winners of the monthly tournament – despite, as *The Golfing Annual* for 1892-93 reported, "no grass".

Contemporaneous with the growth of the public schools, and by some of the same strategies, clubs became indispensable in the Imperial outback. An observer invoked Kipling and ritual to explain their primacy, remarking that the club was ". . . an oasis. It was more than a recreational centre; it was an emblem of exclusiveness . . . For a dispersed and close-knit society, in the club and in other ways, the corporate identity of the overseas Europeans was institutionalized, and ritualized. *All ritual is fortifying. Ritual's a natural necessity for mankind. The more things are upset, the more they fly to it. (Kipling)."*[29] In the midst of the Mesopotamian crisis, the High Commissioner for Iraq, Arnold Wilson reserved as "inviolate" his daily visit to the English club in Basra.[30]

The respite in the club that he and others relished had political dangers, for the clubs made the free mixing of the races and of ideas difficult. The perceptions of the ICS and IPS and kindred services were distorted by the omission from Imperial social life of those who were in tune with what was happening. The British commercial travellers, the educated natives, the missionaries, and other groups were few within club walls. This contributed to British administrators reaching false conclusions, and alienated those who could have been allies: "The Roll of Honour of any Club in India will show that not a single Indian had become the President of a Club before India attained Independence."[31] Sir Percy Cox recognized the problem by sponsoring an Anglo-Arab Club in Baghdad when he was Mesopotamian Commissioner, to be a "common meeting ground".[32] Anglo-Arab did not prosper, and similar attempts elsewhere were only moderately successful.

Desert Dream and *The Sheik's Breath*

The clubs resembled the dressing-rooms of theatres, privileged retreats to which Imperial officialdom withdrew to let its hair down without the natives observing. The barriers were not dropped in even the smallest outposts. The tiniest expatriate settlement supported its exclusive watering-hole. Even in Bushire in the Gulf, when the British population averaged a scant two dozen, there was a club.[33] Clubs such as Bushire were necessarily modest – the only large one in the Gulf resembling a London club was the Alweyah in Baghdad, where Alexander Powell reported one could take shelter on its deep verandahs and order for a cocktail either *Desert Dream* or *The Sheik's Breath*.[34] Here again the verandah seems to have achieved a symbolic status, and had, as it so often did, the obligatory cane chairs.

As citadels, albeit modest ones, British clubs in the Gulf encountered their share of criticism.[35] The Union Club in Mohammerah lasted only the month of June 1923. The local shaikh closed it because of rumours that it was gathering intelligence for the British.[36] (In the late 1980s clubs were closely regulated and watched in the Gulf by the ruling shaikhs, who have long memories.)

While India was the setting where Imperial clublife really flourished, backwaters such as Bahrain also had its clubs. There were those limited to the British, but the Arabs copied the British, as did the Indians. The more traditional native Bahraini clubs included Ahili, Uruba, Firdawsi, the Bahrain, Islah, Nahda, and the Sports. Each had its ethos. Ahili took in rich Sunnis from Manama, the capital. Uruba was for Shia merchants and civil servants. Firdawsi had a large contingent of men with Persian backgrounds. The Bahrain drew from the part of Bahrain known as Muharraq. Islah had members of the ruling family. Nahda members were mostly from the al-Hidd area. There was considerable rivalry in Manama (the capital) clubdom.[37]

The denial of admission to a club irritated the Arabs, while (for example) the denial of vaccination to non-members of the ruling family in Qatar was accepted without resentment. The contradiction, as an observer noted to this writer, is explained when it is understood that to the Arabs their health is of less importance than their dignity, and discrimination by fellow Arabs arouses less bitterness than discrimination perpetuated by Westerners.[38] Of course, exceptions were made by the British for natives of the highest caste, especially when they were fellow old boys. Needless to say Westerners were welcome at some native establishments even if the hospitality was *not* reciprocal. (See *Christian Guests*, page 174.)

The Bahrain Political Agent, Anthony Parsons, ran foul of the division between the prestigious Gymkhana, which excluded Arabs, and the Indian Club, which despite its name admitted them: "I found myself in the embarrassing position of being *ex officio* patron of both clubs: indeed the Indian Club was one of my favourite resorts for a game of tennis. I also discovered that the attitude of the Gymkhana Club towards the Bahrainis was a source of resentment which had penetrated to the Ruler and his family."[39] Parsons persuaded the Gymkhana to open its membership and the ruling shaikh became its patron. This was one occasion of many when the old distinctions proved upsetting in new political circumstances. Another Bahrain Political Agent (1942-43), Edward Wakefield, had an equally rude awakening while earlier serving in India: "I had read, of course, E. M. Forster's *Passage to India*. But it was only when I joined the Lyallpur Club that I realised how cruelly true to life was much of his characterisation . . . never, I am sure, has there existed in England such an elaborate structure of class distinction as British exiles erected for themselves . . .".[40] The clubs

INKY IN ALL HIS GLORY!

(The Magnificent Scene when Harry Wharton & Co. arrive as Hurree Singh's guests for Christmas.)

No. 723. Vol. XX.   Week Ending December 17th, 1921.

Christian guests.

174

proved increasingly troublesome because they were so exceptionally slow to change their outlook.

Sir Charles Belgrave, the British adviser to the shaikh in Bahrain, eventually reached conclusions about clubs that were similar to those held by Parsons and Wakefield. He confirms in his autobiography *Personal Column* that the Bahrain Gymkhana was resented because of its exclusiveness, and adds that the Gulf's clubs tended towards the political rather than social side: "In my part of the Middle East, club membership has provoked strong political feeling."[41] The consequences in the Empire of natives wanting to emulate the British but not being allowed to do so may have been as significant as the consequences of natives rejecting British customs. Had the clubs not generally been segregated, native interest in highly political native clubs might have been dampened.

Discussion of clubs in the Middle East would not be complete without mentioning an unusual exception to the élitist norm, the Royal Union Athletic Club in Basra at the head of the Gulf. This had an altogether different atmosphere from a conventional gentlemen's retreat. The Royal Union started in the compound of the American missionaries there, and besides sports it interested itself in night-schools and carrying on all kinds of social activities for young people. It had a considerable impact on Basra.[42]

Piccadilly Under the Palms

The Raj's departure did not end 'Piccadilly under the palms', any more than it ended public schools. The clubs continued and *boxwallahs* or businessmen continued to face membership committees stacked as they had been in colonial days with civil servants and retired colonels. The Saturday Club in Calcutta advised that national dress would *not* be worn. The secretary of the Tollygunge in Calcutta was still (1989) an Englishman, described by the *Hindustani Times* as "the most influential figure in Calcutta after Mother Theresa." Marxist members of the Bengal legislature belong to the club, apparently not finding the cabalism incompatible with their communism. *The Economist* (22 April 1989) reported that the Muthaiga Club outside Nairobi retains hunting scenes by Sir Alfred Munnings on its walls and the *Daily Telegraph* in the reading-room, while the Harare Club cherishes a photograph of Cecil Rhodes.

In the 1980s, Geoffrey Moorhouse made a nostalgic pilgrimage to the haunts of the Empire, and in Karachi (See *Sind Club,* page 176) he ". . . passed the Sind Club, a very elegant and rambling low place of brown sandstone with a long colonnaded verandah, an arched storey above, and wooden lattice blinds over most of the windows. Here, beyond a superbly immaculate garden well back from the road, the rich and powerful of Karachi discussed their ruling preoccupations, their private passions, their commercial speculations, their devious ways and means of retaining wealth and power, in secrecy from the population at large; just as their old masters had done."[43] Any club man who has travelled the Indian sub-continent knows the truth to this description, and how successfully the clubs have survived. In Bombay,

175

The Sind Club, Karachi.

the hallway of the Willingdon Sports Club displays the photographs in coroneted silver frames of its Viceroy founder and his Vicereine.[43] The Gymkhana in Delhi treasures its library of English classics.[44] In 1982 the Inspector General of Police in the Indian port of Visakhapatnam complained to the Waltair Club there: "Admissions to the Club membership should be more broad-based, keeping in view the democratic setup in our country . . . It is high time that membership of the club is thrown open to the service officers, including the Police . . .".[45]

The clubs found, as did the overseas public schools, a constituency enabling them to continue after the British left.[46] Complainers lamented that standards slipped, that the newspapers were no longer ironed and that coins to be given in change were no longer boiled. Nevertheless, as late as 1963 the Sudan Club barred Sudanese from the premises: "Given the small size of Khartoum, the situation was analogous to the Americans having annexed and fenced off the whole of Hyde Park, called it the British Club and denied entry to all except American citizens."[47] This attitude has part of its origins in the public schools, when the most inconsiderable boys could hope to be important in overseas posts. (See *Big Chief Bunter*, page 177, and *Castaways of Cannibal Island*, page 178. *The Magnet*, 17 September 1938.)

This discussion of Imperial clubs should not create an impression that overseas posts had one club, any more than posts always had only one school. In small towns one club was the rule, but if a city were large enough, there were several clubs serving different clientèles. In Kenya the senior officials frequented the Nairobi "on the Hill" and their juniors were in the Parklands "on the plain".[48] In Calcutta the leading clubs were *Tolly, Bally* and *Slap:* the Tollyganj, the Ballyganj, and the Saturday. The Slap or Saturday Club was not as sedate as the Tolly and Bally. Less prestigious than this 'big three', the Calcutta United Services "had no social life and was normally a short-stay put-up for officers in transit."[49] Unlike the 'Holy Trinity' the Bengal Club admitted Indians and took 'commercial' men or 'box-wallahs' as members. Although the United Services was not top-drawer, when after World War II there was a proposal to amalgamate with the inter-racial Bengal, the suggestion was rejected as

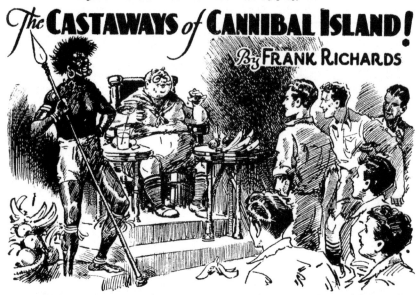

BIG CHIEF BUNTER ! At Greyfriars School Billy Bunter is a mere nobody. Now he's the most important member of Lord Mauleverer's holiday party, bar none !

The **CASTAWAYS** of **CANNIBAL ISLAND!**

By **FRANK RICHARDS**

Harry Wharton & Co. entered the devil-house to find Billy Bunter sitting in his chair of state. On one side of the fat junior were dishes of fruits ; on the other, supplies of cooling drinks. Bunter helped himself from them alternately and grinned.

"outrageous". The discrimination was not only racial: if a man married, the "form" was to resign and seek re-admission so members could decide on his wife's merits.[50] In a metropolis like Calcutta, there was room for specialized clubs. There were in fact two Welsh ones, where members could "sing to their hearts' content" and dine on a curious mixture of Indo-Cymric dishes.[51]

Baraka and Books

The Calcutta Welsh clubs were closer to the native clubs in *foie de jeunesse* than others were. Natives did not erect the pseudo-Florentine palaces of St. James's, but they enjoyed comradery. In trying to explain the spirit of that most prestigious of London clubs, the Athenaeum's historian approvingly invoked the Arab concept of *baraka*, the "spirit of place" which he asserted the Athenaeum had – a club man's notion perhaps of 'morphic resonance'. Cautioning against "dismissing as gratuitous mysticism" such a comparison, he cited a "loyal member" who insisted on having found the spirit amongst the Arabs that characterized Athenaeum members.[52] Native clubs did not emulate the Athenaeum's intellectual austerity, but *baraka* was in

178

evidence. Dame Freya Stark wrote affectionately of one club in Alexandria, "In the middle of this desert of commerce is the Sa'idis club, a charming building with Quranic texts upon its walls, to which everyone belongs. It is of the docks and its workers, and practically no foreigners except those interested in cotton ever visit it. I met its Elders, and drank tea there, charmed with the dignity with which, wherever the Arab civilization reigns, the spirit still triumphs over circumstance, and the most unlikely place develops a ceremonial drawing-room atmosphere of leisure."[53]

Baraka has a resemblance to school spirit. With clubs as with schools, when it came to inter-mural relationships there was considerable rivalry. During World War II a member of the Reform announced "Ghastly news. The Carlton has been bombed. Only thirty-eight of them were there and none has a scratch."[54] Nor did all members of the same club get along. A United Service legend was that Sir William Napier sat at one end of the library writing his *History of the Peninsular War* while at the other end sat Lord Beresford, who was so annoyed with Napier's criticisms of his strategies in the war that he refused to speak to him and exchanged acid notes through a waiter.[55]

While the bar was fundamental, the library – brunt of jokes about sleeping members – has figured prominently in club lore. The libraries of London clubs became national resources,[56] testimonial to the place of clubs in cultural life. As an amenity, libraries were all the more appreciated in remote overseas posts where books were a scarce commodity. The cultural impact which the libraries embodied is in ways comparable to the influence of the nineteenth-century learned societies that has been mentioned. Many Imperial administrators belonged in addition to clubs to such societies, and contributed articles to the societies' journals. In respects the learned societies were *more* influential than the clubs, espousing an 'antiquarian historiography' that effected perception of native culture.

Imperial Learned Societies

The societies' clubhouses were as appropriate settings as were those of the clubs for the staging of Imperial ritual performances. The talk by the returned adventurer was a staple. Wilfred Thesiger describes giving a lecture in the 1930s at the Royal Geographical: "In those days, a lecture at the Geographical Society was a formal occasion, with the President, Council and lecturer in white tie and tailcoat, and the audience in dinner jackets. The lecture was preceded by a dinner with the Society's dining club. Sir Percy Cox, an awe-inspiring man renowned for his ability to keep silent in a dozen languages, was the President, and I sat next to him . . . he lapsed into silence, while I in my confusion ate a plateful of mushrooms, even though on two previous occasions mushrooms had made me violently ill."[57]

The RGS was popular with Imperial administrators, but there were others too notably the Royal Asiatic Society and the Royal Central Asiatic Society (later known as the Royal Society for Asian Affairs). The Royal Asiatic established branches which still prosper in Sri Lanka, Hong Kong, and Malaysia. Some considered that the Royal Asiatic membership was for the erudite and that the Royal Central membership were the more 'contemporary'.[58] This author, a Fellow of the Royal Asiatic and of the Asian Affairs, mentioned the supposed differences to an elderly member of the Royal Asiatic and was told: "Some people said that the difference was that the Royal Asiatic fellows were scholars and the RSAA fellows were spies – and *(long pause)* – you know – I think they were right."

The resemblances between learned societies and clubs is illustrated by the connection that the Royal Asiatic had with the Oriental Club, which was founded in 1824 in the Asiatic's rooms by Sir John Malcolm and other East India Company luminaries.[59] Likewise, the East India Club membership rules requiring applicants to have been employed by the Government or East India Company in "the East", or to be in service in the administration of "Eastern Governments" either in England or abroad, were waived for members of the Royal Asiatic. School registers and club registers need to be examined to see how relationships like these persisted and had Imperial consequences.[60]

The societies performed a similar function to the clubs as a rendezvous for those on leave. The original premises of the Royal Geographic at 1 Savile Road was "the Mecca of all the geographers, the home port of every traveller." Active members included Sir Mountstuart Elphinstone Duff of the India Office (Lt-Governor of Madras) and Sir Henry Bartle Frere of the ICS, Governor of Bombay. Frere served as president in 1873-74.[61] The old boy societies of a number of overseas public schools used the Royal Colonial for meetings.[62]

Learned societies in England and abroad not only performed similar social functions to clubs but physically resembled them, being possessed of comfortable houses. On the one hand, the Athenaeum was a club whose library and atmosphere made it a learned society. On the other hand, the Royal Geographical Society was a society whose atmosphere was that of a club.[63] Those familiar with the Athenaeum and with the RGS, or with the old premises of the Royal Asiatic before its move in 1987, will acknowledge similarities.

Learned societies in England and overseas were made up overwhelmingly of public school men. Indeed, the unique building of the Royal Geographic in Kensington Gore was owed to Curzon's hearing about the availability of Lowther Lodge at the Eton and Harrow match at Lords in June 1912. He mentioned to his fellow Old Etonian James Lowther (Speaker of the House, later Lord Ullswater) that the Society needed a new home and Lowther indicated that his town house could be bought.[64] The Royal Geographic strengthened its public school associations by the part it played in the introduction of geography into public school curriculums. A member of its Council, Francis Galton, established examinations conducted by the RGS and open only to selected schools, with a gold medal awarded for outstanding papers.

The RGS has been studied sufficiently to provide a historian discovering its members in a prosopographical survey with a basis for interpreting the significance of joining. Current RGS membership is not so much different in characteristics from earlier times: dominated by males (80%) who have lived overseas (two-thirds) and belong to other learned societies (two-thirds).[65] The RGS perhaps was pre-eminent as far as the membership of Imperial mandarins was concerned, but it was not the oldest society. Founded much earlier (1784) was the Asiatic Society, not to be confused with the Royal Asiatic or Royal Central Asian, which had a building in Calcutta. Although ICS and IPS members were contributors to its *Proceedings* and used the building as a club when in the city, the Asiatic was not large in membership. Between 1855 through 1883, the membership varied between 162 and 446, declining from 1871 onwards.[66]

A Needed Study

In absolute numbers none of the clubs or societies were sizable, but neither was the public school population. A study of *everyone* who went to an English public school in Victorian and Edwardian times and of *everyone* who belonged to a London club and to a Masonic lodge is not beyond the power of modern computers. On a more limited scale, a study of the club and society memberships of leading headmasters and other public school educators is practicable and overdue. So too are investigations of the school backgrounds of the memberships of specific clubs and learned societies, and the compiling of a list of Masonic lodges meeting in clubs and their memberships. **Club membership is a significant item to be included in any prosopographical survey.**

While the links of clubs and learned societies with the public schools should be considered when discussing causality and the British Empire, this can be carried to extremes. There are those who claim that clubs in London and overseas drew from certain schools and ended up by producing a TYPE, or at least attracting a type. The Turf Club members were supposed to be Etonians and tall and shambling, as well as somewhat rakish and loud. Those who frequented Boodle's allegedly included Rugbeians who were accused of being dull, and the members of White's included Harrovians that were branded as garrulous. The denizens of Brook's were more likely to be Wykehamists than in some clubs and were 'serious'. Actually Etonians were well represented in all the top clubs, and there is no study of what schools were over or underrepresented in clubdom.

Whatever the arguments about these distinctions, there is no denying that the clubs were part of the Imperial and public school mosaic. A visitor to the Turf was told that "It has the feel of a school."[67] The evidence in these two chapters also confirms F. E. Hill's observation that gentlemen's clubs were a vehicle of informal education.[68] Research is needed in this area, and the findings will have implications for the history of British and Imperial education. Harold Silver points out that:

> The history of education is in fact multiple histories, because education is itself no simple and homogeneous concept or category, and because its history can be explored in relation to almost endless variables. Whether education is conceived as itself an indefinite cluster of experiences or as a more narrowly definable process related to a variety of other processes, it has no meaning when presented in isolated and discretely institutional terms.[69]

Because the clubs were such an integral part of the Imperial experience, membership is as important to an understanding of Imperialism as election to them was to the Imperial administrators. The appreciation of Imperial rituals will be enhanced when such affiliations are taken more seriously. The schools, lodges, and clubs of the Empire were the sodality of Imperialism.

NOTES – CHAPTER VII

1. *Letters of an Indian Judge to an English Gentlewoman*, Future/Macdonald, 1983 (1934), 135. For ways that the club ambience suited more nefarious planning, see Masters, *Literary Agents*, 92.

2. No matter how far afield travels took them, they eventually returned. See *e.g.* Wilfred Thesiger, *The Life of My Choice*, Collins, 1987, 432.

3. Hall, *Savile Club*, 29.

4. See Richard Hall, *Lovers on the Nile*, Quartet, 1981, 19, 210.

5. Thornton, *Imperialism*, 13. Peter Mudford, *Birds of a Different Plumage: A Study of British-Indian Relations from Akbar to Curzon*, Collins, 1974, 154- 55. "The club made the station complete. It was a place where the cares and worries of 'severe duty' could be temporarily shelved while the delights of 'the refinement and luxuries of European Society' were savoured." Robert Fermor-Hesketh ed., *Architecture of the British Empire*, Weidenfeld and Nicolson, 1986, 71. See the magnificent photos of the Selangor, Ootacamund, and Adyar Clubs, *Ibid.*, 71-73. The 'refinement' was one reason that the clubs were not open to 'natives'. On reading this in draft copy, Charles Chenevix Trench wrote: "I hope you will not fall into the common error of supposing that most clubs in India excluded Indian officers. When I went to India in 1935, there were, I believe, only two clubs in the whole country which had no Indian members. These were the Bombay Yacht Club and one in Calcutta both preserves of 'boxwallahs', merchants and business, who were far more illiberal in these matters than army officers and Indian Civil Servants." Trench to P. J. Rich, 5 October 1987. See Trench, *Viceroy's Agents*, 51-52. **However,** Morrow asserts: "Indians were rigorously excluded from all British clubs." *Highness*, 256. *Cf.* Johan Khasnor, *The Emergence of the Modern Malay Administrative Elite*, OUP, 1984, 156-60.

6. "The British legacy of urinals in India, magnificent temples of bladder worship are to be found and admired in the splendid clubs like the Gymkhana in Delhi, the Willingdon in Bombay, the Bengal and Calcutta in Calcutta, and the Ootacamund." Trevor Fishlock, *India File*, John Murray, 1983, 131. The urinals in the basement of Gresham's in London were included on a tour given this author by the female club manager. They are truly impressive.

The contract between the bank-like clubhouses of St. James's and the pavilion-like colonial clubhouses is intriguing: is it an architectural statement implying that London is the central bank and the colonial outposts were branches? *Exegi monumentum aere perennius.*

7. Anthony Sattin, *Lifting the Veil: British Society in Egypt, 1768-1956*, J. M. Dent & Sons, 1988, 191.

8. Jan Morris, *Stones of Empire*, OUP, 1986, 55, 57. The *Union Club* erected "arbours" from which to view the Eton v. Harrow match at Lord's. Rome, *Union Club*, 64.

9. Richard Gordon, *The Private Life of Florence Nightingale*, Heinemann, 1978, 2.

10. Stephen Frenkel and John Western, "Pretext or Prophylaxis? Racial Segregation and Malarial Mosquitos in a British Tropical Colony: Sierra Leone", *Annals of the Association of American Geographers*, VI. 78, No. 2, June 1988, 221-22. This ingenious article suggests that residential segregation as a prophylaxis for malaria masked a drive for racial segregation.

11. Hough, *Ace of Clubs*, 14.

12. See *e.g.* GLE:NJR 166 (3796) *The Gymkhana Lodge No. 3796, EC Bombay: A Summary of the First Fifteen Years*, 1917-1932.

13. *Ibid.*

14. E. H. Glassup, "Memories", M. K. Murugesh ed., *Waltair Club Centenary Celebrations, 1882-1982*, Waltair Club, Visakhapatnam (India), 1982, n.p.

15. See Wm. Roger Louis, *The British Empire in the Middle East, 1945-1956: Arab Nationalism, The United States, and Postwar Imperialism*, Clarendon Press, Oxford, 1985, 9.

16. Reciprocity usually existed between clubs that considered themselves of equal standing. The secretary of the Constitutional Club wrote to the Madras Club: "Dear Sir, we have thirty of our members visiting India and would appreciate it if you would show them every hospitality. We cannot of course reciprocate, as you will readily understand." Qtd. Graves, *Armchairs*, xxv. See A. Bertram Cox, *The First Hundred Years: History of the S.A. Tattersalls Club*, Brolgo Books, Adelaide (South Australia), 1980, 29. Also Perry, *The Naval and Military Club, Melbourne*, 138, 212, 322, 406. Reciprocity is an old custom. The Union Club history records an inquiry in 1864 from "Monsieur Bigi of the Club Grammont St. Hubert, Montmartre, inviting the Union to join in a 'system of mutual intercourse', in other words reciprocation. Monsieur Bigi offered a friendly welcome from his members, who he states 'belong chiefly to our most respected class of merchants and citizens'. The chairman of the Union, however, politely declined in the name of the Committee." Rome, *Union Club*, 48. *Cf.* also Graves, *Armchairs*, 77. See Morris, *Stones of Empire*, 55.

17. Gordon, *A Gentlemen's Club*, 39.

18. Forrest, *Foursome in St. James*, 137.

19. *E.g.* the American Arctic explorer Vilhjalmur Stefansson frequently made use of the Athenaeum and obtained the privilege for his friends. This author has donated a number of Stefansson's letters concerning reciprocity to the Royal Geographic Society, in which he was active. See in the RGS Archives, Vilhjalmur Stefansson to Professor Frederick W. Sternfeld, 18 June 1954.

20. "So one way in which to impress your guests is to take them to a club of which they are not members. The question is: How do you become a member? You don't. The solution is to be a member of a good club in your home town that has guest privileges in establishments of a similar caliber around the world." Roger Beardwood. "Some Do's and Don't for Business Lunches", *Wall Street Journal*, 24 February 1987, 11.

21. Forrest, *Foursome in St. James*, 187.

22. Brook's maintained an ultimate exclusiveness by being reciprocal with only **one** club, the Knickerbocker in New York.

23. Clubs on occasion deferred seeking reciprocity until they felt they had facilities up to what visitors would expect. Oscar Whitelaw Rexford, *The History of the University Club of St. Louis, 1872-1978*. University Club of St. Louis, St. Louis (Missouri), 1979, 61, 77.

24. Some clubs were willing to exchange reciprocity with clubs of like interest, despite a difference in social standings. For example, the Naval and Military in Melbourne was a club of considerable stature but was reciprocal with several 'lesser' clubs that had military connections. Perry, *Naval and Military Club*, 406.

25. Graves, *Armchairs*, 134.

26. However: ". . . there is now a reciprocal arrangement between the New Club and the Caledonian, and extremely useful it is too!" Commander G. J. T. Creedy, Secretary, New Club, to P. J. Rich, 4 August 1987.

27. IOR:MSSEurC.273/1-5, Olaf Caroe, "Five Autobiographical Narratives", 34.

28. Dunae, *Gentlemen Emigrants*, 108.

29. A. J. Stockwell, "The White Man's Burden and Brown Humanity: Colonialism and Ethnicity in British Malaya", *The Southeast Asian Journal of Social Science*, Vol. 10, No. 1, 1982, 48. See Mudford, *Birds of a Different Plumage*, 154-55.

30. Marlowe, *Late Victorian*, 115.

31. M. R. Sripada Rao, "The Club", *Waltair Club Platinum Jubilee Souvenir, 1904-1979*, Waltair Club, Visakhapatnam (India), 1979.

32. Gertrude Bell to Sir Hugh Bell, 16 July 1922, Florence Bell ed., *Letters of Gertrude Bell*, 520. *Cf.* Doyle, *Memories and Adventures*, 127-28.

33. IOR:L/PS/11/206/1698, "Report on General Local Conditions".

34. E. Alexander Powell, *The Last Home of Mystery*, John Long, 1929, 297.

35. See Allen, *Plain Tales*, 124. *Cf.* Trench, *Viceroy's Agent*, 51.

36. IOR:R/15/6/523, *Persian Gulf Administrative Reports 1923*, "Administration Report of the Vice-Consulate at Mohammerah for the Year 1923", 61.

37. Faud Khuri, *Tribe and State in Bahrain*, University of Chicago Press, 1981, 173-79, 183, 217.

38. In the Gulf in the late 1980s, it was harder for an expatriate Britisher to join one of the exclusive clubs than for an Arab of comparable background and resources. Time moves on.

39. Parsons, *They Say the Lion*, 120.

40. Edward Wakefield, *Past Imperative: My Life in India, 1927-1947*, Chatto and Windus, 1966, 7. This is confirmed by Oaten, *Memories of India*, 87, but conflicts with the position taken by Trench that only a few Indian clubs discriminated. Trench is at odds with the often stated view that even Anglo-Indians were barred from many of clubs. See, *e.g.* Allen, *Plain Tales*, 123- 24.

41. Charles Belgrave, *Personal Column*, Hutchinson, 1960, 144.

42. Dorothy Van Ess, *History of the Arabian Mission, 1926-1957*, Board of Foreign Missions, Reformed Church in America, n.d., 16 (See Bibliography).

43 Geoffrey Moorhouse, *To the Frontier*, Sceptre, 1988 (1984), 28.

44. Mark Bence-Jones, *Viceroys of India*, Constable, 1982, 273. *Cf.* Morrow, *Highness*, 256.

45. Tulja Raj to Waltair Club, qtd. M. K. Murugesh ed., *Waltair Club Centenary Celebrations*. One member felt the centenary was "... really an occasion to recall the services rendered by the British, not in a narrow way confined to the Club's services, but in a larger sense, bringing about a renaissance and a new era of peace and humanism in the country." Avaula Sambasiva to Waltair Club, *Ibid*.

46. "Tunka Tan Sri has had the singular honour and distinction of being our first Malaysian President elected to office in the year 1965 after a continuous series of expatriate Presidents since the inception of our Club in the year 1890 – our very own President after 75 years of Clubbing and many years of independence. This phenomenon should not appear strange as historically Clubbing was an expatriate hobby and pastime. To be precise, it was and is an adjunct of an English life-style; wherever the British went they **consecrated** exclusive social Clubs which today have become the domain of an enlightened Malaysian Society." President's Speech, President's Ball 1986, *Kelab Taman Perdana Newsletter*, August 1986, 12.

47. Parsons, *They Say the Lion*, 84. "And yet successive Sudanese independent governments had made no move either to close it down and to annex the Club and its premises, or to insist that it be thrown open to Sudanese . . . Needless to say, intermittent guerrilla warfare waged between the Embassy and the Club Committee. The Ambassador was determined to persuade the Club to relax its restrictions on membership; the Committee was equally determined to die in the last ditch in defence of the Club's exclusiveness." *Ibid.*, 84-85. In 1986 the Sudan Club was till only open to holders of British passports. A. H. Bennett, Secretary, Sudan Club, to P. J. Rich, 27 January 1986. In 1988 the club was bombed, apparently by Libyan-funded terrorists.

48. William Boyd, *An Ice-Cream War*, Hamish Hamilton, 1982, 107.

49. See Morris, *Pax Britannica*, 291. *Cf.* Carritt, *Mole in the Crown*, 84-89. Also Mudford, *Different Plumage*, 155.

50. *Ibid.*

51. Rosie Llewellyn-Jones, "Foreigners in India", *Chowkidar*, British Association for Cemeteries in South Asia, Vol. 4, No. 5, Spring 1987, 79-80.

52. F. R. Cowell, *The Athenaeum: Club and Social Life in London, 1824-1974*, Heinemann, 1975, 61-62.

53. Freya Stark, *East is West*, John Murray, 1945, 91.

54. Emile A. Nakhleh, *Bahrain: Political Development in a Modernizing Society*, D. E. Heath, 1976, 49-50. Nakhleh particularly notes the importance of libraries in Bahrain clubs. *Ibid.*, 57.

55. Jackson, *History of the United Service*, 39. Since Sir William was not a member, presumably he was there as a guest.

56. George Woodbridge, *The Reform Club, 1936-1978: A History From the Club's Records*, The Reform Club, 1978, 99-114, 145. "Books have . . . found their way into many rooms: they stretch from floor to ceiling in the Library, the Morning Room, the Smoking Room, the Committee Room, the Map Room and the small Smoking Room, they occupy space between the ground and first floors and in the attic, they invade almost any place in which a bookcase can be squeezed." *Ibid.*, 99. Matthew Arnold did much of his writing in the Athenaeum library. Lejeune, *Gentlemen' Clubs*, 40. The Reform Club had a role in the making of *The Dictionary of National Biography*. The partners in the original publishing house of Smith, Elder, as well as the editor and numerous contributors, were Reform members. *Ibid.*, 109. ". . . the not

inconsiderable body of members for whom the Library continues to be not only the most beautiful of the Club's rooms but the least expendable." *Ibid.*, 114. See Almeric Fitzroy, *History of the Travellers' Club*, George Allen & Unwin, 1927, 136. "The Garrick Club Library is small but its seven and a half thousand volumes constitute one of the major sources for the study of British theatre history." Hough, *Ace of Clubs*, 147.

57. Thesiger, *Life of My Choice*, 171.

58. A merger was declined by the Royal Asiatic in 1925 because the Central was "political". Stuart Simmonds and Simon Digby, *The Royal Asiatic Society: Its History and Treasures*, E. J. Brill, Leiden, 1979, 23. "Now it has always been difficult to explain exactly what is the difference between the Royal Asiatic Society and the Royal Society for Asian Affairs, but I am reminded of the tale of the Civil Service Commissioner who was asked how on earth he could possibly, by the same process, select candidates for the Home Civil Service and for the Diplomatic Service. Without any hesitation he replied: – 'For the Home Civil Service we look for intelligence.'" Sir Michael Wilford, Chairman's Speech, Annual Dinner, Royal Asiatic Society, 5 February 1987, *Asiatic Affairs*, Vol. XVIII, Part II, June 1987, 244.

59. Forrest, *The Oriental*, 5. The Oriental by-laws stress as a purpose the encouragement of knowledge about the Empire, **but** Forrest adds: "I suspect that this gesture, which was not at all what a club is about, was merely an attempt to keep on . . . terms with the Royal Asiatic." *Ibid.*, 26. Fellows of the Royal Asiatic were eligible for membership in the Oriental. In the 1840s a guinea was added to the subscription to build up the library. *Ibid.*, 105. James Hough wrote *Political and Military Events in British India*, and the preface and dedication are dated from the Oriental. In fact, the club committee had to chide him about taking up too much space with his books. *Ibid.*, 107.

60. Possibly the best discussion of the fluctuating membership requirements of a London club is in Forrest, *Foursome in St. James, passim.*

61. Hugh Robert Mill, *The Record of the Royal Geographical Society, 1830-1930*, Royal Geographical Society, 1930, 95, 96, 101.

62. See Reese, *The History of the Royal Commonwealth Society, passim.*

63. Ian Cameron Macdonald. *To the Farthest East of the Earth: The History of the Geographical Society, 1830-1980*, RGS, 1980, 15. *I, Kensington Gore, Newsletter of the Royal Geographical Society*, Autumn 1987, 4. See A. D. R. Caroe, *The House of the Royal Institution*. The Royal Institution, 1962.

64. Mill, *Royal Geographical Society*, 18, 226.

65. See David Rhind and Jacqui Burgess, "The Characteristics and Views of the RGS Fellowship", *Geographical Journal*, Vol. 155, No. 1, March 1989, 106-12. Recently the RGS membership has been between six thousand and seven thousand. In 1830 the Society had four hundred and sixty members and in 1930, six thousand four hundred. All told, up to 1930, there were approximately twenty thousand members. *Ibid.*, 233. Mill provides a revealing breakdown of the growth, the greatest period of expansion being 1922-1930. *Ibid.*, 234.

66. See *Centenary Review of the Asiatic Society, 1784-1884*, The Asiatic Society, Calcutta, reptd. 1986 (1885), 21-28, 83. Of course, London's Royal Society of Arts dates to 1754.

67. Carlton Mole, "Turf at the Top?", *Tatler*, February 1989, 92.

68. Hill, *Man-Made Culture*, 151.

69. Harold Silver, *Education as History: Interpreting Nineteenth- and Twentieth-Century Education*, Methuen, 1983, 4. See P. J. Rich, review of Barbara Smith's *Truth, Liberty, Religion: Essays Celebrating Two Hundred Years of Manchester College. History of Education Review*, Vol. 18, No. 2, 79.

CHAPTER VIII

Protagonists

History consists not only of facts and events. It also consists of the relationships between facts and events and the interpretation, often imaginative, of such relationships. – Michael Baigent and Richard Leigh, *The Temple and the Lodge,* 1989.

Moths had eaten the punkahs of Heristan and the library had been consumed by a billion hungry worms. When he turned on the taps, snakes oozed out instead of water, and creepers had twined themselves around the four-poster bed in which Viceroys had once slept. – Salman Rushdie, *The Satanic Verses,* 1988.

We may not be colonizers any more. But we can be leaders. It is not the function of a public school to produce underdogs. – Michael Campbell, *Lord Dismiss Us,* 1967.

The reader's contemplation of causality while reading this book has now become itself a causal factor.[1] On that epanorthic note this discussion nears its end, having suggested that the public school was a major contributor to the Imperial ritualism and having postulated that many of the leading Imperial administrators relied on school ritualism when it came to maintain authority.[2] (In fact, the Imperial cadre have been called Arnoldians, a term which somewhat over-emphasizes the contribution of Thomas Arnold to the making of the public school.[3])

The clubs have been discussed as an example of how the public school influence permeated other institutions. Other examples could have been used, notably the regiments and the guilds.[4] The effect on the civil service itself could be further investigated, and the public school influence on the Commons could be more precisely delineated – and there is the related but separate issue of how much the public schools influenced state involvement in education.[5] All of these topics involving the public schools can be fruitfully studied with more than one approach, statistical or psychological or economic.[6]

The historical appraisal of the public schools therefore should undergo a transformation in coming years.[7] This may not be a comfortable process. The application of the insights of psychohistory will put the protagonists of the schools on the defensive. They can derive comfort from the thought that whenever one cause is stressed, the consequence is to distort the importance of others.[8] Few social forces are as hard to understand as the English public school; the quest to understand so complex a movement has sometimes been seen as well nigh hopeless.[9]

186

The everlasting book-making about the schools makes some educationists weary.[10] The fact is that the analysis of the schools will never be contained in a "neat parallelogram".[11] Every so often the prevailing paradigm will have to be broken. Such a course is not *carte blanche* for metaphysical flights of fancy, and here causality has been approached in a fairly pragmatic fashion.[12] That does not exclude the need for a draught of the philosophy of history when approaching the topic.

Indeed, for historians an embarrassing contradiction seems to have arisen, because discussion of causality amongst natural scientists has acquired metaphysical undertones at the same time that a few historians have embraced scientism. An outstanding example of this is Dr. Rupert Sheldrake's *A New Science of Life: The Hypothesis of Formative Causation*, which on its appearance in 1981 started the debate about morphic resonance. Apparently the first effort to relate Dr. Sheldrake's work to a discussion of historical causation was made by Dorothy Emmet in *The Effectiveness of Causes* (1984). She wrote:

> Besides 'energetic causation', the mechanisms of which are increasingly discovered in physics and chemistry, and which are shown in the probabilistic outcomes of exchanges of energy, there is 'formative causation', but which natural systems get their organised patterns ('natural systems' here including atoms, molecules, crystals, as well as living organisms). Sheldrake claims that each system has the organisation it has because others of the same kind had it before, and it is transmitted through a 'morphogenetic field' across space and time from earlier specimens to their successors.[13]

So someone *did* see the implications of morphic resonance for the philosophy of history from the very first, but Emmet's reference is the exception. Sheldrake's is a startling hypothesis that may have profound implications for education.[14] On the other hand morphic resonance could be only a mistaken interpretation of nature's and of history's propensity for pastiche.[15] The evidence that has now accumulated should provoke a re-examination of the place of ritual in education *ab oro us que ad mala.*[16]

Common Denominators and Confusions

In all historic periods there are causes which deserve notice as common denominators. This was decidedly the case of the public schools during the years from the Crimean War through World War II. Sir J. T. Coleridge remarked in 1860:

> To have been together at Eton or Harrow, Winchester or Rubgy, is a spell, the influence of which is felt at any period of life, in any climate, after however long an interval: to have been friends there, is a charm which makes the oldest friendship more holy and tender; even merely to have been

at the same school, though at different times, in the same classroom, and knelt in the same chapel, is a link which binds together old and young, great and humble; which makes strangers at once familiar by common topics and the same associations.[17]

No less an Imperial historian than A. P. Thornton claims that the conduct of the Imperialists was attributable to the schools' imprint – the probity, the loyalty, and the self-respect of the Empire's administrators could be traced to the way that schools inculcated these qualities.[18] Much evidence argues that the public school rhetoric was the rhetoric adopted by the Empire. The influence of adolescence should not be underestimated.[19]

Understanding the history of the schools and of the Empire has been complicated by the obtaining of legitimacy through a ritualism of contrived antiquity. This was a Victorian obsession. It coincided with the 'restoration' of Victorian churches. The Roundheads would have been aghast. (See *Wax Figures of Westminster Abbey*, page 189.) Dr. John Rae remarks, "For most boys' independent schools, the need to establish ancient roots and royal associations is paramount . . . The competition to be the oldest independent school brings out the best in headmasters. I particularly like, Queen Emma, mother of Edward the Confessor, who chose as the place of education of her son the monastic seminary that was to become in later times the – School. The School, therefore, in varying forms, has existed since the refoundation of the monarchy in 970."[20] The persistence of this *Illustrated London News* sort of historiography is confirmed by looking at just a few of the entries in the 1987 edition of the *Independent Schools' Yearbook:*

Abingdon *The first documentary references to Abingdon School are of early medieval date.*

Allhallows *The School is an ancient foundation whose precise origin is obscure.*

Barnard Castle School *The St. John's Hospital in Barnard Castle was founded in the thirteenth century by John Balliol . . .*

Bedford School *is first mentioned in a document of Henry II's reign.*

Bristol Cathedral *The origins of the School are in the Grammar School of St. Augustine's Abbey founded in 1140.*

Christ College Brecon *During the thirteenth century, the Dominicans or Black Friars built a Friary with a Church dedicated to St. Nicholas on the west bank of the River Usk in Brecon.*

Colfe's *In 1652 the Rev Abraham Colfe, Vicar of Lewisham, refounded a grammar school, whose origins are in a Chantry School founded at Lewisham Parish Church in the late fifteenth century.*

Dundee High School *The present School traces its origins directly back to a thirteenth century foundation by the Abbot and Monks of Lindores.*

Durham *It probably has a continuous history from Saxon times.*

A reference to education in the records of a parish church that is near a school can

The wax figures in Westminster Abbey.

be helpful in pushing back a school's history, but none can touch the audacity of King's School Canterbury: *The School is as old as English Christianity.* Emphasis on the past was essential in creating rituals that would seem legitimate, and was not confined to the schools but occurred as well in the clubs and lodges. There was a busy network of ritual-making communities, the liturgies of which can be scoffed at by the critical. Barbara Rogers points out bitingly in *Men Only: An Investigation into Men's Organizations* that

> The Freemasons of today love to claim an unbroken and mystical secret tradition which extends over not just Centuries but millennia. But, as we see with a number of men-only organisations claiming tradition as their own, **the masons of today are more like beneficiaries of a hijack,** in the much more recent past, of someone else's tradition. The organisation and practices of the skilled medieval stonemasons who designed and built the great

Gothic cathedrals of Europe are the pretext for modern 'masonry', not a genuine forerunner.[21]

Fabrication did not take away from the influence of the invented tradition. Michael Baigent and Richard Leigh in *The Temple and the Lodge*, the successor volume to two highly speculative books that touch on Templarism and Masonry, *The Holy Blood and the Holy Grail* and *The Messianic Legacy*, assert that myth-making is an inseparable part of history. New myths precipitate fresh historic development which in turn produces new myths. *Myths are a causal factor* – and the schools were a primary source of the mythology of Imperial society. The claim that mythology and ritual had an effect on Imperialism has been made as well about other political systems. Baigent writes about the United States of America that, "Most of the men responsible for creating it were staunch Freemasons, and the new nation was originally conceived as the ideal hieratic political structure postulated by certain rites of Freemasonry. The state as a whole was seen as an extension, and a macrocosm, of the Lodge."[22] That seems extravagant, but in the case of British Imperialism a persuasive ritualism did enable the upper strata of British society to manipulate the country and the Empire. Much of this ritualism was founded on scant precedent, but perhaps rather than condemn it, it should be considered 'recollective'.

As repeatedly demonstrated, the schools networked with many other ritual-making institutions.[23] Public schoolism became the equivalent for the upper reaches of society of the nonconformist religious enthusiasm of the lower reaches. An EREMITICISM characterizing the schools became a characteristic as well of the gentlemen's clubs, the regimental mess, and the Imperial services. Eventually public schoolism influenced popular culture, as Michael Rosenthal has shown in *The Character Factory: Baden-Powell and the Origins of the Boy Scout Movement*. This popular enthusiasm for what was originally the schools' esotericism did not come about in a year or ten years, but arose gradually during the last half of the nineteenth century at the same time as the lengthening of the educational process.[24] The resulting confusion is well illustrated by a picture of the Prince of Wales at the University of Wales, Bangor, in 1923. He combines the symbolism of academia, the Army, and the Scouts – unsuccessfully. (Page 191.) All three institutions owed something to the public schools.

Meeting a Challenge

The public schools met a challenge laid down by Imperial expansion: "Above all, the young would have to be equipped with symbolic means of acting-out their ambivalences and advancing their mastery of themselves. But where would such symbolism come from?"[25] The schools furnished the needed symbolism and this gave the old boys a considerable head start in life.[26] Still, this is only a **partial** explanation of what the public schools were about. Historians are inclined to stretch a cause to cover an entire problem.[27] Individuals do not act monocausally, and there **is no reason**

to imagine that when prosopographically considered old boys will be found collectively to have acted monocausally.[28]

Decolonization remains incomplete for the large part of the globe that was subject to imperialism,[29] while modern leaders seek the elixir that will produce loyalty to the new nation-states.[30] They need the insights of historians if they expect to achieve political legitimacy.[31] The suggestion that ritual can be consciously planned to confer legitimacy raises questions as to how Imperial ritualism was planned, and as to how much of it was fortuitous:

Edward, Prince of Wales, as Chancellor of the University of Wales, at Bangor, 1923.

How does an animal path in the jungle arise? Some animal may break through the undergrowth to get to a drinking-place. Other animals find it easiest to use the same track. Thus it may be widened and improved by use. It is not planned – it is unintended consequence . . . This is how a path is originally made – perhaps even by men – and how language and any other institutions which are useful may arise . . . the aim-structure of animals or men is not "given", but it develops, with the help of some kind of feedback mechanism, out of earlier aims, and out of results which were or were not aimed at.[32]

In any event, the effects of ritualism suggest why history àpropos the Empire cannot be hermetic,[33] has a contemporary value, and should include consideration of the effects of schooling. In *The Prefects* Rupert Wilkinson acknowledged that:

> . . . British public life at all levels made great use of pomp and circumstance, from the Lord Mayor's Banquet to local processions of town aldermen. For its part the State maintained a whole medley of ceremonial . . . public school authority and the British Constitution alike relied heavily on aesthetic pressures to control the individual. Self-restraint, no less than public duty, was made a matter of 'good form' and backed by etiquette.[34]

Disciplines and Agendas

The public schoolmasters did not monopolize ritual-making.[35] Like Lord Meath's pudding, there were many ingredients. The ritual-makers included numerous composers and writers, clergy and generals. Ritual-making is an essential human function.[36] Moreover, public schools were not inevitably [37] a **conservative** causal influence:

> In fact, much of the criticism of the public schools is based on a childish psychological error – to wit, that the adolescent mind is receptive rather than critical. This is simply untrue. The customary left-wing objections to a preponderance of schoolmasters of the conservative persuasion are therefore foolish. In these matters, the senior boys always take the view diametrically opposed to that of their instructors. To install socialist masters would inevitably result in a nation-wide revival of Conservatism.[38]

Ritual serves both the Left and Right, but no matter where it is employed, it is an essential part of the maintenance of power. It would be unacceptable to remove the distributor cap from an automobile and then maintain that the cap was what made the car operate. Nevertheless, the distributor cap *is* necessary, and the public school leadership helped to shape Imperialism – and its inequalities.[39]

Protagonists

Agendas

A priority should be the study of all the *institutions* that, as Edward Said notes, propagated Imperialism across five continents: "The annals of schools, missions, universities, scholarly societies, hospitals in Asia, Africa, Latin America, Europe and America, fill its pages . . .".[40] Constant comings and goings provided opportunities for an astonishing 'cross-fertilization'. Contrast the inside front cover illustration showing a not untypical visit of a foreign potentate, Sir Pertab Singh, to Haileybury, with the inside back cover illustration of George V as the Prince of Wales visiting an Indian public school, Aligarh College. Throughout the Empire, aspiring natives went through the gymnastics necessary to become old boys – literally at times, as seen in the illustration *Gordon College, Khartoum* that is compared with *P.T. at Sherborne School* in Chapter II.

If the public school influence on the Empire has been ignored by historians, one reason is because the schools revelled in an obscure argot. The references to old boyism as a FREEMASONRY carry a double entendre: ". . . the Old Boy Network has been the country's most powerful freemasonry."[41] Mostly this was solemn business, but some of the British saw the humour to the rituals imposed and to the inherent incongruities of old boyism overseas – John Betjeman, when he was a boy at Marlborough, wrote an essay on the "Dinner of the Old Marlburian Centipede Farmers in Unyamwazi, S.A."

Suggestions for further work in the field may seem particularistic in the light of the strictures in preceding pages about a holistic approach, but instead of worrying about a narrowing of viewpoint that might result, specialized studies should be welcomed as the building blocks of further synthesis.[42] Historians were forced out of the garden a long time ago.

Reference has been made to new ideas effecting causality such as Rupert Sheldrake's **morphic resonances,** Richard Dawkins's **selfish genes,** and Edward Lorenz's **chaos.** Before dismissing the usefulness to historians of such speculations, one should consider still another speculation, the surprisingly lyrical one of a more conventional authority Michael Oakeshott – hardly a romantic:

> The didactic or so-called living 'past' is not significantly past at all. It is the present contents of a vast storehouse into which time continuously empties the lives, the utterances, the achievements and the sufferings of mankind . . . There is no official custodian and the place is in considerable disorder.
>
> From time to time, however, it appears that persons have retired there and have spent many happy hours turning over the lumber it contains . . . some (Herodotus or Geoffrey of Monmouth) have a good eye for interesting or colourful or curious objects and these, disjoined from their circumstances, they have arranged on shelves cleared for the purpose . . . a counter has been set up at the back door where people may come and ask these self-appointed librarians of *legenda* for what they want . . . There are some well-

193

known items which are so often used in the world outside that they may be said to be on permanent loan to the present of practical engagement . . . Caesar crossing the Rubicon, Athanasius at Nicea . . . Colonel Custer making his last stand.

This **vocabulary of symbolic characters** (ill-distinguished from mythical figures and from such images as sturdy oaks, snakes in the grass, and the burdensome albatross) contains emblems of all the virtues, vices and predicaments known to mankind, continuously added to and continuously recalled for use.[43]

Tom Brown is one of the powerful resilient images that is constantly being recalled, an Imperial icon that has not only survived but flourished.[44] The American equivalent, the hero of the Horatio Alger stories, shows the difference between two cultures. To qualify as one of the boys of Horatio Alger's stories, Tom would have had little schooling and only by pluck and marrying the boss's daughter have climbed the ladder to Wall Street. The heroes in English stories go to public school.

There is a dispute over whether icons such as Tom Brown are 'real'. Oakeshott for all his appreciation of them believes in separating the representational figures from those of a 'real' past that remains the proper subject of historical inquiry, claiming that there is a way in which symbol and ritual can be separated from 'fact'. The truth is that the search for the 'real' Kim or the arguments over which Rugby boy was the 'real' Tom Brown are less important than the **consequences** of the symbolic Kims and Tom Browns, which have more reality than flesh-and-blood personalities. It is not Dr. Arnold but Tom Brown that has had the greater impact.

What was at the heart of the public school influence? Dr. Mangan argues that a "chosen medium" of the schools was team games, and that "They were the pre-eminent instrument for the training of a boy's character."[45] This is not a sufficient explanation, and he has in fact moved away from it in recent writings. Schools of other nations had a similar emphasis on sports without exerting the influence of the English public schools – the extravagant American style of football puts the Eton wall game to shame. **The argument of *Elixir, Chains,* and *Rituals* is that the genius of the public school is not *athleticism* but *ritualism*.** Sports in the school and Imperial context were ritualistic exercises.[46]

In and Out

It was mentioned earlier how London's Naval and Military Club was nicknamed the "In and Out." (See *"In and Out"*, page 195.) The designation originated with the club's famous gate signs directing traffic, but suggests something more significant. "In and Out" can describe a view held by many of the educational process, but ". . . the input-output approach does not give sufficient attention to the impact of schooling itself."[47] The arms that Rajkumar College, an Indian public school, adopted in 1882, reflect a similar 'in and out' idea. (See *Rajkumar College Arms*, page 195.) As a description

"In and Out", *The Naval and Military Club.*

of what the public schools did, 'in and out' is glib. The schools have to be studied not only as the places where the Imperial mythology was temporarily nurtured before boys went out into the world, but as a *continuing* influence.[48] A reinterpretation of Imperialism acknowledges the ideological influence of these remarkable institutions in the Empire, and of the ways in which the school's emphasis on ritual helped to shape Victorian and Edwardian minds.

Gratifyingly, in discussing of morphic resonance, Dr. Sheldrake does refer at length to ritualism.[49] He has asked recently in *The Guardian*, "If places of power have spirits, then what are they?" He claims that even in a 'new' country such as the United States that the influence is apparent of esoteric traditions of antiquity – some rooted in

Rajkumar College arms.

195

pharonic Egypt and which he asserts "through the Freemasons have had such an influence on the symbolism of the United States."[50]

Imperial and educational studies offer handsome prospects,[51] but the exuberance of employing new approaches could mean that coherence will disappear in the sands of premature revisionism.[52] Prosopography is a good referee. It keeps speculation in bounds. A steady course should be maintained with hopes of deciphering more about how the West achieved its total hegemony. This requires open minds: ". . . it is possible that human behaviour, at least, might not be explicable entirely in physical terms, even in principle."[53] History is a curious pursuit with many actors. (See *God save the Queen!!*, below.)

A call for an open-ended approach is an appropriate place to finish this account, adding a warning that history is **not** about to become a science – but that historians should not be unscientific. No matter how much they may wish, ". . . there is a difference, and we all know there is a difference."[54] There is no way that the past can be repeated to test out observations. The subjective rules. As demonstrated, prosopography is not "scientific history", because it never can cast a wide enough net. However, although history has not become more of a science, science has become less scientific. The tidy-minded will find this exasperating, but those who enjoy riposte will welcome the opportunities.[55] Even with a specialized topic such as the history of the English public schools, the expansion of social history into strange areas creates plenty of creative controversy: "Poke your finger into that hornet's nest of a topic, the public school, and the air is at once full of the wings and stings of the enemies of change and the angry buzzings of outraged nitwits."[56] That was never more true, nor was the subject more exciting.[57]

"God Save The Queen!!"

196

1 W. H. G. Armytage, *Yesterday's Tomorrows: A Historical Survey of Future Societies*, Routledge & Kegan Paul, 1968, 5. See Fischer, *Historians' Fallacies*, 174-75. Also Deborah A. Stone, "Causal Stories and the Formation of Policy Agendas", *Political Science Quarterly*, Vol. 24, No. 2, Summer 1989, 281-300.

2. Philip Mason, *A Thread of Silk: Further Memories of a Varied Life*, Michael Rossall, 1984, 115. Recalled is Wittgenstein's story about the man who, to check a newspaper's veracity, bought a second copy of the same edition. Elliott Sober, "Independent Evidence About a Common Cause", *Philosophy of Science*, Vol. 56, No. 2, June 1989, 275.

3. ". . . somewhat arrogant and somewhat shy, very conscious of their standing as gentlemen but very conscious of their duties too . . . **these are the Arnoldians.**" G. M. Young, *Victorian England*, OUP, 1953, 71.

4. See the discussion in *Rituals of Empire*.

5. See, *e.g.* P. W. J. Bartrip, "State Intervention in Mid-nineteenth Century Britain: Fact or Fiction?", *Journal of British Studies*, Vol. XXIII, No. 1, Fall 1983, 63-83. Consider Himmelfarb, *The New History and the Old*, 16.

6. A number of the 'new' approaches will be discussed in the last book of this trilogy, *Rituals of Empire*.

7. See the discussion in the Bibliographical Essay. Public school historians have not yet come to terms with the new pluralities of historiography. *Cf.* John S. Dryzek and Stephen T. Leonard, "History and Discipline in Political Science", *American Political Science Review*, Vol. 82, No. 4, 1245-1260.

8. J. G. Merquior, "Philosophy of History: Thoughts on a Possible Revival", *History of the Human Sciences*, Vol. 1, No. 1, 24.

9. Stanford University's Carolyn C. Lougee writes: "Whereas historical study had traditionally sought to identify chains of causation in human history . . . (the) new definition of history largely eschews the search for causation . . .". "Social History and the Introductory European Course", *Perspectives*, Vol. 24, No. 6, September 1986, 14. She contends that it is impossible to determine "why" people think in a particular way, and concludes that the best that can be hoped for is to describe the *Zusammenghang* (inter-connections) – and **not** pontificate about the suspected reasons.

10. "However voracious the historian's appetite for vicarious experience", wrote J. H. Grainger, "the activity of the British Empire will glut it." *Patriotisms*, 124.

11. See Peter Berger, Brigitte Berger, and Hansfried Kellner, *The Homeless Mind: Modernization and Consciousness*, Viking, 1973, 10.

12. There seems to be no question about the propriety of seeking cause-effect relationships about an accident that dents the fender of an automobile, but inquiry become suspect when applied to education.

13. p. 99.

14. Stephen R. L. Clark, "A Matter of Habit?", *Times Literary Supplement*, 24-30 June 1988, 702.

15. *Ibid.*

16. See Emmet, *Effectiveness of Causes*, 110.

17. Lecture at the Tiverton Athenaeum, qtd. Vincent Alan McClelland ed., *Private and Independent Education*, "Aspects of Education", *Journal of The Institute of Education*, The University of Hull, No. 35, 1986, 1.

18. A. P. Thornton, *Doctrines of Imperialism*, John Wiley & Sons, New York, 1965, 171. "Men stamped in any of these moulds though it the most obvious and natural thing in the world to pass on their view of the world and its ways entire to the coming generation . . . the ideals and then idols may still throw their shadows far: and so too, very often, do the books which embalm for ever the atmosphere that so kindled the imaginations of the age that had gone. Certainly the works of John Buchan and G. A. Henty were to stand in an honoured place on the shelves of all three generations." Thornton, *Imperial Idea and Its Enemies*, 92. The suggestion also has been made that when the entrepreneurial class was emerging in Victorian England it sought to reject the public school "as an impractical industrialization was simply too strong for the entrepreneurs to be able to resist the aristocratic bias of the new education." Armstrong, *Elites*, 145.

19. ". . . an ingenious theory suggests that the change from ape to man consisted essentially in **neoteny**, which is the reaching of sexual maturity of a larval form. Man is, as it were, a foetal ape, just as the Mexican axolotl is a sexually mature tadpole." Young, *Philosophy and the Brain*, 200. If indeed "We

achieve manhood by never reaching apehood", then adolescence is maturity. "I wonder however whether Rich is not, to some extent, contributing to the myth of public schoolism, conceding to the schools some of that mystery which they strived after . . .". Robin Healey, reviewing *Elixir, Gulf Times,* 22 September 1989, 15.

20. *Letters From School,* 218. For Marxists enjoying Dickensian drag, see Max Egelnick, "The Clerkenwell Festival", *Bulletin of the Marx Memorial Library,* No. 109, Summer 1987, 20.

21. Rogers, *Men Only,* 75.

22. Baigent, *Messianic Legacy,* 255. *Cf.* Rogers, *Men Only,* 134.

23. *E.g.,* "A member of the City of London Corporation, Frederick Clearey, insisted that the Lodge he belonged to, his old school's, 'engenders a very fine spirit, cementing members of the Lodge with the school . . .'". Ibid., 94. Contributing to this murky affection was the way the old boys saw themselves mystically as members of a lifelong corporate community, producing a fervour exceeding that displayed by the alumni of schools in other countries. See Marianne Doerfel, "British Pupils in a German Boarding School: Neuwied Rhine 1820-1913", *British Journal of Educational Studies,* Vol. XXXIV, No. 1, February 1986, 92-93. This idea of 'mystic ties' bolstered the schools' influence in *loco republicae* as well as in *loco parentis.* Anthony Kerr, *Schools of Europe,* Bowes & Bowes, 1960, 219.

24. Berger, *Homeless Mind,* 192. The attribution to the schools of all manner of virtues became self-fulfilling prophecy. See Frode S. Vartdal, "The Covert Behavior of Attributing", *Behaviorism,* Vol. 16, No. 2, Fall 1988, 167-73.

25. C. R. Badcock, *The Psychoanalysis of Culture,* Basil Blackwell, Oxford, 1980, 251.

26. "Psychoanalysts, for example, are coming to realize that a degree of preparation for the contingencies of adult life is decidedly advantageous. The repeated use of certain rituals, both religious and secular, encourages psychological integration, mental stability and social responsibility, while exercising a binding factor . . .". Mary Hope, *The Psychology of Ritual,* Element Books, Shaftesbury (England), 1988, 31.

27. There is not much to be said in favour of monocausality, deliberate or slothful. "The long progression in our self-understanding has been from a simple and usually 'intellectual' view to the view that the mind is a mixed structure, for it contains a complex set of 'talents', 'modules', and 'policies' within." Ornstein, *Multimind,* 9. It is worth considering in this regard the implications of Ornstein's remark that "We are not a single person. We are many." *Ibid.* See W. Stark, *The Sociology of Knowledge: An Essay in Aid of a Deeper Understanding of the History of Ideas,* Routledge & Kegan Paul, 1971, 236-37.

28. An interest in the wide range of influences does not preclude a grasp of the concrete. Nor does an interest in social history preclude considering geopolitical themes.

29. See Karen A. Mingst, "The Ivory Coast at the Semi-Periphery of the World-Economy", *International Studies Quarterly,* Vol. 32, No. 3, September 1988, 259.

30. "The design of mess halls, the forms of compensation, the number of marching bands, housing policy, and recruiting policies also affect cohesion. The orientation of the officers corps and . . . (its) policies are, however, intervening variables. They are both cause and effect. **If military officials are to influence cohesion systematically, they must understand the antecedent causative variables that underlie these intervening variables.** Our research leads us to believe that those antecedent causative variables are poorly understood." Johns, *Cohesion,* 3.

31. "Before they came to India their ideals had already been fixed by the environment they had been brought up in, especially the environment of the public schools." Bernard Porter, *The Lion's Share: A Short History of British Imperialism, 1850-1983,* 2nd ed., Longman, 1984, 44. However, ". . . fortunately, there is more to the spirit of Britain than Britannia." Rupert Sheldrake, "Myth Taken", *The Guardian,* 10 February 1988.

32. Bryan Magee, *Popper,* Fontana Press, 1982, 59.

33. "While the motivating benefits of specialization may be better communications and exchange within a narrow community of research scholars, the benefits of unification, in the pragmatic sense, are the opportunities for holistic planning at levels that retain linkages to the broader realm of knowledge." Michael F. Goodchild and Donald G. Janelle, "Specialization in the Structure and Organization of Geography", *Annals of the Association of American Geographers,* Vol. 78, No. 1, March 1988, 5.

34. p. 59.

35. Durkheim's "obsessive" use of the idea of "representations" is an indication of how ubiquitous he felt

the ritual-making process was: "For him, social life is made possible by a vast symbolism that includes all kinds of representations. When Durkheim praised Saint-Simon as the rightful founder of sociology – in contradistinction to Comte, whom he dethrones – it was on the grounds that Saint-Simon was the first to claim that the social system is a system of ideas. His followers were just as obsessive in this regard. For example, Robert Hertz approached right- and left-handedness, even death itself, not as brute facts, but as collective representations. Mauss approached the phenomenon of voodoo death from the perspective of magical representations, and so on." G. Mestrovic, "The Social World as Will and Idea: Schopenhauer's Influence Upon Durkheim's Thought", *The Sociological Review*, Vol. 36, No. 4, November 1988, 684. Representations in a Durkheimian sense have much in common with rituals. See *Ibid.*, 686-87.

36. ". . . it is reasonable to suggest that as our personal interchanges involve symbolic use of words so we find satisfaction in the symbolic gathering together and exchanging of well-known symbols in singing, music or dance, or even simply in talk. The ramifications of public symbolizing are endless, extending throughout religion, politics, law, warfare and the whole of social life." Young, *Philosophy and the Brain*, 204.

37. See David Owens, "Causes and Coincidences", *Proceedings of the Aristotelian Society*, Vol. XC, Part 1, 1989/90, 49-64.

38. Edward Crispin (Bruce Montgomery), *Love Lies Bleeding*, Century Hutchinson, 1988 (1948), 78.

39. "The intractability of educational inequalities has lent weight to theories of social reproduction. In this view, the education system both reflects and contributes to existing class relations and inequalities . . . inequalities in educational attainments both emerge from and perpetuate those broader inequalities within class societies or which they are a part." Brian Graetz, "The Reproduction of Privilege in Australian Education", *British Journal of Sociology*, Vol. XXXIX, No. 3, September 1988, 360. See Thomas Nagel, "Freedom Within Bounds", *Times Literary Supplement*, 22 February 1990, 169.

40. Edward Said, *Nationalism, Colonialism and Literature: Yeats and Decolonization*, Field Day, 1988, 9.

41. Peter Parker, *The Old Lie: The Great War and the Public-School Ethos*, Constable, 1987, 43. Because the topic involves both a figurative and literal Freemasonry, it is a difficult subject to approach in an objective or empirical fashion. It involves emotions and 'mind-stuff' and prejudices as well as the 'facts' of history. For opponents, "Captain Smith lost the battle for lack of guns" is insufficient. The axe to be ground requires "Captain Smith lost the battle because of a failure of the public schools to produce industrialists." For the proponents, Captain Smith undoubtedly died heroically, a credit to the school. *Cf.* Foster Bailey, *The Spirit of Masonry*, Lucis Press, 1957, 21-22.

42. Kertzer, *Ritual, Politics, and Power*, 173-74.

43. Oakeshott, *On History*, 39-41.

44. Mangan, *Games Ethic*, 133, 155, 159.

45. *Ibid.*, 18.

46. A point agreed upon by Dr. J. A. Mangan in his *Times Higher Education Supplement* review of *Elixir*, 13 April 1990, 22. See Sattin, *Lifting the Veil*, 271.

47. Tony Bilton, *et al, Introductory Sociology*, 2nd ed., Macmillan, 1987, 335.

48. See Peter Medawar, *Memoir of a Thinking Radish: An Autobiography*, OUP, 1986, 28. For an American perspective on the continuing interplay of influences, see John E. Chubb and Terry M. Moe, "Politics, Markets, and the Organization of Schools", *American Political Science Review*, Vol. 82, No. 4, December 1988, 1065-1086.

49. This author's doctoral dissertation related morphic resonance to the rituals of British rule in the Middle East. Dr. Sheldrake has been good enough to remark that this is the first application in English of his hypothesis to historical research. Rupert Sheldrake to P. J. Rich, 4 November 1988.

50. Rupert Sheldrake, "The Seats of Power", *The Guardian*, 1 June 1988. He is surely on the right track.

51. "As the researcher's curiosity roves further and further, huge dormant areas of documentation are revealed." François Furet, *In the Worship of History*, University of Chicago Press, 1982, 45.

52. See Christopher Hill's reply to J. H. Hexter's criticisms in *Times Literary Supplement*, 7 November 1975. Still another danger is that what was experimental becomes enshrined as holy writ. See Michael Billington, "A Satire on Post-Freudian Biographers", review of Alan Bennett's play *Kafka's Dick*, *International Herald Tribune*, 1 October 1986, 7.

53. Sheldrake, *A New Science of Life*, 29-30.

54. Arthur Marwick, *The Nature of History*, 2nd ed., Macmillan, 1985, 101.

55. "No theory has so far succeeded in explaining the distribution of political ideologies, systems and forces on our planet. No one knows why certain regions of the world are dominated by liberal doctrines, others by social democracy or Catholicism." Todd, *Explanations of Ideology*, 1. ". . . the great illusion of revolutionary philosophy, the belief that politics shape society and not the reverse." *Ibid*, 11. "I do believe historians could profitably follow up Dr. Rich's lead and look more closely at who were – and who were not – Freemansons in the Colonial Service." A. H. M. Kirk-Greene, reviewer of *Elixir of Empire*, *Overseas Pensioner*, April, 1990, 39.

56. William Plomer, "The Gothic Arch", Greene ed., *The Old School*, 111.

57. "Equations for each of us, equations for the development of all kinds of animals and plants that were already somehow there in advance, before there was even a universe. That's the conventional assumption. By contrast, I think it is better to think of these fields as having a historical basis, depending on what happened before - containing a kind of memory, representing a kind of habit principle in nature." Rupert Sheldrake, "Cause and Effect in Science: A Fresh Look", *Noetic Sciences Review*, No. 11, Summer 1989, 15. *Felix qui potuit rerum cognoscere causas.*

EPILOGUE: *Floreat Etona?*

In explanations of the great historical movements – among them, European state formation and imperialism – realpolitik still takes precedence over ritual, material forces over the moral suasion of the sign. – Jean and John Cormaroff, *Through the Looking-Glass: Colonial Encounters of the First Kind*, 1988.

This has been an extraordinary year for me personally in that the Board decided we should review the possibility of opening up new markets for the school. Since September I have been in Thailand, Malaysia, Singapore, Hong Kong, Japan and Saudi Arabia. . . I am pleased to report that these ventures have been successful and we now have in Morrison's students from each of these places, with the possibility of more in the future. – The Rector of Morrison Academy, *Morrisonian Club Annual Report, 1989.*

I would like all policymakers, politicians, and teachers, before they support or approve any approach or curriculum, to consider if it is one they would choose for their own children . . . When they are "our children" we assume that they must be pushed and pulled until they get where we want them to go. To make other assumptions for other people's children, to do less for "those kids" as opposed to our kids seems, at the very least, immoral. – Barbara Pollard. *Those Kids – and Ours*, 1989.

The story of the British Empire is incomplete without reference to the public schools. (See *Welcoming the Raj*, page 202. *The Gem*, 20 June 1936. and *'The Cane'*, page 202. *The Magnet*, 13 August 1938.) But if schools are ordained to have social consequences, by no means does an emphasis on the public school mean that a case cannot be made for other factors.[1] In crowding many ideas into a few pages there is some consolation in Arthur Lovejoy's remark in *The Great Chain of Being*, that "The history of ideas is . . . no subject for highly departmentalized minds". With the growth of interest in chaotic, or non-linear studies, the pursuit of multiple causes gains additional respectability.

There certainly are enough problems looking for solutions. Had Thomas Arnold lived to serve for any number of years in the chair of modern history at Oxford which he briefly occupied, there might have been a Rugbeian answer to some of the conundrums of historiography that have been disscussed. Arnold's interest in Vico suggests a more than passing interest in causality. He was also, like so many Victorians, interested in biography. In an article "First Person Past" in *The Times Education Supplement* (7 July 1989), Richard Aldrich and Peter Gordon accuse

Welcoming the Raj.

The Cane.

historians of education of emphasizing the impersonal dimensions of education and neglecting the biographical approach:

> At first sight a biographical approach to education and its history might seem to be reactionary, a turning away from the sociological, quantitative, anthropological and other perspectives which have enhanced the study of the subject in recent years. But it is precisely the careful incorporation of such perspectives into the biographical approach, careful in the sense that the essential humanity of the subject is not lost, which can serve to revitalize it, and to bring it to the attention of a wide public.

What is also needed is a prudent choice of issues. The principal issue facing education today is of equality *vs.* quality. This is a good argument for public school studies. As state schools 'opt-out' in England during the 1990s to become independent, the public schools will present an attractive rôle model. But 'opt-outs' should consider the possible defective consequences. The 'opt-out' schools seem inclined to embrace the ways of the public schools. Audenshaw High School Manchester, one of the first to take the independent route, immediately hired Goodman's to do its catering, the same firm that caters for Eton and Rugby. Puddings are served regularly.

Old Victorians

No matter how lengthy, descriptions of so rich a topic as the schools and Imperialism will resemble a *son et lumière* rather than a floodlighting, and be more Heraclitean than Parmenidean. About the importance of the history of education *vis-à-vis* the body politic there is no doubt. Consideration of élite education has current and international significance. Although there has not been a full length study of the influence of the English public schools on American education, evidence points to the New England private schools looking to English models. This takes on added relevance because in the United States the 'bright flight' is accelerating from state schools into the expanding private ones, with parents seeking an atmosphere that they do not find in the government-sponsored schools. Venerable American private schools like Exeter and Andover are being joined by large numbers of new schools. If the American Congress were to pass a tuition voucher or tax credit plan, the exodus would be even more pronounced. Similar issues exacerbate the educational scene in such different places as Australia and Arabia.

As for Britain, the public school continues to confer a cachet. It will be recalled that when the purchase by the Al Fayed brothers of Harrod's became an issue in the late 1980s, an issue was whether the Al Fayeds were Old Victorians, *i.e.* had attended the posh Victoria College in Cairo. As *The Times* explained, if the Al Fayeds were O.V.s, their right to own an Establishment institution seemed less contestable. Two detectives from Scotland Yard were despatched to Egypt to interview the hapless Mr.

Armand Khalil, secretary of the old boys' association, about the Al Fayeds.

The schools are as much a factor now as they were decades ago, and that applies to their continuing importance in former parts of the Empire as well as in Britain. When *The Independent* interviewed the education spokesmen of the Conservative, Labour and Alliance parties, it ended up with the reminiscences of three old boys rather than with opinions on Froebel or Dewey. A Pauline for the Conservatives recalled how gifted his teachers were at St. Paul's. A Wykehamist for Labour explained that his father had been in the Indian Civil Service (as if that automatically explained going to a public school) and allowed that he dreamed about Winchester. Probably thinking about the voters, he protested that he had been a rebel, wearing "very brief, light blue French shorts" for running. Paddy Ashdown, the Alliance shadow education secretary, looked back on Bedford as a "colonial/military school that you would have expected to service the Empire." Although the story ran in 1987, it could have been written in 1937. The Labourite tried to defuse the issue of socialist policy being overseen by a Wykehamist by lamely remarking: **"I have had people say to me you are the only normal Wykenhamist we have ever met."**

John Thorn, a former headmaster of Repton and Winchester, remarked in his autobiography that "The old-style public school had justified itself in the courage its ex-pupils showed in many wars and in the administrative skills they brought to the old empire. In a world without many wars of that kind and in a Britain without an empire, a new justification was required for their strange institutional ways." Indeed. Promoting a re-designation as "independent schools" has not made public schools independent of public opinion. Their fortunes have soared as Thatcherism has carried the day, but they are dangerously allied with one party. Despite their strength, they remain dependent on a tenuous causal chain, relying on the newly wealthy who wish to convert money into social capital. An editorial in the 1988 *Radleian* fretted about the school's prosperous condition in comparison with the facilities of state schools:

> Is the college still living up to its original ethos – to educate boys to become Christian gentlemen and scholars, aware of aesthetic values in an increasingly materialistic society? This would seem unlikely in the atmosphere of ostentation and in some cases apparently unnecessary indulgence which some detect in the school's policy of refurbishment and in its acquisition of classroom paraphernalia.

The boys' concern is one that the public school leadership should be showing. Discussion about the schools' future at H.M.C. meetings should not become bogged down in civilized minutiae. The facile proponents of the schools who enjoy running with the hares while hunting with the hounds are doing the cause no good. Dr. John Rae is an example. His mildly liberal defence of the status quo masks a predestinarianism worthy of any Calvinist. Now he apparently has decided to capture press attention by hair-raising statements about abolishing the schools altogether, though what the parents whom he persuaded to send sons to Westminster when he was headmaster think of *that* is unreported. The ambiguities of equality and quality have remained unsolved while men have gone to the moon and sent probes beyond the solar system. Antonio Gramsci, who had impeccably radical credentials, wanted to substitute one kind of élite education of another by excluding the "rich but stupid" and recruiting those with aptitude. That is a more creditable suggestion than polemics against privilege which advocate destroying the Etons and Harrows out of spite – but make no mistake, a prime issue remains equality and must be addressed. In *The Sunday Times* (3 September 1989) Edward Peace convincingly argued for selection solely on the basis of ability:

> It would cost several hundred million pounds, but it would be money spent to great purpose. Imagine it: Marlborough and Uppingham, Eton and Stowe, as grand lycées upholding their own standards and serving the whole nation, thus independent but not a preserve of wealth, leading the comprehensive by example . . . what I have in mind is a galaxy of direct grant schools available to anyone talented and motivated enough to meet their standards. It is a truly radical proposal, but with executive courage it could be done.

This is too important a subject to be approached with narrow attitudes. The historian Charles A. Beard cautioned: "To borrow from Croce, when grand philosophy is ostentatiously put out at the front door of the mind, then narrow, class, provincial and regional prejudices come in at the back door and dominate, perhaps only half-consciously, the thinking of the historian."[2] The debate over the public schools has a parallel in the computing world, where the divisions in people's minds between micro and macro computing do more harm than good. So do some of the distinctions elaborated in historical work on the schools. This has been accentuated largely because conservative **historicalism** (in contrast with **historicism,** which after Popper nobody wants to be accused of practising) has tried to "ring in the wagons", repopularizing an arcane particularism that resembles nineteenth-century antiquarianism in drag. In the case of the history of the public schools, it is time for a new paradigm.[3] An attempt has been made here, but neither daytime nor night-time astronomers grasp the entire picture.

Sons of Chronos

Notwithstanding the faults of the public schools, one suspects that if Chronos had had a son, he would have sent him to one. As a lifelong socialist friend of mine (and fellow Old Tonbridgian) remarked, "It's too damned bad they are such damned good schools." Appropriately after the Suez debacle in 1956, the Egyptians did not close Victoria College, "perhaps Britain's most important contribution to Egyptian education."[4] New signs read *Victory* College, but the old boys remained Old Victorians.

The public schools have a keen sense of self-preservation. The Common Market and 1992 hold no fears for them. The members of the Boarding School Association were told by their chairman, Colin Reid, at the May 1989 meeting:

> The single market and all that it betokens could be as influential in shaping the future of our boarding schools as that great expansion of the British Empire which determined what was required of them in the late nineteenth century. Young Germans and Hollanders will arrive by the trainload to learn the *lingua franca* of the new Europe as the natives speak it. The schools that cater for this demand could find themselves with a role potential more exciting than when they educated the men who ruled India.[5]

Young Germans and Hollanders will find that the public schools still manipulate emotions and channel energies into ceremonials. Ritualism was a major part of the Imperial story, and continues to be part of the story of British education. *There is no political life without rituals.* Without belabouring this, the reader should consider the chilling custom of placing Masonic insignia on the reverse of the royal coats of arms that adorned Imperial courtrooms. Displayed on one side was the familiar symbolism of the Empire, but on the concealed side was the more enigmatic emblem of Masonry. (The arms that adorned the Supreme Court in Perth, Western Australia in the last part of the nineteenth century are an illustration.) **The images that ritual sustains have a causal role in determining the behaviour of society.** Malcolm Muggeridge writes:

> I like very much the notion of Pascal that people in authority need to dress up in order to justify their position of eminence. "If judges didn't wear ermine," Pascal said, "who could possibly suppose that they were capable of dispensing true justice?" We could say the same of priests in their vestments, scholars in their gowns, admirals in their gold braid and generals with their red tabs, kings and queens with their crowns and their orbs, and chefs with their tall white hats. In the same sort of way, clowns have to paint their faces in order that people may know they are being funny. **Authority, in other words, requires an image.**[6]

Public school ritualism takes on special interest as a causal explanation of how British social structures are perpetuated. Not understanding the importance of ritualism has contributed to the recent difficulties in state education:

> . . . the real issues were so smudged that it was possible for Harold Wilson to talk about 'grammar school education for all'. Poor Harold has been much mocked for this remark, but already by 1973 there were comprehensive schools up and down the country which judged their own success by grammar school standards. They set out to beat the grammar schools at their own game (sometimes rugby union!). They adopted a

Graffiti in Eton classroom.

uniform, they streamed their pupils into at least a tripartite pattern, and often more divisively, they established prefect systems, they retained corporal punishment and they glorified academic success by publishing their examination results in the local press and by holding speech days at which the graduates on the staff wore gowns.[7]

The grammar schools, which had extensively copied public school rituals, were equally unfortunate also-rans. They have all but vanished from the scene. (Perhaps they will reappear in the 1990s as grant-maintained schools.) The misfortunes of working class education in England demonstrate that Macnaghten's proclamation as an Old Etonian of "my absolute adherence to, and belief in, her education and doctrines" was no vain boast. The devotion has continued, the ecclesial apparatus has been enduring, and the consequences for the competition continue to be profound. (See *Graffiti in Eton Classroom,* page 207.) The troubles with secondary education owed much to confused Labour Party policies, but the return of the Conservatives in 1979 brought no relief. A revolutionary outlook was hardly to be expected. Of three hundred and thirty-nine Tory MPs in the new parliament, fifty-one had attended Eton.[8] Public school old boys continue to be the overwhelming majority of bishops, army officers of the rank of major general or above, judges, company directors, and permanent secretaries in the civil service.[9] The staying-power of the public school influence has been extraordinary. A secret agent in Agatha Christie's thriller *They Came to Baghdad* identifies himself by clicking prayer beads to spell out in Morse *Floreat Etona.* In less dramatic but equally effective ways, the old boys have continued to make themselves known and obeyed in modern Britain. So it is fair that they be scrutinised.

Sir Evelyn Wrench remarked, "Eton understood how to turn ordinary little Britons into Etonians first. England for me became a country inhabited by Etonians and their families and the unfortunate remainder of the population. I signed a letter home 'I am your very loving son Evelyn Wrench, belonging to the greatest and best of schools. *Floreat Etona.* Poor Harrovians, how I pitied them!'"[10] Too bad, of course, for the 'unfortunate remainder'. Someone who enjoyed school far less, the Nigerian writer Dillibe Onyeama, describes his last term in the melancholy book *Nigger at Eton:* "It was as if I knew I was leaving Heaven for good and didn't care."[11] Yet in a way, he admitted, nobody *ever* left.

> *And nothing in life shall sever*
> *The chain that is round us now.*

NOTES – EPILOGUE

1. See Charles A. Beard, "Written History as an Act of Faith", *American Historical Review*, Vol. XXXIX, 27. ". . . scholarship has never been as factionalized and polarized as it is today." Gertrude Himmelfarb, "Social History and Moral Imagination", R. S. Neale ed., *History and Class: Essential Readings in Theory and Interpretation*, Basil Blackwell, Oxford, 1983, 248.

2. Beard, "Written History". See P. J. Rich, review of Jeffrey Richards, *Happiest Days: The Public Schools in English Fiction, History of Education Review*, Vol. 18, No. 12, 79-80.

3. See Himmelfarb, "Social History", 249.

4. Sattin, *Lifting the Veil*, 276.

5. David Tyler, "Boarding Schools Prepare for 1992 Influx", *The Times*, 3 May 1989, 5. "Foreign impressions of England itself might often begin with this single institution." Ruth Dodson, "The Essentially English School." *Ambassador International*, Summer 1989, 60. *Cf.* David Thomas, "Public Schools Attract a New Class of Customers", *Financial Times*, 9 December 1989, 6.

6. Malcolm Muggeridge, *A Twentieth Century Testimony*, Collins, 1979, 38. *Cf.* Kertzer, *Ritual, Politics, and Power*, 181. *Cf.* Stephen Haseler, "How a Nation Has Slipped Into Its Dotage", *The Sunday Times*, 25 February 1990, C6.

7. Robert Spooner, "Secondary Schools", Max Morris and Clive Griggs eds., *Education – The Wasted Years? 1973-1986*, Falmer Press, 1988, 74. See Michael Fielding, "Liberté, Egalité, Fraternité, ou la mort: towards a new paradigm for the comprehensive school", Clyde Chitty ed., *Redefining the Comprehensive Experience*, Institute of Education, University of London, 1987, 50-67.

8. Clive Griggs, "Fee-paying Education: The Favoured Sector", Morris and Griggs eds., *Education – The Wasted Years?*, 188.

9. *Ibid.*

10. John Evelyn Wrench, *Uphill: The First Stage in a Strenuous Life*, Ivor Nicholson & Watson, 1934, 25.

11. Dillibe Onyeama, *Nigger at Eton*, Leslie Frewin, 1972, 239.

BIBLIOGRAPHICAL ESSAY

There have been a number of bibliographies of the public schools, although none have been published as a separate volume. A good early one is to be found in the 1924 *Public Schools Book.* A useful work is Phyllis M. Jacobs' *Registry of Universities, Colleges and Schools of Great Britain and Ireland* (Athlone Press, 1967). The lack of a full length bibliography of the schools can be accounted for partly by the way in which bibliography is regarded only as an auxiliary discipline, drudgery done for others. Actually, a full bibliographical study of the public school literature would itself be creative, as there are titles which have been missed by **all** the authors in the field.

The most promising potential bibliographer of the schools may have been a gentleman who was instrumental in the founding of the Bibliography Society in 1892. He was Talbot Baines Reed, a typefounder who wrote both *The Old English Letter Foundries* and popular school stories such as *The Fifth Form at St. Dominic's.* Had Reed not died in 1893, an account of work done on public school bibliography might be longer and more distinguished. The interest of those actually working in the school libraries in bibliography evidences itself intermittently: the Eton College library joined the society in 1898. There is no guide to the libraries of public schools, although some are extensive.

So an up-to-date bibliographical examination of the school literature is needed. Dr. Mack's outstanding two volumes, good as they are, have strange omissions – such as the *Taunton Report.* A lack which has become more apparent with the passage of time was of material about overseas schools or which was published overseas, of which *Sketchy Memories* is an example. Much of the 'missing' public school bibliography falls into the overseas category. Also, Mack and other historians are more comfortable with journals and organizations that reflect their own proclivities. In London, I prefer the splendour of the Society of Antiquaries to the squalour of the Marx library. I quote more from the *Journal of the Writing Equipment Society* than from the more plebian *Pencil Collector.* One gets the impression that old boys are more likely to be collectors of writing equipment than pencil collector. (However, see the discussion of Conrad Gessner as a pencil pioneer in *The Pencil Collector,* Vol. XXXII, No. 3, March 1988.)

At the very least, a bibliography of extant school lists is in order and would serve general historians. As long ago as 1905, R. A. Austen Leigh wrote to the *Saturday Review* (2 September 1905) to complain about the failure to collate and transcribe material that might have survived in the "archives of country houses" or had been "written by the boys themselves and sent home for the edification of their parents". A

British Museum – additional library.

useful survey to update and improve the bibliography of Dr. Mack's two volumes would start with an outstanding general collection such as Oxford's or Cambridge's, but would include the libraries of individual public schools as well as a search of past booktrade catalogues. A list of manuscript holdings, particularly of papers of headmasters and assistant masters, is another priority.

There are many unanswered questions about public school bibliography. For example, just how extensive are the holdings about the schools of the city companies that have been associated with the schools? A study of public school librarians as a group and of the development under their leadership of public school libraries would be invaluable. A prosopographical investigation of the early members of antiquarian publishing consortiums might produce interesting results as far as the schools attended by the founders are concerned.

A neglected area of public school studies is that of the Victorian periodical press. It has become clear that the number (at least twenty-five thousand) and the variety of Victorian magazines is far more than has been commonly realized: "But the emerging need for a more general study of the press is part of the same historiographical development that calls us to the more general study of Victorian life, to the recognition of a great many more or less hidden lives which have until recently escaped the close attention of the historian and the litterateur." (Joanne Shattock and Michael Wolff, ed., "Introduction", *The Victorian Press: Samplings and Soundings,* Leicester University Press, 1982, xiv.) How many headmasters and assistant masters contributed to the journals? Here is another prosopographical category.

The Society for the Study of Victorian Periodicals provides a meeting ground for all scholars of the period. Attention should also be called to several other useful organizations: *The Association for the Bibliography of History, the Society for Educational Biography,* and *The Cambridge Bibliographical Society. Dragon's Teeth,* the "Anti-Racist Children's Book magazine", takes up issues aired nowhere else.

All this suggests that bibliographical research in the field has barely begun. **Moreover, the bibliographies that do exist of books about the public schools reflect the neglect of historians in relating the schools to the mainstream problems of British historiography.** Some books are cited here not so much for their value as history as for their value in calling the reader's attention to areas that are relatively unexplored. The publication of *Elixir* produced letters from students asking about suggestions for research, including some from students in the sixth forms of public schools. There are many topics which come to mind, and this bibliography suggests some of them. The Welsh public schools, the Scottish public schools, and the Irish schools deserve attention.

Because the London clubs published registers, prosopographical studies *vis-à-vis* the school, affiliations of members could be done. The civil service in a small colony such as Belize would be an ideal prosopographical study, again with attention to school affiliations. This writer has already studied the school affiliations of the British in the Arabian Gulf, with some surprising results.

There is no accepted taxonomy for materials about the public schools, other than the usual hierarchy that gives a primacy to primary sources. The sources which could be said to be as much techniques as sources – photographs, objects of art – are underused by public school historians. In the final book of this trilogy, *Rituals of Empire,* an effort is made to redress that. A related problem is the time-honoured distinction made between published and unpublished materials by the use of inverted commas for unpublished works. The advent of desktop publishing and microfiche and online reproduction renders distinctions increasingly dubious, although retained here.

SELECTED BIBLIOGRAPHY

Omissions are primarily of school magazines, newsletters, some secondary texts, and other material documented in the footnotes but of limited general interest. Publication is in London unless otherwise stated. Masonic titles are often marked "For Private Circulation Only", but can sometimes be found in bookshops because the relatives of deceased members have not returned items to the lodge. The bibliographies may be helpful in *Elixir of Empire* and in the author's doctoral dissertation *The Role of Ritual in the Arabian Gulf, 1858-1947: The Influence of English Public Schools,* The University of Western Australia, 1989 (available from University Microfilms).

Abbreviations: (original date of publication). CUP: Cambridge University Press. ed.: editor. GLE: Library of United Grand Lodge of England, London. IOR: India Office Library and Records, London. OUP: Oxford University Press. RGS: Royal Geographical Society archives. A fuller bibliography and index to all three volumes of the triology appear in *Rituals of Empire.*

Allen, Charles, ed., *Plain Tales from the Raj: Images of British India in the Twentieth Century,* Futura, 1986 (1975).

Allen, Robert J., *The Clubs of Augustan London,* Harvard University Press, Cambridge (Massachusetts), 1933.

Andersen, Roger, *The Power and The Word: Language, Power and Change,* Paladin, 1988.

Anonymous, *Letters of an Indian Judge to an English Gentlewoman,* Futura/MacDonald, 1983 (1934), 135.

Anstruther, Ian, *The Knights and the Umbrella: An Account of the Eglinton Tournament* 1839, Alan Sutton, 1986. The beginnings of ritualism?

Appignanesi, Lisa, and Sara Maitland, *The Rushdie File,* Fourth Estate, 1989.

Apple, Michael W., *Education and Power,* Ark ed., Ark, 1985.

Armstrong, Albert, *Public School Power,* Armstrong Publications, Hatfield (Hertfordshire), 1987. A most remarkable book. (!!!)

Armstrong, John A., *The European Administrative Elites,* Princeton University Press, 1973. Compares the effects of various educational systems on national civil services.

Armytage, W. H. G., *Yesterday's Tomorrows: A Historical Survey of Future Societies,* Routledge & Kegan Paul, 1968.

Arnold, Matthew, *Democratic Education, Collected Works on Education,* R. H. Super ed., University of Michigan Press, Ann Arbor, 1962.

Atkins, J. B., *Incidents and Reflections,* Christophers, 1947.

Ayer, A. J., *More of My Life,* OUP, 1985.

Selected Bibliography

Badcock, C. R., *The Psychoanalysis of Culture,* Basil Blackwell, Oxford, 1980.

Baigent, Michael, Richard Leigh, and Henry Lincoln, *The Messianic Legacy,* Corgi, 1987. To be used with caution.

Baigent, Michael, and Richard Leigh, *The Temple and The Lodge,* Jonathan Cape, 1989. Imaginative and too much so.

Bailey, Foster, *The Spirit of Masonry,* Lucis Press, 1957.

Bamford, T. W., *Rise of the Public Schools,* Nelson, 1967. Still the best general introduction.

Barnett, Correlli, *The Audit of War: The Illusion & Reality of Britain as a Great Nation,* Macmillan, 1986.

Bartlett, Neil, *Who Was That Man?,* Serpent's Tail, 1988.

Barton, J. E., *et al, The Headmaster Speaks,* Kegan Paul, 1936.

Bazalgette, Jack, *The Captains and the King's Depart: Life in India 1928-46,* Amate Press, 1984.

Beame, John, *Memoirs of a Bengal Civilian,* Chatto & Windus, 1961.

Belgrave, Charles, *Personal Column,* Hutchinson, 1960.

Belhaven, Lord, *The Uneven Road,* John Murray, 1955.

Bell, Gawain. *Shadows on the Sand: The Memoirs of Sir Gawain Bell,* C. Hurst, 1983.

Bence-Jones, Mark, *Viceroys of India,* Constable, 1982.

Benedict, Ruth, *Patterns of Culture,* Routledge & Kegan Paul, 1961.

Benson, A. C., ed., *Cambridge Essays on Eduction,* CUP, 1918.

Berg, David N., and K. K. Smith eds., *The Self in Social Inquiry: Researching Methods,* Sage, 1988 (1985).

Berger, Peter, and Thomas Luckmann, *The Social Construction of Reality,* Allen Lane, Harmondsworth, 1967.

Berger, Peter, Brigitte Berger, and Hansfreid Kellner, *The Homeless Mind: Modernization and Consciousness.* Viking, 1973.

Berque, Jacques, *Cultural Expression in Arab Society Today,* trs. Robert Stookey, University of Texas Press, Austin, 1978.

Berridge, Virginia, and Griffith Edwards, *Opium and the People: Opiate Use in Nineteenth-Century England,* Yale University Press, 1987.

Bilton, Tony, *et al, Introductory Sociology,* 2nd ed., Macmillan, 1987.

Bintliff, John, *Extracting Meaning From The Past:* Oxbow, Oxford, 1988.

Birkin, Andrew, *J. M. Barrie & The Lost Boys,* Constable, 1986. Inadvertently, psychohistory.

Blunt, Wilfrid, *Slow on the Feather: Further Autobiography,* 1938-1959, Michael Russell, 1986.

Boulding, Kenneth E., *The Image: Knowledge in Life and Science,* University of Michigan Press, Ann Arbor, 1961 (1956).

Boyd, William, *An Ice-Cream War,* Hamish Hamilton, 1982.

Bradshaw, Percy V., *'Brother Savages and Guests': A History of the Savage Club, 1857-1957,* W. H. Allen, 1958.

Braithwaite, R. B., *Scientific Explanation*, CUP, 1953.

Brander, Michael, *The Victorian Gentleman*, Cremonesi, 1975.

Briggs, Asa, *Marx in London, BBC*, 1982.

Brodie, Fawn M., *No Man Knows My History: The Life of Joseph Smith, The Mormon Prophet*, 2nd ed. rev., 1986. A remarkable account of the creation of a religion, illustrating the sources of the Latter Day Saints' ceremonies and rituals.

Brown, L. Carl, Norman Itzkowitz eds., *Psychological Dimensions of Near Eastern Studies*, Darwin Press, Princeton (New Jersey), 1977.

Browning, Oscar, *An Introduction to the History of Educational Theories*, Kegan Paul, Trench, Trubner, 1903.

Bruce, Anthony, *The Purchase System in the British Army, 1660-1871*, Royal Historical Society, 1980.

Byrde, Penelope, *The Male Image: Men's Fashions England, 1300-1970*, B. T. Batsford, 1979.

Burke, T. E., *The Philosophy of Popper*, Manchester University Press, 1983,

Burnett, J. F., ed., *Destiny Obscure: Autobiographies of Childhood, Education, and Family From the 1820s to the 1920s*, Penguin, Harmondswoth, 1984.

J. F. Burnett ed., *Independent Schools Yearbook*, A. C. Black, 1987.

Bush, M. L., *The English Aristocracy: A Comparative Synthesis*, Manchester University Press, 1984.

Calhoun, Daniel, *The Intelligence of People*, Princeton University Press, New Jersey, 1973.

Cambray, Philip G., *Club Days and Ways: The Story of The Constitutional Club, London: 1883-1962*, Constitutional Club, 1963.

Campbell, Michael, *Lord Dismiss Us*, William Heinemann, 1987.

Caroe, A. D. R., *The House of the Royal Institution*, The Royal Institution, 1963.

Carritt, Michael, *A Mole in the Crown*, Central Books, 1985. Carritt was the complete anomaly, a Communist Indian Political Service officer.

Cecil, Lord David, *The Leisure of an Egyptian Official*, Century Publishing, 1984 (1921). The Raj on a camel.

Chitty, Clyde, ed., *Redefining The Comprehensive Experience*, Institution of Education, University of London, 1987.

Churchill, Winston, S., *My Early Life: A Roving Commission*, Collins, 1977 (1930).

Cleverley, John, ed., *Half a Million Children: Studies of Non-Government Education in Australia*, Longman Cheshire, Melbourne, 1978.

Cohen, Abner, *The Politics of Elite Culture: Expressions in the Dramaturgy of Power in a Modern African Society*, University of California, Berkeley, 1981.

Coleridge, Gilbert, *Eton in the Seventies*, Smith, Elder, 1912.

Collenette, V. G., *Elizabeth College, 1563-1963*, Guernsey Press, St. Peter Port (Guernsey), 1963.

Collins, Robert O., and Francis M. Deng eds., *The British in the Sudan, 1898-1956: The Sweetness and the Sorrow*, Macmillan, 1984.

Selected Bibliography

Colson, Percy, *White's: 1693-1950*, William Heinemann, 1951.

Cowell, F. R. *The Athenaeum: Club and Social Life in London, 1824-1974*, Heinnemann, 1975.

Cox, A. Bertra, *The First Hundred Years: History of the S.A. Tattersalls' Club*, Brolga Books, Adelaide (South Australia), 1980.

Crispin, Edward (Bruce Montgomery), *Love Lies Bleeding*, Century Hutchinson, 1988 (1948).

Cryer, N. B., *Masonic Halls of England: The South*, Lewis Masonic, Shepperton, 1989. Rare photographs. Part of a series.

Dahl, Roald, Boy: *Tales of Childhood*, Penguin, Harmondsworth, 1984.

Dance, E. H., *History the Betrayer: A Study in Bias*, Greenwood, Westport, (Connecticut), 1960.

Dancy, John, *The Public Schools and the Future*, Faber and Faber, 1963.

Darwin, Bernard, *British Clubs*, William Collins, 1943.

Davidoff, Leonore, *The Best Circles: Social Etiquette and the Season*, Creset, 1986 (1973).

Dawkins, Richard, *The Blind Watchmaker*, Penguin, Harmondsworth, 1988 (1986).

Delaney, Paul, *The Neo-pagans*, Macmillan, 1988.

Didsbury, Howard F., Jr., ed., *Challenges and Opportunities: From Now to 2001*, World Future Society, Bethesda (Maryland) 1986.

Dillistone, F. W., *The Power of Symbols*, SCM Press, 1986.

Dixon, Bob, *Catching Them Young (2): Political Ideas in Children's Fiction*, Pluto, 1977.

Doyle, Sir Arthur Conan, *Memories and Adventurers*, OUP 1989 (1924).

Dunae, Patrick, *Gentleman Emigrants: From the British Public School to the Canadian Frontier*, Douglas & McIntyre, 1981. A significant contribution to the development of the theory of the importance of the public school to the Imperial idea.

Duncan, Malcolm C., *Masonic Ritual and Monitor*, 3rd ed., David McKay, New York, n.d.

Elliman, Michael, and Frederick Roll, *The Pink Plaque Guide to London*, GMP, 1986.

Ellis, Havelock, *An Open Letter to Biographers*, Oriole Press, Berkely Heights (New Jersey), 1931.

Elton, G. R., *The Practice of History*, Fontana, 1989 (1967).

Eco, Umberto, *Travels in Hyperreality*, Picador, 1987. (Appeared in 1986 as *Faith in Fakes*.)

Evans, E. W., *The British Yoke: Reflections on the Colonial Empire*, William Hodge, 1949.

Fekete, John, ed., *Life After Postmodernism: Essays on Value and Culture*, Macmillan, 1988.

Fermor-Hesketh, Robert, ed., *Architecture of the British Empire,* Weidenfeld and Nicolson, 1986.

Feuchtwanger, E. J., *Democracy and Empire: Britain 1865-1914,* Edward Arnold, 1985.

Firminger, Walter K., *The Second Lodge of Bengal in the Old Times, Being a History of the Early Days of Lodge Industry and Perseverance No. 109 of England,* Thacker, Spink, Calcutta, 1911.

Fischer, David Hackett, *Historians' Fallacies: Toward a Logic of Historical Thought,* Harper, New York, 1970.

Firth, R. H., *The Junior: A History of the Junior United Service Club,* Junior United Service Club, 1929.

Fishlock, Trevor, *India File,* John Murray, 1983.

Fitzroy, Almeric, *History of the Travellers' Club,* George Allen & Unwin, 1927.

Forrest, Denys M., *Foursome in St. James: The Story of the East India, Devonshire, Sports and Public Schools Club,* East India Club, 1982.

Forrest, Denys, *The Oriental: Life Story of a West End Club,* B. T. Batsford, 1968.

Fox, Adam, *A Brief Description of the Worshipful Company of Skinners,* Privately Printed for the Company, rev. ed. 1968.

Fraser, George Macdonald, ed., *The World of the Public School,* Weidenfeld & Nicolson.

Freeman, Arnold D., *Boy Life and Labour: The Manufacture of Inefficiency,* P. S. King, 1914.

Fromm, Erich, *Beyond the Chains of Illusion: My Encounter with Marx and Freud,* Abacus, 1986 (1962).

Fuller, Roy, *The Ruined Boys,* Andre Deutsch, 1959.

Furet, Francois, *In the Workshop of History,* University of Chicago Press, 1982.

Gambetta, Diego, *Were They Pushed or Did They Jump?: Individual Decision Mechanisms in Education,* CUP, 1987.

Gann, L. H., and Peter Duignan, *The Rulers of British Africa, 1870-1914,* Croom Helm, 1978. Includes an interesting discussion of the public school backgrounds of the British in Africa.

Gathorne-Hardy, Jonathan, *The Public School Phenomenon,* Hodder & Stoughton, 1977. A slightly different American edition appeared as *The Old School Tie: The Phenomenon of the English Public School,* Viking Press, New York, 1978.

Gathorne-Hardy, Jonathan, *The Rise and Fall of the British Nanny,* Weidenfeld and Nicolson, 1985.

Gibson, Ian, *The English Vice: Beating, Sex and Shame in Victorian England and After,* Duckworth, 1978. An exhaustive treatment of an unpleasant subject, with considerable public school material.

Giles, G. C. T., *The New School Tie,* Pilot Press, 1976.

Gill, Anton, *How to be Oxbridge: a Bluffer's Handbook,* Grafton Books, 1985.

Gleick, James, *Chaos: Making a New Science,* Heinemann, 1988.

Selected Bibliography

Glinga, Werner, *Legacy of Empire: A Journey Through British Society,* Manchester University Press, 1986.

Goldthorpe, J. E., *An Introduction to Sociology,* 3rd ed., CUP, 1985.

Gordon, Richard, *A Gentlemen's Club,* Arrow, 1988.

Gordon, Richard, *The Private Life of Florence Nightingale,* Heinemann, 1978.

Grainger, J. H., *Patriotisms: Britain 1900-1939,* Routledge & Kegan Paul, 1986.

Graves, Charles L., *Mr. Punch's History of Modern England,* Vol. IV, Cassell, 1922.

Graves, Richard Perceval, *Robert Graves: The Assault Heroic, 1895-1926,* Macmillan, 1987.

Graves, Robert, *Goodbye to All That,* Penguin, Harmondsworth, 1986 (1929).

Greene, Graham, ed., *The Old School: Essays by Divers Hands,* Jonathan Cape 1984 (1934). Still the best of anthologies.

Griffiths, Arthur, *Clubs and Clubmen,* Hutchinson, 1907.

Guttsman, W. L., ed., *The English Ruling Class,* Weidenfeld & Nicolson, 1969.

Haggard, V. E. D., *The Brewing Years: The Story of the Old Malthouse,* the Old Malthouse, Swanage, 1981.

Haley, Bruce, *Healthy Body and Victorian Culture,* Harvard University Press, Cambridge (Massachusetts), 1978. It is difficult to understand why this book is not cited in Dr. Mangan's *Athleticism* or his *Games Ethic and Imperialism.*

Hall, A. D., *The Savile Club, 1868 to 1923,* Committee of the Club, 1923.

Hall, Edward T., *The Silent Language,* Fawcett, 1969 (1959).

Hall, Richard, *Lovers on the Nile,* Quartet, 1981.

Hamrow, Theodore S., *Reflections on History and Historians,* University of Wisconsin Press, Madison, 1987.

Hamilton, William B., ed., *The Transfer of Institutions,* Duke University Press, Durham (North Carolina), 1964.

Heald, Tim, *Networks,* Hodder and Stoughton, 1983.

Hearnden, Arthur, *Red Robert: A Life of Robert Birley,* Hamish Hamilton, 1984.

Heathcote, T. A., *The Indian Army: The Garrison of British Imperial India, 1822-1922,* Davie & Charles, 1974.

Heller, Agnes, *A Theory of History,* Routledge & Kegan Paul, 1982.

Hess, Robert D. and Judith V. Torney, *The Development of Political Attitudes in Children,* Adine, Chicago, 1967.

Heussler, Robet, *Yesterday's Rulers: The Making of the British Colonial Service,* Syracuse University Press, 1982.

Hexter, J. H., *The History Primer,* Allen Lane, 1971.

Hill, Christopher, *History and the Present,* 65th Conway Memorial Lecture, South Place Etical Society, 1988.

Hill, Frank Ernest, *Man-Made Culture: The Educational Activities of Men's Clubs,* American Association for Adult Education, New York, 1938.

Hill, J. W., *Eton Medley,* Winchester Publications, 1948.

Himmelfarb, Gertrude, *The New History and the Old,* Belknap Press of Harvard

University Press, Cambridge (Massachusetts), 1987. Elegantly written if ultimately unpersuasive.

Hobson, J. A., *Imperialism*, George Allen & Unwin, 3rd Ed., 1961. The most useful edition of a classic.

Hollinghurst, Alan, *The Swimming-Pool Library*, Penguin, Harmondsworth, 1988.

Homas, Albert, *Wait & See*, Michael Joseph, 1944.

Honey, J. R. de S., *Tom Brown's Universe: The Development of the Public School in the 19th Century*, Millington Books, 1977.

Hope, Mary, *The Psychology of Ritual*, Element Books, Shaftesbury (England), 1988.

Horne, Donald, *The Great Museum: The Re-Presentation of History*, Pluto, 1984. Seminal in considering ritual *vis-à-vis.* history.

Hough, Richard, *The Ace of Clubs: A History of the Garrick*, Andre Deutsch, 1986.

Humphries, Stephen, *Hooligans or Rebels? An Oral History of Working-Class Childhood and Youth, 1889-1939*, Basil Blackwell, Oxford, 1981.

Hunt, Roland, and John Harrison, *The District Officer in India, 1930-1947*, Scolar Press, 1980.

Irvine, Rebecca, *A Girl's Guide to the English Public Schoolboy*, Severn House, 1985.

Jackson, Louis, C., *History of the United Service Club*, United Service Club, 1937.

Jackson, Robert, *Thirty Seconds at Quetta: The Story of an Earthquake*, Evans, 1960.

Jameson, Frederic, *Nationalism, Colonialism and Literature: Modernism and Imperialism*, Field Day, Derry (Northern Ireland), 1988.

Johan, Khasnor, *The Emergency of the Modern Malay Administrative Elite*, OUP, 1984.

Johns, John H. *Cohesion in the US Military*, National Defense University Press, Washington, 1984.

Jung, C. G., *Synchronicity: An Acausal Connecting Principle*, Ark, 1987 (1952).

Kabbani, Rana, *Europe's Myths of Orient*, Macmillan, 1986. A rather pale also-ran to Said's *Orientalism.*

Kerr, Anthony, *Schools of Europe*, Bowes & Bowes, 1960.

Kertzer, David I., *Ritual, Politics, and Power*, Yale University Press, 1988. One of the building blocks in considering the importance of ritual in historiography.

Khasnor, Johan, *The Emergence of The Modern Malay Administrative Elite*, OUP, 1984.

Knightly, Charles, *The Customs and Ceremonies of Britain*, Thames and Hudson, 1986.

Khuri, Fuad, *Tribe and State In Bahrain*, University of Chicago Press, 1981. Considers influences of native clubs.

Ladurie, Emmanuel, Le Roy, *The Territory of the Historian*, Harvester Press, Brighton, 1979.

Selected Bibliography

Lambert, Angela, *Unquiet Souls: The Indian Summer of the British Aristocracy, 1880-1918,* Macmillan, 1984.

Langen, Sussane K., *Philosophy in a New Key: A Study in the Symbolism of Reason, Rite, and Art,* 3rd ed., Harvard University Press, 1957 (1942).

Lant, Jeffrey L., *Insubstantial Pageant: Ceremony & Confusion at Queen Victoria's Court,* Hamish Hamilton, 1979.

Lavery, James, *Victoriana,* Ward Lock, 1966.

Lawless, R. I., ed., *The Gulf in the Early 20th Century: Foreign Institutions and Local Responses,* Occasional Paper Series No. 31, Centre for Middle Eastern and Islamic Studies, University of Durham, 1986.

Lawrence, John, *Freemasonry – A Religion?,* Kingsway, Eastbourne, 1987.

Lawton, Henry, *The Psychohistorian's Handbook,* Psychohistory Press, New York, 1988.

Lelyveld, David, *Aligarth's First Generation: Muslim Solidarity in British Indian,* Princeton University Press, 1978.

Lee-Milne, James, *The Enigmatic Edwardians: The Life of Reginald, 2nd Viscount Esher,* Sidgwick & Jackson, 1986.

Leinster-Mackay, Donald, *The Educational World of Daniel Defoe,* University of Victoria, British Columbia, 1981. A book which should have a wider audience and be more appreciated.

Leinster-Mackay, Donald, *The Rise of the English Prep School,* Falmer Press, 1984.

Lever, James, *Victoriana,* Ward Lock, 1966.

Levine, George, *et al, Speaking for the Humanities,* American Council of Learned Societies Occasional Paper No. 7, New York, 1989.

Lewis, W, *Marlborough College 1873-1943,* OUP 1943.

Library Resources Co-ordinating Committee, *A Guide to History, Libraries and Collecting,* 3rd ed., University of London, 1988.

Lloyd, Christopher, *Explanation in Social History,* Basil Blackwell, 1986.

Lloyd, T. O., *The British Empire, 1558-1983,* OUP, 1984.

Longford, Elizabeth, *A Pilgrimage of Passion: The Life of Wilfrid Scawen Blunt,* Alfred Knopf, New York, 1980.

Louch, T. S., *The First Fifty Years: The History of the Weld Club (1871-1921),* Perth (Western Australia), 1964.

Loewenberg, *Peter, Decoding the Past: The Psychohistorical Approach,* University of California Press, Berkeley 1985 (1969).

Louis, Wm. Roger, *The British Empire in the Middle East, 1945-1951,* Clarendon Press, Oxford, 1985.

Lovejoy, Arthur O., *The Great Claim of Being; A Study of the History of an Idea,* Harvard University Press, Cambridge (Massachusetts), 1978 (1936).

Lovelock, James, *The Ages of Gaia,* OUP, 1988.

MacAloon, John J., *This Great Symbol: Pierre de Coubertin and The Origins of the Modern Olympic Games,* University of Chicago Press, 1984.

Macdonald, Ian Camerson, *To the Farthest End of the Earth: The History of the Royal Geographical Society, 1830-1980,* RGS, 1980.

Macintyre, Stuart, *Ormond College: Centenary Essays,* Melbourne University Press, 1984.

Mack, Edward C., *Public Schools and British Opinion Since 1860,* Columbia University Press, 1941 (reprinted Greenwood Press, Westport Connecticut, 1971). In this work of distinction, it is hard to find any subsequent development in public school studies which is not anticipated.

Mackenzie, J. M., *Propaganda and Empire: The Manipulation of British Public Opinion 1880-1960,* Manchester University Press, 1984.

Maconochie, Evan, *Life in the Indian Civil Service,* Chapman and Hall, 1926.

McLaren, Peter, *Schooling as a Ritual Performance: Towards a Political Economy of Educational Symbols and Gestures,* Routledge & Kegan Paul, 1986. To Dr. McLaren goes the honour of having written the first full length study of a school employing ritual as a conceptual framework.

Magee, Bryan, *Popper,* Fontana Press, 1982.

Mangan, J. A., *Athleticism in the Victorian and Edwardian Public School: The Emergence and Consolidation of an Educational Ideology,* CUP 1981. An important book putting the case for athleticism in the public schools.

Mangan, J. A. ed., *'Benefits Bestowed'?: Education and British Imperialism,* Manchester University Press, 1988.

Mangan, J. A., and James Walvin, eds., *Manliness and Morality: Middle-class Masculinity in Britain and America, 1800-1940,* Manchester University Press, 1987.

Mann, Erika, *School for Barbarians: Education Under the Nazis,* Lindsey Drummond, 1939.

Marlowe, John, *Late Victorian,* Cresset Press, 1967. The only biography of Sir Arnold Wilson.

Martin, Mady, *Martyn Sahib: The Story of John Martyn of The Doon School,* Dass Media, New Delhi, 1985.

Marwick, Arthur, *The Nature of History,* 2nd ed., Macmillan, 1985 (1970, 1981).

Mason, Philip, *A Matter of Honour: An Account of the Indian Army, Its Officers and Men,* Jonathan Cape, 1974. (Philip Woodard.)

Mason, Philip, *A Thread of Silk: Further Memories of a Varied Life,* Michael Rossall, 1984.

Masters, Anthony, *Literary Agents: The Agent as Spy,* Basil Blackwell, Oxford, 1987. Contains a surprising number of references to public schools.

Melden, A. I., *Free Action,* Routledge & Kegan Paul, 1961.

Medawar, Peter, *Memoirs of a Thinking Radish: An Autobiography,* OUP, 1986.

Middleton, Warren, ed., *The Betrayal of Youth,* CL Publications, n.d.

Midwinter, Eric, *Schools in Society: The Evolution of English Education,* Batsford, 1980.

Milford, L. S., *Haileybury College: Past and Present,* T. Fisher Unwin, 1909.

Mill, Hugh Robert, *The Record of the Royal Geographical Society, 1830-1930,* Royal Geographical Society, 1930.

Miller, David, ed., *A Pocket Popper,* Fontana, 1983.

Selected Bibliography

Mitchell, Nora, *The Indian Hill-Station: Kodaikanal,* University of Chicago, Department of Geography, Research Paper No. 141. A monograph whose importance has been missed by writers about India and the Empire.

Monier-Williams, Monier, *Memorial of Old Haileybury College,* Archibald Constable, 1894.

Montgomery, R. J., *Examinations: An Account of Their Evolution as Administrative Devices in England,* Longmans, 1965.

Moorhouse, Geoffrey, *To the Frontier, Sceptre,* 1988 (1984).

Morris, James, *Farewell the Trumpets: An Imperial Retreat,* Penguin, Harmondsworth, 1984.

Morris, Jan, *Pax Britannica: The Climax of an Empire,* Penguin, Harmondsworth, 1984.

Morris, Jan, *The Spectacle of Empire,* Faber and Faber, 1982.

Morris, Jan, *Stones of Empire,* OUP, 1986.

Morris, Max, and Clive Griggs, eds., *Education – The Wasted Years?, 1973-1986,* Falmer Press, 1988.

Morrow, Ann, Highness, *The Maharajahs of India,* Grafton Books, 1986. The Indian public schools are given their due as part of the effort to shore up the legitimacy of Indian monarchies.

Mudford, Peter, *Birds of a Different Plumage: A Study of British-Indian Relations from Akbar to Curzon,* Collins, 1974.

Muggeridge, Malcom, *A Twentieth Century Testimony,* Collins, 1979.

Murugesh, M. K., ed., *Waltair Club Centenary Celebrations, 1882-1982.* Waltair Club, Visakhapatnam (India), 1982, n.p.

Musgrave, P. W., ed., *Sociology, History and Education,* Methuen, 1970.

Nakhleh, Emile A., *Bahrain: Political Development in a Modernizing Society,* D. C. Heath, Lexington (Massachusetts), 1976. Offers interesting observations on the influence of clubs in a developing society.

Nasir, Sari J., *The Arabs and the English,* 2nd ed., Longman, 1979.

Neale, R. S., *Class and Ideology in the Nineteenth Century,* Routledge & Kegan Paul, 1972.

Neale, R. S., ed., *History and Class: Essential Readings in Theory and Interpretation,* Basil Blackwell, Oxford, 1983.

Needleman, Jacob, *The Sword of Gnosis: Metaphysics, Cosmology, Tradition, Symbolism,* Arkana, 1986 (1974).

Nevill, Ralph, *London Clubs: Their History & Treasures,* Chatto & Windus, 1919.

Nobbs, Jack, Bob Hine, and Margaret Fleming, *Sociology,* 2nd ed. rev., Macmillan, 1983.

Novick, Peter, *That Noble Dream: The Objectivity Question and the American Historical Profession,* CUP, 1988.

Oakeshott, Michael, *On History and Other Essays,* Basil Blackwell, 1985 (1983).

Oaten, Edward Farley, *My Memories of India,* Sobal Genguli ed., Jamaki

Prakejham, Patna (India), 1984. Details of Imperial Freemasonry.

O'Connor, Anthony, *Clubland: The Wrong Side of the Right People*, Brian & O'Keefe, 1976. The manager's view.

Ollard, Richard, *An English Education: A Perspective of Eton*, Collins, 1982.

Onyeama, Dillibe, *Nigger at Eton*, Leslie Frewin, 1972.

Ornstein, Robert, *Multimind: A New Way of Looking At Human Behaviour*, Macmillan, 1988 (1980).

Orwell, George, George Orwell: *Collected Works, Vol. II*, Secker & Warburg, 1980.

Ottaway, A. K. C., *Education and Society*, 2nd ed. rev., Routledge & Kegan Paul, 1964.

Outhwaite, William, *New Philosophies of Social Science: Realism, Hermeneutics and Critical Theory*, Macmillan, 1987.

Palmer, Arnold, *Movable Feasts: Changes in English Eating Habits*, OUP, 1984.

Parker, Eric, *Floreat: An Eton Anthology*, Nisbet, 1923.

Parker, Peter, *The Old Lie: the Great War and the Public School Ethos*, Constable, 1987.

Parsons, Anthony, *They Say the Lion – Britain's Legacy to the Arabs: A Personal Memoir*, Jonathan Cape, 1986.

Pattison, Robert, *The Child Figure in English Literature*, University of Georgia Press, Athens (Georgia), 1978.

Peat, F. David, *Synchronicity: the Bridge Between Matter and Mind*, Bantham, Toronto, 1988.

Perry, Warren, *The Naval and Military Club, Melbourne: A History of its First Hundred Years, 1881-1981*, Lothian, Melbourne, 1981. A model club history.

Petrie, Charles, *The Carlton Club*, Eyre & Spottiswoode, 1955.

Petrie, Charles, *Scenes of Edwardian Life*, Severn House, 1975 (1965).

Pitt-Aikens, Tom, and Alice Thomas Ellis, *Loss of the Good Authority: The Cause of Delinquency*, Viking, 1989.

Pollock, Linda A., *Forgotten Children: Parent-Child Relations from 1500 to 1900*, CUP, 1985.

Ponsonby, Arthur, *The Decline of Aristocracy*, T. Fisher Unwin, 1912.

Porter, Bernard, *The Lion's Share: A Short History of British Imperialism, 1850-1983*, 2nd ed., Longman, 1984.

Potter, David C. *India's Political Administrators, 1919-1983*, Clarendon Press, Oxford, 1986.

Powell, E. Alexander, *The Last Home of Mystery*, John Long, 1929.

Public Schools Alpine Sports Club Year Book, 1930.

Quigly, Isabel, *The Heirs of Tom Brown: The English School Story*, OUP, 1984. Among the best of the works about English public school fiction.

Rae, John, *Letters From School*, Fontana/Collins, 1988.

Selected Bibliography

Rajkumar College, *Centenary Souvenir, 1882-1982*, Rajkumar College, Raipur, 1982.

Raven, Simon, *The Old School: A Study in the Oddities of the English Public School System*, Hamish Hamilton, 1986. Like all of Raven's books, must be taken with a grain of salt.

Reed, John R., *Old School Ties: The Public Schools in British Literature*, Syracuse University Press, 1964. By far the best consideration of the public school novel.

Reese, Trevor R., *The History of the University Club of St. Louis, 1872-1978*, University Club of St. Louis, St. Louis (Missouri), 1978.

Richards, Jeffrey, *Happiest Days: The Public Schools in English Fiction*, Manchester University Press, 1988. A sophisticated and original consideration.

Roberts, Marie, *British Poets and Secret Societies*, Croom Helm, 1986.

Rogers, Barbara, *Men Only: An Investigation Into Men's Organisations*, Pandora, 1988. A fervid feminist's view indeed. Vitriolic.

Rome, R. C., *The Union Club: An Illustrated Descriptive Record of the Oldest Members' Club in London, founded circa 1799*, B. T. Batsford, 1948.

Rose, Kenneth, Curzon: *A Most Superior Person*, Macmillan, 1985. Contains an excellent account of Curzon's Eton connections and of his friendship with Oscar Browning. A most superior biography.

Rosenthal, Michael, *The Character Factory: Baden-Powell and the Origins of the Boy Scout Movement*, Collins, 1986. One of the first works to perceive clearly the connection between the public schools and the mass youth movements.

Rowse, A. L., *Homosexuals in History: A Study of Ambivalence in Society, Literature and the Arts*, Weidenfeld and Nicolson, 1977.

Rushdie, Salman, *The Satanic Verses*, Viking, 1988. Its notoriety should not detract from the book's value as a commentary (among other virtues) on East-West relationships.

Ryan, Alan, *The Philosophy of The Social Sciences*, Macmillan, 1988 (1970).

Said, Edward, *Nationalism, Colonialism and Literature: Yeats and Decolonization*, Field Day, 1988.

Said, Edward, *Orientalism*, Penguin, Harmondsworth, 1978. A landmark essential for anyone who wishes to understand the complexity of Imperialism.

Salter, Brian, and Ted Tapper, *Power and Policy in Education: The Case of Independent Schooling*, Falmer Press, 1985.

Sams, Hubert Arthur, *Pauline and Old Pauline 1884-1931*, privately printed (CUP), 1933.

William Sanderson, *Two Hundred Years of Freemasonry: A History of the Britannic Lodge No. 33, Annis Domini 1730-1930*, George Kenning, 1930.

Sattin, Sattin, *Lifting the Veil: British Society in Egypt, 1768-1956*, J. M. Dent & Sons, 1988. Provides an unusual view of the British influence in the Middle East.

Schaff, Adam, *History and Truth*, Permagon Press, Oxford, 1976.

Scott, J. M., *The Book of Pall Mall*, Heinemann, 1965.

Scott, Paul, *A Division of the Spoils*, Granada, 1985 (1975).

Sedgwick, Eve Kosofsky, *Between Men,* Columbia University Press, New York, 1985.

Serjeant, R. B., and R. L. Bidwell, eds., *Arabian Studies V,* C. Hurst, 1979.

Sendak, Maurice, *Caldecott & Co.: Notes on Books & Pictures,* Reinhardt, 1988.

Shar, Sirdar Ikbal Ali, *The Golden East,* John Long, 1931.

Sheldrake, Rupert, *A New Science of Life: The Hypothesis of Formative Causation,* Paladian, 2nd ed., 1987 (1981).

Sheldrake, Rupert, *The Presence of the Past: Morphic Resonance and the Habits of Nature,* Collins, 1988.

Shepherd, Simon, and Mick Wallis, *Coming on Strong,* Unwin Hyman, 1989.

Sherry, Norman, *The Life of Graham Greene, Volume One: 1904-1939,* Jonathan Cape, 1989.

Shrosbree, Colin, *Public Schools and Private Education: The Clarendon Commission 1861-64 and the Public Schools Acts,* Manchester University Press, 1988.

Silver, Harold, *Education as History: Interpreting Nineteenth- and Twentieth-Century Education,* Methuen, 1983.

Simmonds, Stuart, and Simon Digby, *The Royal Asiatic Society: Its History and Treasures,* E. J. Brill, Leiden, 1979.

Simon, Brian, *The Two Nations and the Education Structure, 1780-1870,* Lawrence & Wishart, 1981.

Slater, Brian, and Ted Tapper, *Power and Policy in Education: The Case of Independent Schooling,* Falmer Press, 1985.

Smith, Jonathan Z., *Imagining Religion: From Babylon to Jamestown,* University of Chicago, 1982.

Smith, Tony, *The Pattern of Imperialism: The United States, Great Britain, and the Late-industrializing World Since 1815,* CUP, 1981.

Sprent, Peter, *Taking Risks: The Science of Uncertainty,* Penguin, Harmondsworth, 1988.

Stannard, David E., *Shrinking History: On Freud and the Failure of Psychohistory,* OUP, 1980.

Stark, Freya, *East is West,* John Murray, 1945.

Stark, W., *The Sociology of Knowledge: An Essay in Aid of a Deeper Understanding of the History of Ideas,* Routledge & Kegan Paul, 1971.

Steepmuller, Francis, ed. and trans., *Flaubert in Egypt: A Sensibility on Tour,* Little Brown, Boston (Massachusetts), 1973.

Stevenson, David, *The Origins of Freemasonry: Scotland's Century, 1590-1710,* CUP, 1988. In a field notable for pseudo-scholarship, a significant scholarly advance on previous work. Ingenious.

Steward, J. I. M., *Myself and Michael Innes: A Memoir,* Victor Gollancz, 1987.

Stewart, J. M., *Changes and Chances: Memories of Shrewsbury and Other Places,* Abbey Press, Abingdon upon Thames, 1971.

Storr, Anthony, *The School of Genius,* Andre Deutsch, 1988.

Strange, T. Bland, *Gunner Jingo's Jubilee,* Remington, 1893.

Selected Bibliography

Strawson, Gale, *The Secret Connection: Causation, Realism, and David Hume,* Clarendon Press, Oxford, 1989.

Street, J. M., *Changes and Chances: Memories of Shrewsbury and other places,* Abbey Press, Abingdon Upon Thames, 1971.

Street, Pamela, *Arthur Bryant: Portrait of a Historian,* Collins, 1979.

Symonds, Richard, *Oxford and Empire: the Last Lost Cause?,* Macmillan, 1986. Acknowledges the public school influence on Oxford.

Taylor, A. J. P., *A Personal History,* Hamish Hamilton, 1983.

Thane, Pat, and Anthony Sutcliffe eds., *Essays in Social History,* Clarendon Press Oxford, 1986.

Thesiger, Wilfred, *The Life of My Choice,* Collins, 1987. Psychologically revealing, although its recurring Eton and club motifs went largely unnoticed in reviews.

Thomas, Malcolm I., *The Brisbane Club,* Jacaranda Press, Milton (Queensland), 1980.

Thomas, Bernard, ed., *Repton, 1557 to 1957,* B. T. Batsford, 1957.

Thorn, John, *The Road to Winchester,* Weidenfeld and Nicolson, 1989.

Thornton, A. P., *Doctrines of Imperialism,* John Wiley & Sons, New York, 1965.

Thornton, A. P., *The Imperial Idea and Its Enemies: A Study in British Power,* 2nd ed., Macmillan, 1985.

Thorpe, Mary, and Charlotte Thorpe, *London Church Staves,* Elliot Stock, 1895.

Tidrick, Kathryn, *Heart-beguiling Arabia,* OUP, 1967. Notes the old boy ties with Arabs.

Todd, Emmanuel, *The Explanation of Ideology: Family Structures and Social Systems,* Basil Blackwell, 1985.

Tooley, Michael, *Causation: A Realist Approach,* Clarendon Press, Oxford, 1988.

Toynbee, Arnold, *Acquaintances,* OUP, 1967.

Trench, Charles Chenevix, *Viceroy's Agent,* Jonathan Cape, 1987. An opinionated but useful account of the Indian Political Service.

Trollope, Anthony, *Dr. Wortle's School,* OUP, 1984 (1880).

Trusted, Jennifer, *Inquiry and Understanding: an Introduction to Explanation in the Physical and Human Sciences,* Macmillan, 1987 (1979).

Turnbull, Colin, *The Human Cycle,* Triad/Paladin, 1985.

Van Ess, Dorothy, *History of the Arabian Mission, 1926-1957,* Board of Foreign Missions, Reformed Church in America, n.d. Typescript in Sage Library, New Brunswick (New Jersey).

Wakefield, Edward, *Past Imperative: My Life In India, 1927-1947,* Chatto and Windus, 1966.

Walford, Geoffrey, *Life in Public Schools,* Methuen, 1986.

Warnock, Mary, *A Common Policy for Education,* OUP, 1988.

Watson, Lyall, *Neophilia: The Tradition of the New,* Sceptre, 1989.

Waugh, Alec, *Public School Life: Boys, Parents, Masters,* W. Collins, 1927 (1922).

Welsh, William A., *Leaders and Elites*, Holt, Rinehart and Winston, New York, 1979.

Whitmore, Hugh, *Breaking the Code:* A Play Based on Andrew Hodges' *Alan Turing, the Enigma*, Amber Lane Press, 1987.

Wiener, Martin J., *English Culture and the Decline of the Industrial Spirit, 1850-1980*, Penguin, Harmondsworth, 1985.

Wilkinson, Rupert, *The Prefects: British Leadership and the Public School Tradition*, OUP, 1964. The American edition is known as *Gentlemanly Power*, OUP, New York, 1964.

Wilson, Arnold, *More Thoughts and Talks: The Diary and Scrap-book of a Member of Parliament from September 1937 to August 1939*, Right Book Club, 1939.

Wilson, Arnold, S. W. Persia: *A Political Officer's Diary, 1907-1914*, OUP, 1941. Much about Clifton.

Winstone, H. V. F., *The Illicit Adventure: the Story of Political and Military Intelligence in the Middle East from 1898 to 1926*, Jonathan Cape, 1982.

Woodbridge, George, *The Reform Club, 1936-1978: A History From the Club's Records*, The Reform Club, 1978.

Wrench, John Evelyn, *Uphill: The First Stage in a Strenuous Life*, Ivor Nicholson & Watson, 1934.

'Y', The Autobiography of an Englishman, Paul Elek, 1975.

Young, G. M., *Victorian England*, OUP, 1953.

Young, J. Z., *Philosophy and the Brain*, OUP, 1988.

Zinkin, Maurice and Taya Zinkin, *Britain and India: Requiem for Empire*, Chatto & Windus, 1964.

JOURNALS AND NEWSPAPERS

All Journal, Ambassador International, American Antiquity, American Historical Review, American Speech, Annals of the Association of American Geographers, Armed Forces & Society Asiatic Affairs, Art in America.

Behaviorism, Biography, British Journal of Educational Studies, British Journal of Sociology, Bulletin of the Institute of Historical Research, The British Journal of Aesthetics.

Canadian Journal of History of Sport, Chowkidar. (British Association for Cemeteries in South Asia), The Coat of Arms, Connections, Commentary, Cultural Studies.

The Daily Express

Ecology Law Quarterly, The Economist, Education, (Institute for Scientific Co-operation, Tubingen), Education Research and Perspectives, Educational Communication and Technology.

FLS Children's Folklore Newsletter, Forum for Social Economics.

The Gem, Gender and Education, Geographical Journal, The Guardian.

Harper's Franklin Square Library, Harvard Educational Review, Harvard Law Review, Harvard Library Bulletin, Harvard University Gazette, Historical Methods, Historical Studies in Education, History of Education, History of Education Quarterly, History of European Ideas, History of the Human Sciences, History Workshop.

International Herald Tribune, Ideas and Production, The International Journal of the History of Sport, International Political Science Review, International Studies Quarterly, Institute for Social Research Newsletter.

JAMA (Journal of The American Medical Association), The Journal of American History, Journal of British Studies, Journal of Contemporary Asia, Journal of Curriculum Studies, Journal of Design History, Journal of Historical Sociology, Journal of Imperial and Commonwealth History, Journal of The Institute of Education, (The University of Hull), Journal of Mississippi History, The Journal of Psychohistory, Journal of the Royal Asiatic Society, Journal of Social History, The Journal of the Society for Army Historical Research, Journal of the Society for Naval Research.

The Listener, Learning and Motivation.

The Magnet, Man, Mythprint. Mississippi History.

National Trust Magazine, New Scientist, The New York Review of Books, The New York Times, The New Yorker, Noetic Sciences Review.

The Observer, 1 Kensington Gore (Newsletter of the Royal Geographical Society), Organization of American Historians' Newsletter.

Perspectives, The Photo Historian, Political Science Quarterly, Proceedings of the Suffolk Institute of Archaeology and Natural History, Proceedings of the Wesley Historical Society, The Psychohistory Review, Punch.

Research, The Royal Bank Letter, Rutland Review.

Scientific American, Siam Society Journal, Social History of Medicine, The Society for Journal of Psychical Research, Society for Historians of American Foreign Relations Newsletter, The Sociological Review, Sociology, Sociology of Education, The Southeast Asian Journal of Social Science, Studies in History and Philosophy of Science.

Tatler, The Sunday Times, Times Higher Education Supplement (abbreviated THES) Times Literary Supplement, (abbreviated TLS), Transactions of the London & Middlesex Archaeological Society, Triange, Trollopiana.

Victorian Periodicals Review, Victorian Studies.

Wall Street Journal, Weather, The Westminster Review.

ARCHIVES AND DISSERTATIONS

Some of the more obscure titles can be found in the libraries of the United Grand

Lodge of England (GLE) and the Royal Commonwealth Society. The India Office Library and Records, London, was of great use. (IOR). American missionary records from the Arabian Gulf are in The Sage Library of The Reformed Church of America, in New Brunswick, New Jersey. The following dissertations were found particularly helpful:

Frank Martin Brodhead, "Social Imperialism and the British Youth Movement, 1880-1914," PhD, Princeton University, 1978.

Martin Moir, "A Study of the History & Organization of the Political and Secret Department of the East India Company, the Board of Control and Indian Office", PhD, University of London, 1966.

INDEX

Abbotsholme School 61

Abingdon School 188

Abrams, Philip, "Notes on the Difficulty of Studying the State" 140

Ackerly, J. R., homosexual sympathies 139

Adamson, Prof. J. H., Mormonism and Freemasonry views 143

Aden Golf Club 172

administrators
class divisions blurred overseas 85; examinations for public service 102; financial rewards 122, 140; lead in food effect on 92-3; learned societies attendance 179-80; public schools imprint 188; recruitment 75, 82-3, 84, 88-9, 100, 105; sexual inequality encouraged by structure of Empire 130; sexuality influenced by public school 126-7; *see also* colonialism, British Empire *and* Imperialism

adolescence
behaviour in gentlemen's clubs 40, 151; influences received during 69; life of the Empire an extension of 44, 56, 138; permanent theory of C. Connolly 39, 44; significance of attending public school 99, 198; *see also* sexuality

Agar, W. E., 'living memory' experiments 55

agricultural history 57

Albany, The (club) 170-1

Aldrich, Richard, "First Person Past" article 201

Al Fayed brothers, purchase of Harrods 203

Alger, Horatio, stories 194

Alington, Cyril, playing fields of Eton quote, view 111

Allen, Charles, *Plain Tales From the Raj* 115, 140, 183, 184

Allen, Robert J., *The Clubs of Augustan London* 161

Allhallows School, Imperial influence on teachers and pupils 63-4; origins of 188; *Rousdon Mansion: Present Home of School* 71

Alpine Sports Club 161

Altholz, Josef L., "The Simony Press" article 114

Althusser, Louis, social apparatus theory 49

Amery, Leo, education and political attitudes 44

Ampere, Andre, attack on the Idealogues 93

Andersen, Roger, *The Power and the Word* 49, 161

Anstruther, Ian, *The Knight and the Umbrella* 25

Arabian Gulf
Arabs, club membership denial 173; British clubs in 173, 175; British serving in 140; Bushire Club 173; club membership 184; *Clubs of the British Residents and Agents of the Arabian Gulf* 164; *Magicians of Arabia* 13; Mohammerah, Union Club 173; *Persian Gulf Administrative Reports* 183; traditional Bahraini clubs 173; *see also* individually named countries

235

193-4, 197, 201; monocausality 190-1, 198; morphic resonance 33, 51, 55, 56, 59, 61, 63, 65, 68-9, 70, 81, 86, 92, 187; multidimensional subject 47, 105; preparatory school study 99; prosopography association with 73-5, 80-1; public schools influence 15, 20, 59, 111; readers of this book a factor 186; religious influence in public schools 95-9; scientific discussions metaphysical overtones 187

Cavalry Club 160, 164

Cecil, Lord David, *The Leisure of an Egyptian Official* 151, 162

Chaeronea, Battle of 123-4, 126

Chamberlain, Joseph, religion Unitarian 96

Chamberlain, Neville, Ark Club membership 160

Champs-Elysees Club 171

Chandler, Timothy J. L., "The Development of Sporting Tradition at Oxbridge" 115; "Emergent Athleticism" 88

chaos theories 47-8, 80

Charles, John, Eton educated, later head of Newcastle prep school 35

Charterhouse School, building for masters 161; move to Godalming 66

Checkland, S. G., *The Rise of Industrial Society in England* 164

childhood history 139

China
"Goddess of Democracy" in Peking's Tiananmen Square 24; Shanghai Clubs 171

Chinese Society of the Green Dragon 138

Chitty, Clyde, *Redefining the Comprehensive Experience* 209

Christ College, Brecon 188

Christie, Agatha, *They Came to Baghdad* 208

Christ's Hospital, height of boys recorded 57

Chubb, John E., "Politics and the Organization of Schools" 199

Chums, illustration 25; public school stories 17, 32

Churchill, Sir Winston, Ark Club membership 160; crammers attended 102; influence of Harrow School 95; *My Early Life* 114

Church of England, influence, on education 46, 47

Church of Scotland, General Assembly debate on freemasonry 133

Church Preferment Gazette 96

CIA 133

City of London Club, freemasons' lodge meetings held at 153

civil service, public schools influence 186

clairvoyance 72

Clarendon Commission 34

Clark, Prof. B., OUP edition of *The Making of a Schoolgirl* 22

Clark, D. T. D., quoted 116

Clark, Jonathan, review of Longford's *New Oxford History of England* 70

Clark, Stephen R. F., "A Matter of Habit" 70, 197

Clarke, Patricia, place of imperial governess research 91

Clarke, Roger, "Beware Falling Masonry" 142

classics, unexpurgated at Eton 126

Clearey, Frederick, spirit of the Lodge, view 198

Cleveland Street affairs (1889-90) 127

Cleverley, John ed., *Half a Million Children: Studies of Non-Government Education in Australia* 53

Clifton School, chapel plaques removal protest 97; memories of Sir Arnold Wilson 58

climatology 27, 53

clubs, gentlemen's
addresses and details listed in school registers 151; architecture 79, 166-7,

Phenomenon. Does the NFL Drive the Market?" 53

Eardley-Wilmot, F. M., styled 'the military Arnold' 104
East India Company, London Club 155-6; officers 155-6, 164
East India, Devonshire, Sports and Public Schools Club 156, 159, 171, 180
East India United Services Club 155-6, 164
Eccentric Club, freemason lodge for members 153
Eco, Umberto, novels 31; quoted 54; *Travels in Hyperreality* 71
education
  biographical approach to history 203; comprehensive schools 206, 208; cultural influence of public schools 39; elitism 44, 47, 48, 52, 59, 78, 100, 105, 111, 203, 205; equality vs quality 203-5; grammar schools 206, 208; history of, material available 74-5; history of relationship to political history 29-30, 36, 39, 56, 69, 79-80, 203; imperial attitudes produced by 79; inequalities 199; influence on individuals 69, 79; informal from gentlemen's clubs 181; mandarin class training 52; metaphysics reappearance in discussion of 69, 187; military regimental schools 116; morphic resonance implications 187; opt-out state schools 203, 208; popular not encouraged 59; prosopography *see* prosopography; school origins 188; secondary 87; selection on basis of ability 205; social conditioning 116; state education 57, 203-6, 208; Taunton Commission (1868) 47; technical v general 61, 63; *see also* public schools
Edward VII, King, in Masonic apron 97, *(illus)* 98, 133; *see also* Wales, Prince of

Edward VIII, King, dancing for *(illus)* 40; gavel 152; procession *(illus)* 191
Edwardians, club membership, ideology of belonging 150; public schools ideological influence 195
Edwards, Griffith, *Opium and the People* 121, 140
Edwards, Menlove, homosexual sympathies 139
Edwards, Thomas, "Reconstruction: Changing Historical Paradigms in Mississipi History" 53
Egelnick, Max, "The Clerkenwell Festival" article 198
Egypt
  Alexandria, Union Club 171; Cairo, Turf Club 169; Cairo, Victoria College 203-4, 205
élitism
  club membership restrictions on natives of country 172-5; education 44, 47, 48, 52, 59, 78, 100, 105, 111, 203, 205; imperial awards 68, 78; prosopography 87; regiments of Imperial élite 79; religion and 96; *see also* education *and* public schools
Elizabeth I, Queen, visit to Eton commemorated 106
Elizabeth College, Guernsey, study of boys attending 80
Elkins, Stanley, *The Founding Fathers: Young Men of the Revolution* 75
Ellesmere College, admission policy 76-7; book on 75
Elliman, Michael, homosexual tendencies 139
Elliott, Sir Claude, Eton debarring foreign boys from taking scholarship exams 151
Elliott, J. H., "Conspicuous Consumption" 113
Ellis, Alice Thomas, *Loss of the Good Authority* 25
Ellis, Havelock, *An Open Letter to*

243

244

152-3; membership of 74, 87, 181; overseas associations with schools and clubs 148, 169; spirit of 198

French, Thomas, founder of St John's college in Agra, India 100-1, *(illus)* 101

Frenkel, Stephen, article "Malaria Prophylaxis and Racial Segregation" 182

Frere, Sir Henry Bartle, membership of RGS 180

Freud, Sigmund 75

Fromm, Erich, *Beyond the Chains of Illusion* 141

Froude, James Anthony, *Oceana or England and Her Colonies* 36

Fuller, Roy, *The Ruined Boys* 115

Furet, Francois, *In the Workshop of History* 70, 199

Fussell, Paul, article "A Radical Road to Happiness" 50

Gabriel, Col. R. C., letter quoted 165

Gallagher, J., Victorian imperial enthusiasm, quote 39

Galton, Francis, established RGS examinations 180

Gambetta, Diego, *Were They Pushed or Did They Jump?* 51

Gann, L. H., *The Rules of British Africa (1870-1914)* 161

Gardner, Brian, *The Public Schools* 107

Garrick Club, atmosphere 155; library 185; Masonic gavel treasure 151

Gathorne-Hardy, Jonathan, "frustrated benevalent dictators" quote 47; *The Old School Tie* 16, 27, 95, 114, 118; *The Public School Phenomenon* 52; *The Rise and Fall of the British Nanny* 95, 114

Gay, Professor Peter, *Freud for Historians* 118

gay behaviour *see* homosexuality

Gee, James Paul, "The Legacies of Literacy" 52

Geertz, Clifford, study of Balinese cockfighting 16

Gellner, Ernest, "Incestuous Initiation" 141

Genealogists, Society of 85

genetics
causal vehicles for preserving genes 92; history 57; morphic resonance hypothesis and 33, 55, 56, 59, 61, 63, 65, 69, 70, 81, 86, 92

gentlemen's clubs *see* clubs

Germania, symbolism 24

Gérôme, J. L., painting *The Snake Charmer (illus)* 129, 141-2

Gessner, Conrad, pencil pioneer 210

Gibbon, Edward, *Decline and Fall* 56

Gibbon, Ian, *The English Vice* 141

Giles, G. C. T., *The New School Tie* 53

Gill, Anton, *How to be Oxbridge: A Bluffer's Handbook* 115

Gillis, A. R., "Feminist Scholarship, Relational and Instrumental Control" 113

Giroux, Henry A., "Schooling, Culture and Literacy in the Age of Broken Dreams" 52

Glassup, E. H., "Memories" 182

Glasgow Acadamy: *The First Hundred Years* 88

Gleick, James, *Chaos: making a New Science* 53, 72, 89

Glinga, Werner, club membership, quote 160; *Legacy of Empire* 27, 160, 161, 162, 165

Godley, Sir Arthur (Lord Kilbracken), recruitment to public service, views 83

Goldthorpe, J. E., *An Introduction to Sociology* 142

Goleman, Daniel, *"For Each Sibling There Appears to be a Different Family* 114

Gonzales-Reigosa, Fernando, "Greek Homosexuality" 141

Goodchild, Michael F., "Specialization in

the Structure and Organization of Geography" article 198

Gordon, Peter, "First Person Past" article 201

Gordon, Richard, *A Gentleman's Club* 52, 155, 163, 183; *The Private Life of Florence Nightingale* 182

Gothic Revival 15, 25

Graetz, Brian, "The Reproduction of Privilege in Australian Education" 199

Grainger, J. H., *Patriotisms; Britain 1900-1939* 48, 50, 51-2, 87, 161, 197

grammar schools 87

Gramsci, Antonio, cutural hegemony, view 36, 49, 52, 54, 75; education views 205

Grant, Duncan, homosexual sympathies 139

Grant-Maintained Schools 12, 24

Graunbaum, Adolf, "The Pseudo-Problem of Creation in Physical Cosmology" 70

Graves, Charles, *Leather Armchairs* 162, 163, 164, 183

Graves, Richard Perceval, *Robert Graves: the Assault Heroic* 141

Graves, Robert, *Goodbye to All That* 44, 53, 58, 70, 115, 139

Green, John Richard, *Short History of the English People* 41

Green, Vivian, chaplain at Sherborne 119

Greene, Charles Henry, headmaster of Berkhamsted 95

Greene, Graham, father headmaster at Berkhamsted 95; memories of schooldays 138; *The Old School* 34, 51; *A Sort of Life* 114

Gresham's Club 182

Griffiths, Arthur, *Clubs and Clubmen* 163

Griffiths, Richard, *Jours de Gloire* 70

Griggs, Clive, *Education – The Wasted Years* 209; "Fee Paying Education: The Favoured Sector" article 209

Guards Club 160, 164

Guba, Egon G., "Epistemological and Methodological Bases of Naturalistic Inquiry" 49, 88

Gulf *see* Arabian Gulf

Guttsman, W. L. ed., *The English Ruling Class* 140

Hachen Jr., David S., "The Delicate Balance: Technology and Control in Organizations" 113

Hagan, John, "Feminist Scholarship, Relational and Instrumental Control" 113

Haggard, V. E. D., *The Brewing Years* 115

Haileybury College.
associations with St. John's College, Agra 101; old boy functions 151; pudding purveyor George James Coleman 107, *(illus)* 108

Hailsham, Lord (Quinten Hogg), Ark Club membership 160

Haldane, J. B. S., idea of God, quote 27

Haley, Bruce, *Healthy Body and Victorian Culture* 117

Hall, A. D., *The Savile Club* 161, 182

Hall, Edward T., *The Silent Language* 71

Hall, Phyllis A., "Teaching Analytical Thinking" 50

Hall, Richard, *Lovers on the Nile* 182

Hall, Roland, article "Causal Powers" 50

Hamcrow, Theodore S., *Reflections on History and Historians* 25

Hamilton, David, "Adam Smith and the Moral Economy of the Classroom System" 113

Hamilton, William B., *The Transfer of Institutions* 71

Hamilton, W. Mark, "The New Navalism and the British Navy League" 89

Hampe, M., "Two Consequences of Richard Dawkins' View of Genes and Organisms" 51, 113

Hansell, Peter and Jean, publications about dovecotes 91

Harcourt, Lewis, affair with boy at Eton 126

Hardy, H. H., director of studies, Sandhurst 104

Harris, Ruth, "Melodrama, Hysteria and Feminine Crimes of Passion" 140

Harman, Willis, "Spirituality, Science and the Transformation of Consciousness" 51

Harrison, John, *The District Officer In India* 89

Harrods purchase by Al Fayed brothers 203-4

Harrow School
club membership by old boys 181; homosexual friendships 123; memories of Arthur Bryant 58, 59

Harvey, Thomas, Eton old boy, imperial connections 35

Haseler, Stephen, "How a Nation Slipped into its Dotage" 209

Haskell, Thomas L., quoted 52

Hatfield, Mrs. P., archivist of Eton College, quote 22

Hattie, John, New Zealand state schools 143

Havet, José, "Cartoons – A neglected Source of Insight Into International Development" 70

Haymarket tennis club *(illus)* 146, 147

Haythronthwaite, John, son attended Haileybury, head of St. John's School, Agra 101

headmasters
bribery for admission of pupil 122-3; club membership sought for old boys 149; club Nobody's Friend membership 154; freemasonry pageantry, influence on 97; importance of role in Victorian England 95; Sandhurst reorganisation in 1857, consultation with 103

Headmasters' Conference 75

Heald, Tim, *Who We Know and How We Use Them* 161

Healey, Robin, review of *Elixir of Empire* 198

Hearnden, Arthur, *Red Robert: A Life of Robert Birley* 71, 161, 163

Hearl, Trevor, military education, views 104; military education and the school curriculum 116

Hearn, Jeffrey, review of *Making a Man of Him: Gender and Education* 87

Heathcote, T. A., *The Indian Army* 140

hegemony 36, 49, 52, 54, 75, 196

Henn, Percy, founding warden of Australian college 100

Henty, G. A., novels 58, 63, 197

heraldry 25

Hess, Robert D., *The Development of Political Attitudes in Children* 114

Heussler, Robert, *Yesterday's Rulers* 73, 162

Heward, Christine, *Making a Man of Him* 75, 77

Heywood, Colin, "Boundless Dress of the Levant" 50; "Wittek and the Austrian Tradition" 50

Hexter, J. H., criticism of Christopher Hill 199; *The History Primer* 143

Hildebrant, Kurt, approach to history 30

Hill, Christopher, "Causal Necessitation, Moral Responsibility" 141; *History and the Present* 50; reply to criticisms 199

Hill, Frank Ernest, clubs vehicle of education, view 181; *Man-Made Culture* 151, 161, 185

Hill, J. W., *Eton Medley* 49

Hilton, James, *Goodbye Mr. Chips* 78

Himmelfarb, Gertrude, *The New History and the Old* 50, 87, 113, 118, 197; "Social History and Moral Imagination" 209

Hine, Bob, *Sociology* 70

history
antiquarian approach 57; biographical approach 203; causality, importance of

15-16, 27, 29, 31, 41-2, 48, 49, 52-3, 54-5, 68-9, 92, 187, 193-4, 197, 201; causes involved in any situation numberless 56-7, 105; climatology interpretation 27, 53; cross-discipline, importance to study of 47-8; diet and smell interpretations 93, 105; education, material available 74-5; empathy 16, 81; epidemiology interpretation 27-8; food commodities causal contribution 105-6, 110; German notion of *Verstehen* 31; iconology contribution to studies 15; monocausality 190-1, 198; myth-making and 190; of childhood 139; of emotion 118, 139; political historians' perspective 41-2, 52-3; political relationship to educational history 29-30, 36, 39, 57, 69, 79-80; prosopography and 196, 212; psychohistory *see* Psychohistory; public schools influence 15, 29, 39; revisionism 69, 196; specialities proliferation 30-31, 42, 48, 50, 57, 75, 93, 105; social history and causal concerns 29, 39, 41-2, 48, 49, 68, 196; subjective sifting of information 93, 196; *see also* culture

Hitler, Adolf, defeat, cause of, view 145

Hobson, J. A., *Imperialism* 28

Hofstadt, Dan, custard, importance of in school diet 107-8

Hollinghurst, Allan, *The Swimming Pool Library* 3, 88, 114

Hollis, Sir Roger, head of MI5 140

Holmes, Sherlock, methods of deduction 27, 74, 91, 137

Homas, Albert, *Wait and See* 116

homosexuality
  gay studies 57; homo-eroticism in public schools 46; in public school literature 118, 119, 125, 139; in public schools 46, 88, 118, 123-30, 139; Order of Chaerorea, secret society 123-4, 126; public school old boys with artistic and literary talent 139, 141; *see also* sexuality

Honey, John, *Tom Brown's Universe* 76, 84, 153, 163, 170

Hong Kong clubs 171

honours, medals and orders 68, 78

Hope, Mary, *The Psychology of Ritual* 198

Hornby, James, headmaster of Eton 34

Hough, James, *Political and Military Events in British India* 185

Hough, Richard, *The Ace of Clubs* 163, 164, 182, 185

Houseman, A. E., possible member of secret homosexual society 125

House of Commons, public schools' influence 186

Housman, Laurence, member of secret homosexual society 123-4

Huberman, A. Michael, "Assessing Local Causality in Qualitive Research" 53

Hughes, Linda, "Turbulence in the 'Golden Stream': Chaos Theory and the Study of Periodicals" 53

Hughes, Thomas, Savile Club founding member 151; *Tom Brown at Oxford* 100; *Tom Brown's Schooldays* 79, 94, 99, 103, 126, 151

Hume, David, causality depends on conjunction 56, 113; *History of England* 41; *Treatise on Human Nature* 41

Humphries, Stephen, *Hooligans or Rebels?* 53

Hunt, Roland, *The District Officer in India* 89

Hurlingham Club, lodge meetings at 153

Huxley, Thomas Henry, membership of Athenaeum 150

Hyam, Ronald, "Empire and Sexual Opportunity" 130, 141, 142

Presland, Eric, "Power and Consent" 140

Price, Cormell, headmaster at United Service College 127

Primrose League 52

Prince Alfred College, Adelaide, metal badge for old boys 61

Prior, Charles, education in Bahrain 111

Private Patrons' Gazette (later Church Patronage Gazette) 96

prosopography

antiquarian publishing investigation 212; avoidance of pseudo-scientific language 84; causality, association with 73-5, 80-1; causes to be identified 91-2; club, lodge and society memberships 149-50, 181, 212; difficulties in using the technique 75, 79; élitism and necromancy in choice of subject 87-8; experiences neither totally private nor totally subjective 81; food habits 105-10; gentlemen's clubs membership 159; medical histories 105; powerful instrument of discovery 69, 73, 86, 87, 196, 212; psychohistory and 119, 127; public schools consideration 190-1; and Royal Geographical Society membership 180-1

Prosser, Evans, head of Ellesmere College 76

Proust, Marcel, *Swann's Way* 56

psychohistory 42, 44, 118, 139, 186; acceptance as descriptive term 118-9; interplay of political intrigue and sex 121; prosopographical 119, 127; public schools effects 118; radical and conservative camps, journals on 119

Psychology, International Society of Political Psychology 42; Victorians unaware of 57

public schools

admissions policies 76-7, 122-3; agents of British imperialism 16-7, 35-6, 49, 54, 87; antiquity contrived 66-7, 71, 188-9; bibliographic study 210-3;

boarding influence on boys 94-5, 99; books analysing 22, 39, 52, 75, 210-3; books, cloak and dagger content 119, 125, 197; books popularising 31, 36, 45, 58, 63, 99; books sexuality in 118, 125; Borstals influenced by 46; cabalism *see* cabalism; cadet corps 103, *(illus)* 103; capitalist ploy 122; categorization of 77-80, 84, 88, 89-90, 107, 115; causal considerations 15, 20, 59, 111; choice of 76, *(illus)* 77; clubs *see* clubs, gentlemen's; colonialism, dependence on 13; common denominators 187-8; crammers 101-2; cultural influences of 39, 64-6, 111, 195; discrimination against women 42; documents and records 57; élitism *see* élitism; European Community in 1992, opportunities for 206; fees 122, 140; flagellation *see* flagellation; food in *see* food; freemasonry *see* freemasonry; generalism vs specialism 61, 63; Harrods purchase by public school educated Al Fayed Brothers 203-4; historians' approach 212; history, influence on 15, 29, 31, 47; history of 74, 82, 186-7, 205; homosexuality *see* homosexuality; ideology reflected in careers of boys 84; imperial expansion effect 13, 28, 31, 188, 190-1; imperial icon Tom Brown 194; imperialist values of teachers handed down 35-6, 87; India destination, contribution of individual schools 75; influencing life-long conduct 46, 47, 59, 69, 80-1, 83, 86, 188, 195; learned societies' membership 180; libraries 212; magazines popularise 17, 32, 64, 99, 122; museums 63; mythology source of 190; Nazis influenced by 53; old boys' fraternities 65-6, 81; old school ties 61, 99; parents living abroad 95; Peter Pan syndrome encouraged 126-7; political factor of 52; practical rather than academic products of 156; preparatory schools *see* preparatory schools; prominent positions held by old boys 208; prosopography application 190-1; prosperity under Thatcher governments 204-5; psychohistory application 186; railway locomotives named after 39; recruitment to public services 75, 82-3, 84, 88-9; regimental societies 104; registers 74-7, 80, 81-2, 87, 90, 151, 181; religion, chapels in 96-7; religious antiquity claim for 188-9; religious influence 95-7, 98, 188-9; reputations waxing and waning 79; rites of initiation 57-8; rituals and British imperial rule 13, 28, 30, 31, 44, 47, 55, 56, 59, 66, 83, 194; rituals faked to make them seem older 67-8, 148; rituals importance of 15, 28, 29, 47, 61, 66, 206; rituals, origins of 15, 42, 44, 45-6; Scotland 84; secrecy and esoteric language 132-3, 136; selection for, on basis of ability 205; sexuality *see* sexuality; social imperialism, expression of 31, 47; social needs of family met 94-5; sporting rituals 45, 47, 59, 61, *(illus)* 62, 76, 77, 88, 170; statistics publication 75-7; status, strategies to achieve 76, 77-80, 105; tainting of youth, criticism by Daniel Defoe 64-5; traditions, sanctity of 66; 'traitors' 137; universities influenced by 100-1; vocabulary and accents 31

Public Schools Club, limited membership 155

public schools, overseas 111, 137-8, 143, 148; bibliography of 210; *see also* under individually named countries

Public Schools Yearbook 75, 210

puddings *see* food

Punch, cartoon of 1911 Britannia 22, *(illus)* 23; illustrations 25, 28; tribute to Queen Victoria in 1897 *(illus)* 28

Qatar, Doha Club 161, Library and staff.

Quigly, Isabel, *The Heirs of Tom Brown* 50

Quinton, Anthony, clubs and imperialism, quote 13

racism, in public school literature 118

Radcliffe, Raymond, Eton educated, later a teacher 35

Radley School, prosperity 204

Rae, John, *Letters from School* 140; public schools, quotes 24, 91, 122, 123-4, 140, 188, 204

railway locomotives named after public schools 39

Rajkumar College, 194-5

Rao, M. R. Sripado, *Waltair Club Platinum Jubilee Souvenir* 183

Rattigan, Terence, *Cause Célèbre* 119; schooldays at Harrow 119

Raven, Simon, *The Old School* 89, 90

Reading Grammar School, Prince of Wales setting cornerstone 13, *(illus)* 14

Reed, John R., *The Old School Ties* 52, 89

Reed, Talbot Baines, Bibliography Society founded by 210

Reese, Revor R., *The History of the Royal Commonwealth Society* 116, 185

Reform Club 179, atmosphere 154, 184; *Eighty Days Around the World* by Jules Verne 166; library *(illus)* 43, 44

Reid, Colin, European Community and public schools, views 206

religion

allegiance to various churches 96; causal influence, prosopographical considerations 95-7, 98; élitism and 96; headmasters influenced by freemasonry pageantry 97; organised voluntary social institutions replace in seventeenth century 147; Oxford Movement 96; public schools origins in, claims 188-9; public schools religio-political ecumenism 96; public schools right to present clergy to livings 96; Union of Modern Churchmen 96

Rendall, Montague, *Acquaintances* 58-9

Repton School, former headmaster John Thom's autobiography 204; memories of discipline handed out by Geoffrey Fisher 46-7

Rexford, Oscar Whitelaw, *The History of the University Club of St Louis* 183

Reynolds, Stanley, "From Boers to Boys Own" article 50

Rhind, David, "The Characteristics and Views of the RGS Fellowship" 185

Rich, Bruce M., "The Multilateral Development Banks, Environmental Policy and the USA" 113

Rich, P. J., "The Bahrain Public School Scheme" 117; *Chains of Empire* 6, 13, 52, 59; *Elixir of Empire* 6, 17, 20, 39, 49, 198, 199, 200, 212, 214; morphic resonance and rituals of British rule 199; review of the *Happiest Days* by Jeffrey Richard 209; review of *Manliness and Morality* ed. by Mangan 115; review of *Truth, Liberty, Religion* by Barbara Smith 185; *Rituals of Empire* 6, 13, 49, 61, 197, 213; *The Role of Ritual in the Arabian Gulf* 214

Richards, Jeffrey, *Happiest Days* 209; "Passing the Love of Women" 141

ritology, challenge to entrenched presumptions 32

rituals

antiquity contrived 66-8, 188-9; Aztec 32; British Empire 13, 28, 31, 39, *(illus)* 40, 44, 83, 137-9; British public life 192; Christianity invoked for imperialism 96-7; clubs, gentlemen's 44, 47, 150-3, 155, 172; colonialism, importance of 31-2, 169-70, 172, 191; communities strengthened by 80; eating habits 109; essential human

function 192; fraternal orders 31; freemasonry *see* freemasonry; imperial, planned or fortuitous 191-2; magical and supernatural connotations 28; makers of, diverse 192; manipulation of emotions 31; new nation states need for 191; origins of in public schools 15, 42, 44, 45; politics 30, 61, 191, 192; preparatory schools 99; psychological integration encouragement 198; public schools *see* public schools; reinforcement of value systems 56; royal power assisted by 44-5, 52; schools repositories of systems 15; social structures perpetuation 206; spirit of places of power 195-6; sporting 45, 47, 59, 61, *(illus)* 62; talismans substratum of ideology 68; uniforms image of authority 206; Victorian 13, 25, 28

Rogers, Barbara, discrimination against women, views 42; *Men Only: An Investigation Into Men's Organisations* 90, 115, 160, 189, 198

Rolls, Frederick, *The Pink Plaque Guide to London* 139

Roman Catholic controlled schools 84

Rome, R. C., *The Union Club* 164, 182, 183

Rongstad, L. James, *How to Respond to The Lodge* 143

Rose, Kenneth, *Curzon: A Most Superior Person* 161, 163

Rosee, Pasque, coffee house opened in London (1652) 147

Rosenburg, David, "The Causal Connection in Mass Exposure Cases" article 48

Rosenthal, Michael, *The Character Factory* 71, 126, 190

Rosicrucians, public schools support and imperial versions 31, 66

Ross, Gordon, "Breathless Hush in the Close" 115

259

Rowse, A. L., *Homosexuals in History* 141

Royal Asiatic Society 57, 179-80, 185

Royal Automobile Club 162; school lodges meeting at 152

Royal Central Asiatic Society 179-80

Royal Colonial Institute, respectability 149

Royal Commonwealth Society 116, 185

Royal Cruising Club 154

Royal Geographical Society 57, 150, 179, 180-1, 183, 185

Royal Institution 185

royal power
  rituals help to maintain 44-5, 50; support for freemasonry 44

Royal School of St Peter, antiquity of 66

Royal Societies Club 148

Royal Society for Asian Affairs 179-80, 185

Royal Yacht Squadron Club 154

Rubinstein, W. D., "The Victorian Middle Classes: Wealth, Occupation and Geography" 113

Rugby School
  associations with St. John's College, Agra 101; characteristics, generalizations about 75; club membership by old boys 181; food, chef's pudding *(illus)* 106, 107; influence of Thomas Arnold 29, 95, 96; influence on author Salman Rushdie 16; memories of R. G. Collingwood 58, 59; Oxford University, importance to 100; Register 162; Siam minister of education, Prince Dhani Nivat an old boy of 25; Tom Brown, an imperial icon 194

Rumi, Jalaludin, Persian poet 113

Rusbridger, Alan, review of Martin Short's *Inside the Brotherhood* 135, 143

Rushdie, Salman, membership of Pitt Club, Cambridge 145; *The Satanic Verses* 16, 186

Russian Society of the Green Glove 138

Ryan, Alan, *The Philosophy of the Social Sciences* 53

Sadomasochism in public schools 128-9; in literature of 118

Said, Edward, cover illustration for *Orientalism* 129, 130; *Nationalism, Colonialism and Literature* 193, 199

St. Andrew's Golf Club 172

St. Paul's School, Conservative spokesmen's memories of 204; day school, influence on boys 94

Saint-Simon, Claude, founder of sociology, Durkheim's view 199

St. Vincent, Lord, United Services Club, influence quote 159

Salt, Henry, Eton educated, later a teacher 35

Salter, Brian, *Power and Policy in Education* 51, 52, 71

Sams, Hubert Arthur, *Pauline and Old Pauline* 161

Sandbach, Henry, Eton old boy imperial connections 35

Sanderson, William, *Two Hundred Years of Freemasonry* 152

Sandhurst Military Acadamy 102, 103-4, 121, 140

Sapire, David, "Determinism, The Report Past, and Causal or Determinal Structure of the Universe" 70

Sassoon, Siegfried, homosexual sympathies 139

Sattin, Anthony, *Lifting the Veil* 182, 199, 209

Saunders, Kate, "Running Circles Round Men" 161

Savage Club
  atmosphere 155; book on, by Percy V. Bradshaw 162; freemasons lodge for members 153

Savile Club 166; atmosphere 154

Sayer, George, Eton educated, later

master at Bradfield 35
Schaff, Adam, *History and Truth* 70, 142
Schatzberg, John D., "The Super Bowl
Phenomenon. Does the NFL Drive the
Market?" 53
Schoenwald, Richard L., "Norman O.
Brown and the legacy of Freud" 140
science
aggregatability of data 88; chaos
studies 47-8, 80; holism and synthesis
48; metaphysical overtones arising
from causality discussions 187, 196
Scott, J. M., *The Book of Pall Mall* 163
Scott, Paul, *A Division of the Spoils* 89;
Raj Quartet 81, 89
Scottish public schools 84
scouting, boys, 30, 50, 59, 126
Searle, John R., "Is the Brain's Mind a
Computer Program?" 51
secrecy *see* cabalism *and* freemasonry
secret service 133, 135, 136, 137, 142
secret societies 138, 142
Sedgwick, Eve Kosofsky, *Between Man*
139
Seeley, John Robert, *The Expansion of
England* 36
Selwyn, Edward, Eton educated, later
head of Uppingham 35
Sendak, Maurice, *Notes on Books and
Pictures* 25
Senghaas, Dieter, *Wisenschafts-
imperialismus* 52
Senior club, merged with Naval and
Military Club 157, *see* United Service
Club
Sergeant, R. B. ed., *Arabian Studies* 89
Seton-Kerr, Heywood, Eton old boy,
imperial connections 35
Seymour-Smith, Martin, biography of
Kipling 127-8, 141
sexuality
British Empire and association with
power 130; distortion by public schools
126-7; in public school literature 118,

125; *see also* adolescence, homo-
eroticism *and* sexuality
Shah, Idries, *The Natives are Restless* 144
Shah, Sirdar Ikbal Ali, *The Golden East*
161
Sharp, Allen, "The Case of Devil's
Hoofmarks" 27
Sharpe, Evelyn, *The Making of a
Schoolgirl* 22
Shattock, Joanne, *The Victorian Press* 212
Shawnigan Lake School, British
Columbia, pancake greezing custom 67
Sheldrake, Dr. Rupert, Britannia
symbolism, views 22, 24, 140; "Cause
and Effect in Science" article 200;
creativity quote 5; morphic resonance
application to British rule 199; morphic
resonance hypothesis 55, 56, 59, 61,
63, 65, 69, 71, 81, 86, 92, 187, 193;
"Myth Taken" article 198; *A New
Science of Life* 32-3, 71, 187, 200; *The
Presence of the Past* 32, 51, 70, 71, 72,
89, 90; ritualism, views 195-6; "The
Seats of Power" article 199; theories
57, 81, 200
Shepherd, Simon, *Coming on Strong* 140;
"Gay Spy Sex Orgy: the State's Need
for Queers" 140
Sherborne School: PT in Quad *(illlus)* 62
Sherry, Norman, *The Life of Graham
Greene* 140, 143
Short, Martin, *Inside the Brotherhood*
135; "The Wives' Tale" 142
Shrewsbury School, rebuilding, efforts to
make seem old 66
Shrosbree, Colin, *Public Schools and
Private Education* 59, 71
Sigelman, Lee, "Self-Selection, Socializ-
ation and Distinctive Military Values"
115
Silver, Harold, *Education as History* 30,
181, 185.
Simmonds, Stuart, *The Royal Asiatic
Society* 185

261

264

Motu proprio